T0340228

The Theory of the Firm

Firms are a ubiquitous feature of the economic landscape, with much of the activity undertaken within an economy taking place within their boundaries. Given the size of the contribution made by firms to economic activity, employment and growth, having a theoretical understanding of the nature and structure of firms is crucial for understanding how an economy functions.

The Theory of the Firm firstly offers a brief overview of the 'past' of the theory of the firm. This consists of a concise discussion of the classical view of production, followed by an outline of the development of the neoclassical – or 'textbook' – approach to firm level production. Secondly, the 'present' of the theory of the firm is discussed in three sections. The first section considers the post-1970 theory of the firm literature per se, while the second section scrutinises the relationship between the three most prominent of the modern sets of theories: the reference point, property rights and transaction cost approaches. The third section looks at the theory of privatisation. The unique aspects of this book include its discussions of the post-1970 contributions to the theory of the firm; the integration of the theory of the entrepreneur with the theory of the firm; and the theory of privatisation.

This volume offers an intuitive introduction to the theories of the firm as well as simple formal models of the most important contributions to the literature. It also outlines the historical evolution of the traditional and modern theories of the firm. This book will be of great interest to those who study the history of economic thought, industrial economics and organisational studies.

Paul Walker is an economist in Christchurch, New Zealand. He received his PhD in Economics from the University of Canterbury, Christchurch, New Zealand. His research is mainly on the history of economics and the theory of the firm.

Routledge Studies in the History of Economics

A full list of titles in this series is available at: www.routledge.com/series/SE0341

177 Economic Theory and its History
Edited by Giuseppe Freni, Heinz D. Kurz, Andrea Lavezzi, Rodolfo Signorino

178 Great Economic Thinkers from Antiquity to the Historical School
Translations from the series
Klassiker der Nationalökonomie Bertram Schefold

179 On the Foundations of Happiness in Economics
Reinterpreting Tibor Scitovsky
Mauizio Pugno

180 A Historical Political Economy of Capitalism
After Metaphysics
Andrea Micocci

181 Comparisons in Economic Thought
Economic Interdependency Reconsidered
Stavros A. Drakopoulos

182 Four Central Theories of the Market Economy
Conceptions, Evolution and Applications
Farhad Rassekh

183 Ricardo and the History of Japanese Economic Thought
A selection of Ricardo studies in Japan during the interwar period
Edited by Susumu Takenaga

184 The Theory of the Firm
An overview of the economic mainstream
Paul Walker

The Theory of the Firm

An overview of the economic mainstream

Paul Walker

LONDON AND NEW YORK

First published 2017
by Routledge

2 Park Square, Milton Park, Abingdon, Oxfordshire OX14 4RN
52 Vanderbilt Avenue, New York, NY 10017

Routledge is an imprint of the Taylor & Francis Group, an informa business

First issued in paperback 2019

British Library Cataloguing in Publication Data
A catalogue record for this book is available from the British Library

Library of Congress Cataloging in Publication Data
Names: Walker, Paul, 1959- author.
Title: The theory of the firm: an overview of the economic mainstream / Paul Walker.
Description: Abingdon, Oxon; New York, NY: Routledge, 2017.
Identifiers: LCCN 2016014898| ISBN 9781138191532 (hardback) |
ISBN 9781315640440 (ebook)
Subjects: LCSH: Industrial organization (Economic theory)
Classification: LCC HD2326. W354 2017 | DDC 338.6–dc23
LC record available at https://lccn.loc.gov/2016014898

ISBN: 978-1-138-19153-2 (hbk)
ISBN: 978-0-367-87679-1 (pbk)

Typeset in Times New Roman
by Sunrise Setting Ltd, Brixham, UK

Contents

Preface and acknowledgements

The theoretical literature on the firm is diverse and growing, albeit from a small base, and no overview of the length presented here could possibly encompass all the different approaches that have been taken, across both time and the spectrum of economic thought, to the analysis of production and/or the firm. We therefore restrict our survey to, in the main, the major 'mainstream' approaches to the firm, both 'past' and 'present'. We concentrate on the mainstream theory because these theories, obviously, dominate the literature while aspects of the pre-1970 mainstream theory are still the most common, often the only, 'theory of the firm' taught to students. Few of the post-1970 theoretical advancements have made it into the standard economics textbooks, particularly undergraduate textbooks.

While the intention here is to provide a concise, reasonably critical, yet readable survey that is primarily focussed on the contemporary advancements within the theoretical literature on the firm, we also wish to understand the evolution of ideas that has resulted in these theories. Consequently, we consider, albeit briefly, the theoretical approaches of the pre-1970 literature (the 'past') as well as the approaches of the post-1970 period (the 'present'). Consideration of the history of the theory of the firm allows us to see the changes that have taken place with regard to economists' thinking on production or firms over the last 200 years or so.

Even for critics of the orthodoxy, an appreciation of the mainstream theory is needed to understand the reasons for and the advantages/disadvantages of the non-standard approaches taken in the heterodox literature.

It has been assumed that the reader will have been exposed to the standard introductory/intermediate 'textbook' treatment of the firm and thus little time need be spent on a discussion of the details of this material. If a review of this material is desired see, for example, in increasing order of difficulty, Varian (2014: Chapters 19 to 23), Cowell (2006: Chapters 2 and 3), Gravelle and Rees (2004: Chapters 5 to 10) and Mas-Colell *et al.* (1995: Chapter 5).

In terms of the mathematics required, we try to follow the advice of A. W. Zotoff: "In spite of the maxim, 'Il ne s'agit pas de faire lire, mais de faire penser', we think that mathematical problems should not be given to economists to solve, and that mathematical economics should be treated as simply as possible, with all results worked out in detail" (Zotoff 1923: 115). We thus attempt to provide as much detail as is needed for a senior undergraduate to follow any mathematical argument relatively easily.

An extensive bibliography is provided to guide readers who wish to further their reading on topics of interest and as a starting point for reading on material not covered directly in the text. See, for example, Chapter note 3, page 6, for information on other surveys of the mainstream theory and the pertinent empirical evidence, in addition to coverage of some applications and extensions of the mainstream approaches to the firm. For another example see Chapter note 6, page 7, for references that provide, along with their own bibliographies, a starting point for reading on the heterodox literature.

Acknowledgements

We wish to thank (without implicating) Graeme Guthrie and Simon Kemp for their comments on, and for pointing out errors in, previous drafts of the manuscript. All of the remaining errors are the fault of the author.

We are grateful to the following people and publishers for permission to incorporate material which has been published previously (all urls accessed 27 April 2016):

Professor Vikramaditya S. Khanna for permission to reproduce Table 1 on page 27 of Vikramaditya S. Khanna, 'The Economic History of Organizational Entities in Ancient India', University of Michigan Law School Program in Law & Economics Working Paper No. 14, updated version 2/2006.

Professor Timothy Van Zandt for permission to reproduce results from Timothy Van Zandt, 'An Introduction to Monotone Comparative Statics', Notes, INSEAD, 14 November 2002.

Cambridge University Press for permission to reproduce Figure 10.7 on page 368 of Mark Blaug, *Economic Theory in Retrospect*, 5th edn., Cambridge: Cambridge University Press, 1997. www.cambridge.org/

Cambridge University Press for permission to reproduce Figure 1.1. Microeconomics with endogenous entrepreneurs, firms, markets and organizations, on page 2 of Daniel Spulber, *The Theory of the Firm: Microeconomics with Endogenous Entrepreneurs, Firms, Markets, and Organizations*, Cambridge: Cambridge University Press, 2009. www.cambridge.org/

Oxford University Press for permission to reproduce the figure from page 44 of D. H. Macgregor, *Economic Thought and Policy*, Oxford: Oxford University Press, 1949. https://global.oup.com/academic/

The Econometric Society for permission to reproduce Figures 1 and 2 from Herbert A. Simon, 'A Formal Theory of the Employment Relationship', *Econometrica*, 19(3) (July, 1951), 293–305. http://onlinelibrary.wiley.com/journal/10.1111/(ISSN)1468–0262.

Wiley for permission to use material from Paul Walker, 'The (Non) theory of the Knowledge Firm', *Scottish Journal of Political Economy*, 57(1) (February, 2010), 1–32. http://onlinelibrary.wiley.com/journal/10.1111/(ISSN)1467–9485.

Wiley for permission to use material from Paul Walker, 'Thc 'Reference Point' Approach to the Theory of the Firm: An Introduction', *Journal of Economic Surveys*, 27(4) (September, 2013), 670–95. http://onlinelibrary.wiley.com/journal/10.1111/(ISSN)1467–6419.

Wiley for permission to use material from Paul Walker, 'Contracts, Entrepreneurs, Market Creation and Judgement: The Contemporary Mainstream Theory of the Firm in Perspective', *Journal of Economic Surveys*, 29(2) (April, 2015), 317–38. http://onlinelibrary.wiley.com/journal/10.1111/(ISSN)1467–6419.

Taylor and Francis for permission to use material from Paul Walker, 'From Complete to Incomplete (Contracts): A Survey of the Mainstream Approach to the Theory of Privatisation', *New Zealand Economic Papers*, 5(2) (June, 2016), 212–29. www.tandfonline.com/toc/rnzp20/current#.VdifrPaqpBd.

A note on the numbering of equations, theorems and figures

The numbering system utilised in the book consists of two numbers $x.y$ where the first number, x, is the page on which the equation, theorem, or figure and so on appears while the second number, y, is the number of the equation, theorem or figure on that page. As an example, Figure 111.3 would be the third figure on page 111.

1 Introduction

Firms[1] are a ubiquitous feature of the economic landscape with much of the activity undertaken within an economy taking place within their boundaries. McMillan (2002: 168–9), for example, estimates that less than a third of all the transactions in the US economy occur through markets, and instead over 70 percent are made within firms. Lafontaine and Slade (2007: 629) state that the "[d]ata on value added, for example, reveal that, in the United States, transactions that occur in firms are roughly equal in value to those that occur in markets". With regard to the number of firms and their importance to employment Otteson (2014: 30) takes the United States as an example and reports that: "[i]n 2008, the United States had some 31.6 million businesses across thousands of industries employing some 120 million people". The scale of activity within firms ranges from that of global giants to that of sole proprietorships. Kikuchi, Nishimura and Stachurski (2012: 2) note that

> [...] in 2011, Royal Dutch Shell operated in over 80 countries, had annual revenue exceeding the GDP of 150 nations, and paid its CEO 35 times more than the president of the United States. In the same year, the total number of employees at Wal-Mart exceeded the population of all but 4 US cities. In addition to such giants, tens of millions of smaller firms operate around the world.

Bowen (1955: 1) highlights the importance of firms to people's well-being by noting that

> The business enterprise is one of the most pervasive and influential institutions of our society, and one in which innumerable important decisions and responses are made. These decisions and responses, in small and large enterprises, are links in the chain of factors determining the range of products available to consumers, the level of national income, the degree of economic security, the rate and direction of economic progress, and the distribution of income. These decisions and responses also significantly influence the character of human relations in industry, the quality of the lives of those who work in industry, and even the power structure of our society.

Micklethwait and Wooldridge (2003: xv) argue that "[t]he most important organization in the world is the company: the basis of the prosperity of the West and the best hope for the future of the rest of the world".

Given the size of the contribution made by firms to economic activity, employment, innovation, growth, income and well-being, having a sophisticated theoretical understanding of the nature and structure of firms is a crucial component of a proper understanding of how an economy functions.[2] And yet

> The theory of the firm has been a neglected area of study in mainstream economics. Despite Ronald Coase bringing the issue up for discussion in 1937, it was not on the research agenda until the 1970s. Even now, as both Coase and Oliver Williamson, the founder of and prominent scholar in the transaction cost-focusing analysis of firm organization, have received the Nobel Prize in economics, the area remains in the periphery of economic analysis.
>
> (Bylund 2011: 189)

This distinct lack of interest by the majority of economists in the theory of the firm has also been commented on by Fleckner (2016: 5, footnote 2),

> Probably the best evidence of the traditional disinterest in the theory of the firm is the fact that the firm has no prominent place, if it is broached at all, in books on the history of economic thought. Two examples: In Sandmo 2011, a new and very readable book, none of the almost 500 pages are devoted to the theory of the firm (the selection of topics is explained on pp. vii, 2–3, 11–2); in Heilbroner 1999, one of the best-selling books in economics of all time, firms are mentioned more frequently, especially those whose shares are publicly traded, but there is no discussion of the issues that are typically associated with the theory of the firm (which, given the broad scope of the book, is not meant to be a criticism; neither Heilbroner nor Sandmo would have been well advised to focus on the firm).

When considering the state of contemporary price theory Coase and Wang (2011: 1) remark

> But the gain in rigor achieved in modern price theory comes with a heavy price tag. The most obvious and serious omission in price theory is that it sees no role for production, let alone entrepreneurship. How goods and services are actually produced, how new goods and services and new ways of production are constantly invented in the economy, how production and innovation are organized, and what forces are at work are rarely on the research agenda in economics. It is extraordinary that the process of production is virtually invisible in economic theory.

While Coase himself commented in a 2013 interview that: "Modern economics shows little interest in production" (Wang 2014: 118). Oliver Hart argues "[...]

that the theory of the firm is one of the less developed and agreed-upon areas of economics" (Hart 2011: 102). With regard to the more general area of organisational economics, for which the theory of the firm is a foundational component, Gibbons and Roberts (2013: 1) say that: "However, organizational economics is not yet a fully recognized field in economics – for example, it has no *Journal of Economic Literature* classification number, and few doctoral programs offer courses in it".

With this book we hope to help remedy this neglect, if only a little, by showing that ongoing developments in the theory of the firm[3] justify moving the analysis of the firm from the margins of economic inquiry to its centre.[4] We aim to do this by providing a short overview of these developments. Our objective is to show how the theory of the firm has been formulated within the 'mainstream'[5] of economics, both 'past' and 'present'. We emphasise the mainstream theory because it is these theories that dominate the teaching of and literature on the theory of the firm. In terms of undergraduate teaching, aspects of the pre-1970 mainstream theory – the 'past' – constitute the most common, often the only, 'theory of the firm' taught to students. Few of the post-1970s advancements have made it into the standard undergraduate economics textbooks. Part of our purpose here is to help address this shortcoming. In graduate courses, and in the research literature, the post-1970 mainstream theories – the 'present' – provide the dominant theoretical frameworks. We aim to offer an accessible and concise introduction to the major theories that make-up the contemporary literature.

An analysis of the past of the theory of the firm is undertaken to help cultivate an understanding of the historical developments that have resulted in the contemporary theories. This inquiry helps to add depth to our knowledge of ideas that are commonly used today but whose origins lie in past debates to do with production and the firm. It also allows us to see how and why changes in thinking took place. We will argue that over time a more sophisticated understanding of firms has been developed, which has in turn led to the development of related areas such as the theory of privatisation. We will also look at some of the possible ways that the mainstream theory of the firm could evolve to continue this trend into the future.

Foss and Klein (2006) have noted that there has been a close relationship between advances in the general economic mainstream and the development of the theory of the firm,

> [...] the evolution of the theory of the firm has never taken place far away from the economic mainstream. On the contrary, it has in fact been much driven by advances in the mainstream, and the relatively limited borrowing from other disciplines that has taken place has usually been strongly adapted to conform to central mainstream tenets. To be sure, the theory of the firm may have been revolutionary in the (somewhat limited) sense of introducing new explanation to economics, but it is generally true to say that it has not been revolutionary in the sense of representing a radical break with any of the main tenets of mainstream economics.
>
> (Foss and Klein 2006: 3–4).

One implication of this is that the heterodox approaches to the firm have had little direct effect on the development of the economic theory of organisations. Thus, this survey's concentration on the mainstream literature may do little damage to the story of the emergence of the theory of the firm but it does mean that little will be said of those non-mainstream or heterodox ideas, such as those from the overlap between economics and management, or the Marxist approaches, or the Austrian inspired theory of the firm, or the relevant contributions from business history, that have developed outside of the orthodoxy.[6]

1970 is used as a convenient, if not entirely accurate, dividing line between what constitutes the 'past' and the 'present' of the theory of the firm since it was around this time that the present mainstream – largely Coaseian based – approaches to the firm started to develop with works such as Williamson (1971, 1973, 1975), Alchian and Demsetz (1972), Jensen and Meckling (1976) and Klein, Crawford and Alchian (1978). The major difference between the mainstream theories of the past and the mainstream theories of the present, at least as far as they are conceived of here, is that the focus – in terms of the questions the theory attempts to answer – of the post-1970 mainstream literature is markedly different from that of the earlier (neoclassical) mainstream theory. The theory of the firm for Ronald Coase, Oliver Williamson, Bengt Holmström or Oliver Hart is a very different thing from that of Arthur Pigou, Lionel Robbins, Jacob Viner, Joan Robinson or Edward Chamberlin.

The questions that the theory seeks to answer have changed from being about how the firm acts in its various markets: how it prices its outputs or how it combines its inputs; to questions about the firm's existence, boundaries – including the boundary between state and private enterprise – and internal organisation. That is, within the mainstream theory there has been a movement away from seeing the theory of the firm as simply developing one component (albeit an important component) of price theory, namely the element concerned with the factor and product market behaviour of producers, to the theory being concerned with the firm as an important economic institution in its own right.

In addition, there are recent contributions to the theory of the firm which exploit ideas that on the surface make it seem as though they are developing an approach which undermines the mainstream theories. But it will be argued in this book that these new theories can be more usefully interpreted as following a course which extends, rather than subverts, the orthodox literature. In particular these contributions allow for the integration of the theory of the entrepreneur[7] with the theory of the firm. Questions to do with the importance of "judgement" (decision making in situations involving Knightian uncertainty[8]) to the role of the entrepreneur with regard to the existence and organisation of firms, as well as the importance of the entrepreneur to the formation of firms, and through them the creation of markets are beginning to be examined.

The rest of this book consists of five more chapters. Chapter 2 examines the 'past' of the theory of the firm. This chapter concentrates mainly on a discussion of the classical theory of production and the development of the neoclassical model of the 'firm'. Consideration is also given to two of the first, be they largely unsuccessful in terms of affecting the trajectory of the mainstream economics literature, theoretical attempts to look inside the 'black box' that is the neoclassical firm. The theories briefly examined are the behavioural and managerial models of the firm. Following on from this comes an outline of Harold Demsetz's, 'non-Coaseian', interpretation of the neoclassical model.

The third chapter of this book consists of a short survey of the founding works – Knight (1921b) and Coase (1937) – on which the present versions of the mainstream theory of the firm are based, while the fourth chapter deals with the 'present' mainstream theories themselves.

The fourth chapter's first section covers the post-1970 Coaseian/Knightian inspired theories of the firm. Within this category two general groups of theories are identified: principal–agent models and incomplete contract models. In both groups, simple formal models of the major contributions are presented. Following on from this we consider three of the more recent contributions to the theory of the firm. Given their recent origins, these theories are not as well known as the other contributions considered in this section and they have yet to be integrated into standard discussions of the theory of the firm. The reference point approach to the firm developed by Hart and Moore (2008) is looked at first with this discussion being followed by an analysis of the theory put forward in Daniel Spulber's book *The Theory of the Firm: Microeconomics with Endogenous Entrepreneurs, Firms, Markets, and Organizations*. The last of the three approaches considered is the 'entrepreneurial judgement' perspective associated with Foss and Klein's 2012 book *Organizing Entrepreneurial Judgment: A New Approach to the Firm*. These contributions offer a number of possible springboards to future advances in the theory of the firm. Specifically it is the last two of these theories that open pathways to the integration of the theory of the entrepreneur with the theory of the firm.

The second section of the fourth chapter involves a discussion of the relationship between the three main contemporary theories of the firm: the reference point, property rights and transaction costs approaches.

The theory of privatisation is concisely summarised in the third section of the fourth chapter. The close relationship between the theory of the firm and the theory of privatisation – that is, both sets of theories are concerned with the boundaries of firms – is emphasised.

The fifth chapter examines the use of partial versus general equilibrium modelling within the contemporary theory of the firm. It is noted that since the 1970s partial equilibrium analysis has come to dominate general equilibrium analysis as the preferred approach to modelling the firm.

The last chapter is the conclusion.

Notes

1 Spulber (2008: 5, footnote 8) gives the origin of the word "firm" as "[t]he word 'firm' derives from the Latin word "firmare" referring to a signature that confirmed an agreement by designating the name of the business".

2 Certainly such a view has been put forward in the past. Bowen (1955: 6–7) argues

> Many economists, but by no means all, believe that greater and more exact knowledge of the decisions and responses of business enterprises would enhance our ability to predict the outcome of changes in basic economic variables and of changes in public policy. For example, it is frequently asserted that if economists knew more about the factors determining rates of investment in enterprises, they should be able to predict the level of national income with greater assurance. Or if they knew more about the goals or motives of enterprises, and the processes by which decisions and actions are related to these goals, they should be able to explain prices and outputs with greater reliability. Similarly, if economists knew more about the responses of enterprises to changes in taxation, interest rates, price control, and public regulations of various kinds, they should be able to offer better advice on economic policies.

3 For much more complete surveys of the literature on the theory of production/the theory of the firm see, in chronological order, Cannan (1917), Wolman (1921), Carlson (1939), Stigler (1941), Boulding (1942), Samuelson (1947), Papandreou (1952), Bowen (1955) [this book contains a relatively comprehensive selected bibliography covering works on the business enterprise in English for the period, roughly, 1940–1955], Boulding (1960), Simon (1962), Cyert and March (1963: chapter 2), Alchian (1965a), Frisch (1965), Dano (1966), Machlup (1967), Ferguson (1969), Cyert and Hedrick (1972), Williamson (1977), Milgrom and Roberts (1988), Tirole (1988: 15–61), Hart (1989), Holmström and Tirole (1989), Wiggins (1991), Moore (1992), Borland and Garvey (1994), Hart (1995), Holmström and Roberts (1998), Foss (2000), Foss, Lando and Thomsen (2000), Khachatrian (2003), Garrouste (2004), Roberts (2004: 74–117), Furubotn and Richter (2005: 361–469), Gibbons (2005), Mahoney (2005), Menard (2005), Garrouste and Saussier (2008), Müller (2009), Aghion and Holden (2011), Hart (2011), Zenger, Felin and Bigelow (2011) and Kállay (2012).

For surveys of the empirical literature see Joskow (1988), Shelanski and Klein (1995), Vannoni (2002), Klein (2005), Lafontaine and Slade (2007) and Hubbard (2008).

Some topics that are often seen as being closely related to the mainstream theory of the firm but which we ignore include issues such as corporate finance and corporate governance. On these issues see Shleifer and Vishny (1997), Bolton and Scharfstein (1998), Zingales (2000), Tirole (2001, 2006) and Hermalin (2013).

For an application of the property rights approach to the firm to corporate tax avoidance see Borek, Frattarelli and Hart (2013). For a survey of joint ventures and the property rights theory of the firm see Gattai and Natale (forthcoming).

The conditions under which different forms of firm ownership are optimal are discussed in Hansmann (1996, 2013), but are not considered here.

Another topic ignored here is the multinational firm; for overviews of this literature see Markusen (1995), Barba Navaretti *et al.* (2004), Gattai (2006) Antràs and Yeaple (2013) and Antràs (2014, 2016).

For an early example of the application of the theory of the firm to farm management research see Schultz (1939). For a discussion of the modern approach to the economics of farms see Allen and Lueck (2002).

In addition, *The Handbook of Organizational Economics* (Gibbons and Roberts 2013) contains a number of chapters relevant to both theoretical and empirical issues to do with the theory of the firm.

4 That a 'theory of the firm' is important to GE is nothing new, this idea has been argued by some since the early days of the neoclassical theory of firm level production. In 1942 Kenneth Boulding wrote:

> These volumes [a reference to Robinson (1933) and Chamberlin (1933)] mark the explicit recognition of the theory of the firm as an integral division of economic

> analysis upon which rests the whole fabric of equilibrium theory. General equilibrium is nothing more than the problem of the interaction of individual economic organisms, under various conditions and assumptions; as a necessary preliminary to its solution, an adequate theory of the individual organism itself is necessary.
>
> (Boulding 1942: 791)

5 Colander, Holt and Rosser (2004: 490) argue that the

> Mainstream consists of the ideas that are held by those individuals who are dominant in the leading academic institutions, organizations, and journals at any given time, especially the leading graduate research institutions. Mainstream economics consists of the ideas that the elite in the profession finds acceptable, where by elite we mean the leading economists in the top graduate schools. It is not a term describing a historically determined school, but is instead a term describing the beliefs that are seen by the top schools and institutions in the profession as intellectually sound and worth working on.

While Dequech (2007: 281) says "[. . .] that mainstream economics is that which is taught in the most prestigious universities and colleges, gets published in the most prestigious journals, receives funds from the most important research foundations, and wins the most prestigious awards". In this survey we do not distinguish the 'orthodoxy' from the 'mainstream'. The terms are used interchangeably in what follows. See Colander, Holt and Rosser (2004, 2005) for a more sophisticated discussion of the concepts which draws a distinction between them.

6 Here the term 'heterodox' is used in a general way to cover dissenting schools of economic thought such as the Austrians, the Evolutionary approach, the (Old) Institutionists, Marxists and Post-Keynesians, among others.

Since the 1990s there has emerged a small Austrian literature on the firm, see for example Dulbecco and Garrouste (1999), Ioannides (1999), Witt (1999), Yu (1999), Lewin and Phelan (2000), Sautet (2000), Jankovic (2010), Bylund (2011, 2014b, 2016) and Carson (2014). For general discussions of this literature see Foss (1994, 1997), Foss and Klein (2009, 2010), Klein (2010), Langlois (2013) and Foss, Klein and Linder (2015).

For discussions of the contributions from the resource-based theory of the firm see Penrose (1959), Wernerfelt (1984), Conner (1991), Lockett, O'Shea and Wright (2008), and Foss and Stieglitz (2010). On influence of E. A. G. Robinson on Penrose (1959) and her impact on the resource-based view see Jacobsen (2013).

On the knowledge-based view see Richardson (1972), Kogut and Zander (1992, 1996), Conner and Prahalad (1996) and Demsetz (1997). For critiques of knowledge-based theories see Foss (1996a, 1996b).

For examples of the capabilities literature see Barney (1991) and Jacobides and Winter (2005).

The most important work in the evolutionary economics approach to the firm can be found in Nelson and Winter (1982).

Any discussion of the insightful but largely neglected paper, Malmgren (1961), is missing from this overview, but see Foss (1996c). The relationship between the work of Malmgren and G. B. Richardson and their impact on the modern approaches to the theory of the firm is discussed in Arena (2011: Chapter 5).

An early discussion of entrepreneurship and vertical integration is given in Silver (1984).

For a discussion of some of the critics of the theory of the firm see Foss and Klein (2008).

Sawyer (1979: Chapter 9) considers 'radical critique and radical alternatives' to the theory of the firm. Sawyer briefly discusses Galbraith's 'theory of countervailing power' (Galbraith 1963), Baran and Sweezy on *Monopoly Capital* (Baran and Sweezy 1966), Rothchild's 'Price Theory and Oligopoly' (Rothchild 1947) and Galbraith's *The New Industrial State* (Galbraith 1969). Hagendorf (2009) gives a Marxian critique of the theory of the competitive firm. The Marxian notion of the 'conflict theory of the firm' is examined in Baker and Weisbrot (1994).

For an overview of research into the growth of firms see Coad (2007, 2009).

From business history comes Alfred D. Chandler's classic works on the origins of the modern large-scale business enterprise, Chandler (1962, 1977, 1990). For a brief history of the development of the limited liability company see Hickson and Turner (2006). Walsh (2009) offers a 'Mengerian theory' of the origins of the modern business firm.

The *Handbook on the Economics and Theory of the Firm* (Dietrich and Krafft 2012) contains a number of chapters covering material not discussed later on.

7

> The word "entrepreneur" originates from a thirteenth-century French verb, entreprendre, meaning "to do something" or "to undertake". By the sixteenth century, the noun form, entrepreneur, was being used to refer to someone who undertakes a business venture. The first academic use of the word by an economist was likely in 1730 by Richard Cantillon, who identified the willingness to bear the personal financial risk of a business venture as the defining characteristic of an entrepreneur. In the early 1800s, economists Jean-Baptiste Say and John Stuart Mill further popularized the academic usage of the word "entrepreneur". Say stressed the role of the entrepreneur in creating value by moving resources out of less productive areas and into more productive ones. Mill used the term "entrepreneur" in his popular 1848 book, Principles of Political Economy, to refer to a person who assumes both the risk and the management of a business. In this manner, Mill provided a clearer distinction than Cantillon between an entrepreneur and other business owners (such as shareholders of a corporation) who assume financial risk but do not actively participate in the day-to-day operations or management of the firm.
>
> (Sobel 2007: 154–5)

In his 1931 English translation of Cantillon (1755) Henry Higgs rendered "entrepreneur" as "undertaker".

8 On the nature of "uncertainty" and the, now famous, difference between it and "risk" Frank Knight has written,

> But Uncertainty must be taken in a sense radically distinct from the familiar notion of Risk, from which it has never been properly separated. The term "risk", as loosely used in everyday speech and in economic discussion, really covers two things which, functionally at least, in their causal relations to the phenomena of economic organization, are categorically different. [...] The essential fact is that "risk" means in some cases a quantity susceptible of measurement, while at other times it is something distinctly not of this character; and there are far-reaching and crucial differences in the bearings of the phenomenon depending on which of the two is really present and operating. [...] It will appear that a *measurable* uncertainty, or "risk" proper, as we shall use the term, is so far different from an *unmeasurable* one that it is not in effect an uncertainty at all. We shall accordingly restrict the term "uncertainty" to cases of the non-quantitative type.
>
> (Knight 1921b: 19–20)

and

> To preserve the distinction which has been drawn in the last chapter between the measurable uncertainty and an unmeasurable one we may use the term "risk" to designate the former and the term "uncertainty" for the latter.
>
> (Knight 1921b: 233)

and

> The practical difference between the two categories, risk and uncertainty, is that in the former the distribution of the outcome in a group of instances is known (either through calculation a priori or from statistics of past experience), while in the case of uncertainty this is not true, the reason being in general that it is impossible to form a group of instances, because the situation dealt with is in a high degree unique.
>
> (Knight 1921b: 233)

Knight's detailed discussion of risk and uncertainty is contained in Chapters VII and VIII of Knight (1921b).

2 The 'past'

The brief overview of the 'past' of the theory of the firm given here consists of a concise discussion of the classical view of production, which does not contain a theory of the firm or even a theory of firm level production, followed by a look at the development of the neoclassical – or textbook – approach to firm level production. The behavioural and managerial models of the firm are discussed next; these being significant since they are some of the first models to look inside the black box that is the neoclassical firm. Finally, there will be a short outline of Harold Demsetz's view of the neoclassical model.

2.1 Background

While it can be argued that the theory of the firm has existed for only 80–90 years, in practice 'firms' have existed for several thousand years.[1,2] Taking ancient India as an example Khanna (2005) argues that the *Sreni* – which was a complex organisational entity that shared similarities with companies, guilds, and producers' cooperatives – was being used as early as 800 BC and was in more or less continuous use from that time until AD 1000, at which time the Islamic invasion of India started.[3]

The *Sreni* were separate legal entities which could hold property separately from their owners, create their own regulations controlling the behaviour of their members, contract, sue and be sued in their own name (Khanna 2005: 8–9). Table 11.1 gives a more detailed summary of characteristics of the *Sreni*. The *Sreni* shares a number of these characteristics with the modern business company. The *Sreni* were utilised in occupations involving workers such as carpenters, ivory workers, bamboo workers, money-lenders, barbers, jewellers and weavers (Khanna 2005: 10).

In other regions of the world firms, of some description, go back much further than 800 BC. Firms were, for example, involved in long-distance trade between the city-state of Assur and Anatolia since at least the beginning of the second millennium BC. Jursa (2014: 27) notes that documents from around 1850 BC detail profit-oriented trade in commodities such as textiles and metals. While the centre of this Old Assyrian trade was the city of Assur, Assyrian traders used a network of around 40 colonies and trading stations in Anatolia to conduct trade (Michel 2008: 78). Assyrian merchants exported expensive woollen textiles, tin and lapis lazuli to Anatolia. These commodities were sold for silver and gold, which was shipped back to Assur.[4]

Table 11.1 Summary of the characteristics of the Sreni (Khanna 2005: Table 1, p. 27; table footnotes removed)

Characteristics	*Present in Ancient Indian Sreni?*
Separate entity	Yes
Centralized management	Yes
Transferability of interest	Probably yes
Limited liability	Probably not
Agent has power to bind entity?	Yes
Management elected?	Yes (though at times appears hereditary)
Can management be removed?	Yes
Duty of loyalty	Probably yes
Duty of care	Yes
Liability insulation	Yes (though apparently not very detailed)
Screens on shareholder suits and internal enforcement activity	Yes (though apparently not very detailed)
Internal rules have binding effect	Yes
Some reimbursement for legal defence	Yes
Formation is easy	Yes
Register with state	Yes
State approval needed	Yes
Use of incentive payments	Yes (though apparently not very detailed)
Entry is easy	Some conditions, but no caste bars.
Sharing of assets and liabilities	Terms of agreement and additional rules
Exit is easy	Yes, but with obligations potentially
Board/committee independence	Probably yes
Other board qualifications	Yes (though apparently not very detailed)
Voting regulation	Yes (though apparently not very detailed)
Open debate in meetings & shareholder resolutions	Yes, with some limits (though apparently not very detailed)
Transparency is valuable and disclosure is encouraged	Probably yes (though apparently not very detailed)

The institutions of trading have been well documented.

> Most of these traders had become more independent by having become managers of a "joint-stock fund" (called *naruqqum*, "money bag"), usually set up in Assur. This phenomenon appeared for the first time around 1900 BC and seems to have been an Old Assyrian invention that went beyond individual partnerships and cooperation in a joint caravan. The arrangement, rather similar to that of the early medieval *compagnia*, meant enlisting a number (usually about a dozen) of investors (*ummiānum*, "financiers"), who supplied capital rated in gold, usually in all ca. 30 kilos, ideally consisting of shares of 1 or 2 kilos of gold each. It was entrusted to a trader (the *tractator*), usually for ca. ten years, for the generally formulated purpose of "carrying out trade". The contract contained stipulations on a final settlement of accounts, on paying dividends, on the division of the expected profit, and on fines for premature withdrawal of capital (meant to secure the duration of the business). Investors or shareholders

mostly lived in Assur, but successful traders in Anatolia too invested in funds managed by others, perhaps also as a way of sharing commercial risks. In such cases a contract would to be drawn up in Anatolia that obliged the *tractator* "to book in Assur x gold in his joint-stock fund in the investor's name". Among the investors we find members of the *tractator's* family, but also business relations and others, probably a kind of "merchant-bankers", and other rich citizens, who aimed at fairly safe, long-term investments.

(Veenhof 2010: 55)

Silver (1995: 50) notes that,

Private firms (bītātu) were prominent in late-third-millennium Akkad (the region south of Baghdad), in the Old Assyrian trade with Cappadocia [. . .] and, somewhat later, at Nippur. In the mid-second millennium the firm of Tehip-tilla played a major role in the real estate transactions and other business activities at Nuzi. A list of about the some time from Alalakh in northwest Syria refers to sixty-four firms participating in leatherworking, jewelry, and carpentry.

Turning to the nature of firms in ancient Greece there were some relatively large 'firms' but they were few in number (Bresson 2014: 45). Most of the commercial operations that did exist were small and of limited duration. The (in theory) infinitely lived firm did not exist, partners would agree to cooperate for just a single business operation. Although there may have been many investors or several active partners, their cooperation lasted for only one voyage or one operation. The development of permanent firms for commerce was unnecessary since low transaction costs meant that market transactions were sufficient for business operations. If looking for 'firms' in ancient Greece, then they were more easily found in the rural sector. Farms were longer lived, hierarchical organisations, often family owned and operated with a slave workforce (Bresson 2014: 57–9).[5]

Sobel (1999: 21) points out that during the Roman Republic contracting out of economic activities to private firms was the norm:

The republican Senate left virtually all economic activities to private individuals and companies, known collectively as the publicani. Tax collection, supplying the army, providing for religious sacrifices and ceremonies, building construction and repair, mining, and so on were all contracted out. There was even a contract for summoning the assembly in session and one for feeding the sacred geese.

Micklethwait and Wooldridge (2003: 4) also note the private nature of tax collection in Rome, pointing out that 'companies' were formed for this, and other purposes:[6]

The *societates* of Rome, particularly those organized by tax farming *publicani*, were slightly more ambitious affairs. To begin with, tax collecting was entrusted to individual Roman knights; but as the empire grew, the levies became

> more than any one noble could guarantee, and by the Second Punic War (218–202 B.C.), they began to form companies – *societates* – in which each partner had a share. These firms also found a role as the commercial arm of conquest, grinding out shields and swords for the legions. Lower down the social scale, craftsmen and merchants gathered together to form guilds (*collegia* or *corpora*) that elected their own managers and were supposed to be licensed.

Some of these ancient firms were of reasonable size. Silver (1995: 66–7) notes, "We may note here that during the Ur III period a new mill at Girsu required the services of 679 women and 86 men (Maekawa 1980: 98)" and "A number of cities possessed large workshops employing hundreds of women in spinning and weaving. For example, a late-third-millennium text from Eshnunna lists 585 female and 105 male employees in a weaving house" (Silver 1995: 143). With regard to the size of firms in ancient Greece Bresson (2014: 45) writes "[. . .] large [handicraft] workshops, with possibly a few dozen workers (sometimes up to 120 as in the case of the metic Kephalos in Athens in the fourth century, as mentioned by Lysias 12.19 [Todd 2000]) could indeed exist, but they were rare".

Ancient firms also diversified their activities.

> Large commercial houses flourished in Babylonia from the seventh to the fourth century. The House of Egibi, for example, bought and sold houses, fields, and slaves, took part in domestic and international trade, and participated in a wide variety of banking activities.
>
> [. . .]
>
> Earlier, in the late third-millennium Sumer, the rulers and governors controlled vertically integrated firms that used wool of the sheep they raised in their weaving workshops. At the same time, an Umma businessman (- bureaucrat?) named Ur-e-e busied himself with manifold operations, including raising livestock; transactions involving cheese, oil, leather, carcasses, wool; the weaving and finishing of cloth; shipments by boat of fish and grain; and even the construction of boats.
>
> (Silver 1995: 67)

Thus the 'firm' is an ancient and important empirical feature of the economic landscape but a feature which has been largely overlooked by economic theorists. The dichotomy between theory and practice could not be more stark. Even the most cursory of examination of the development of the contemporary theory of the firm would reveal that theorists have not long considered firms to be important economic entities. As Foss, Lando and Thomsen (2000: 632) note:

> It is only relatively recently, [. . .], that economists have felt the need for an economic theory addressing the reasons for the existence of the institution

> known as the (multi-person) business firm, its boundaries relative to the market, and its internal organization – to mention the issues that are generally seen as the main ones in the modern economics of organization [...].

Foss and Klein (2006: 6) also note that the theory of the firm has been a neglected area of study in economics until quite recent times,

> [...] few economists were working on the development of theories of the firm, in the modern sense, until recently. And if we by "economic theory" understands what has been called "mainstream economics", "neoclassical economics", "microeconomics", etc., it is hard to dispute that economic organization was in general a much neglected subject area until relatively recently in the history of economic doctrines.

Such neglect has resulted in a situation in which the theories of the firm that do exist can be, and are, criticised for being rudimentary and bearing little relationship to the organisations that we see in the world. With regard to the state of the modern theory of the firm Oliver Hart has written,

> An outsider to the field of economics would probably take it for granted that economists have a highly developed theory of the firm. After all, firms are the engines of growth of modern capitalistic economies, and so economists must surely have fairly sophisticated views of how they behave. In fact, little could be further from the truth. Most formal models of the firm are extremely rudimentary, capable only of portraying hypothetical firms that bear little relation to the complex organizations we see in the world. Furthermore, theories that attempt to incorporate real world features of corporations, partnerships and the like often lack precision and rigour, and have therefore failed, by and large, to be accepted by the theoretical mainstream.
>
> (Hart 1989: 1757)[7]

This lack of an adequate theory of the firm, or even an adequate theory of firm level production, is an issue that had been commented on long before the late-1980s, albeit to no avail. More than 80 years before Hart, when surveying the history of the theory of production, Edwin Cannan argued that,

> Before the middle of the eighteenth century a theory of production can scarcely be said to have existed. Durable objects being looked upon as the sole or chief kind of wealth, the functions of industry and trade seemed to be the 'circulation' of wealth. When the physiocratic school turned the attention of economists to the consumable goods obtained by means of agriculture, the idea of circulation gave way to the idea of an annual reproduction, which gradually grew into the modern conception of production and consumption.
>
> (Cannan 1917: 28–9)

Cannan also explains that " 'production' and 'distribution' do not seem, however, to have been used in England before 1821 as titles of divisions of political economy; and, before Adam Smith wrote, they were not in any sense technical economic terms" (Cannan 1917: 26).[8]

But the theories of production that Cannan analysed were not theories of the firm, if we use the current mainstream approaches to modelling firms as the definition of such theories.[9] It was noted by Cannan that

> One of the most familiar and striking features of the theory of production, as taught in the text-books of the second half of the nineteenth century, is the practice of ascribing production to the co-operation or concurrence or joint use of three great agents, instruments, or requisites of production, Labour, land, and capital.
>
> (Cannan 1917: 32)

Such an approach has more in common with the later neoclassical production function[10] approach to production than the Coaseian inspired approaches utilised in the current mainstream theories of the firm.

The theories that Cannan was discussing aimed to explain the creation, and distribution, of the wealth of a nation[11] rather than explaining the existence, boundaries and organisation of firms.[12] Therefore the theories being analysed are macroeconomic theories of the production of an entire economy rather than microeconomic theories of firm production. O'Brien (2003: 112) remarks that

> Classical economics ruled economic thought for about 100 years [roughly 1770–1870]. It focused on macroeconomic issues and economic growth. Because the growth was taking place in an open economy, with a currency that (except during 1797–1819) was convertible into gold, the classical writers were necessarily concerned with the balance of payments, the money supply, and the price level. Monetary theory occupied a central place, and their achievements in this area were substantial and – with their trade theory – are still with us today.

Foss and Klein (2006: 7–8) note that classical economics was largely carried out at the aggregate level with microeconomic analysis acting as little more than a handmaiden to the macro-level investigation,

> Economics began to a large extent in an aggregative mode, as witness, for example, the "Political Arithmetick" of Sir William Petty, and the dominant interest of most of the classical economists in distribution issues. Analysis of pricing, that is to say, analysis of a phenomenon on a lower level of analysis than distributional analysis, was to a large extent only a means to an end, namely to analyze the functional income distribution.

O'Brien (2004: 63) makes the same basic point by noting the differences in emphasis between classical and neoclassical economics:

> The core of neo-Classical economics is the theory of microeconomic allocation, to which students are introduced in their first year in an elementary and largely intuitive form, and which receives increasingly sophisticated statements during succeeding years of study. On top of this, as a sort of icing on the cake, comes the macroeconomics theory of income determination, with, in little attached boxes so to speak, theories of growth and trade appended. But the approach of the Classical economists was the very reverse of this. For them the central propositions of economics concerned macroeconomic problems. Their focus above all was on the problem of growth, and the macroeconomic distribution conclusions which followed from their view of growth. On the one hand, international trade, at least for Smith, was inextricably bound up with all this: on the other, the microeconomic problems of value and microdistribution took their place as subsets of the greater whole.

Lionel Robbins remarked that the classical theories of production and distribution were about determining the total wealth, or total product, of the nation:

> The traditional approach to Economics, at any rate among English-speaking economists, has been by way of an enquiry into the causes determining the production and distribution of wealth. [A footnote at this point refers the reader to Cannan (1917) for more information.] Economics has been divided into two main divisions, the theory of production and the theory of distribution, and the task of these theories has been to explain the causes determining the size of the "total product" and the causes determining the proportions in which it is distributed between different factors of production and different persons.
>
> (Robbins 1935: 64)

As an example of a missed opportunity to construct a classical economics based theory of the firm consider Adam Smith who opens his magnum opus, *An Inquiry into the Nature and Causes of The Wealth of Nations*, with a discussion of the division of labour[13] at the microeconomic level, the famous pin factory example,[14] but quickly moves the analysis to the market level.[15] When discussing Smith's approach to the division of labour[16] McNulty (1984: 237–8) comments,

> Having conceptualized division of labor in terms of the organization of work within the enterprise, however, Smith subsequently failed to develop or even to pursue systematically that line of analysis. His ideas on the division of labor could, for example, have led him toward an analysis of task assignment, management, or organization. Such an intra-firm approach would have foreshadowed the much later – indeed, quite recent – efforts in this direction by Herbert Simon, Oliver Williamson, Harvey Leibenstein, and others, a body

> of work which Leibenstein calls "micro-microeconomics". [. . .] But, instead, Smith quickly turned his attention away from the internal organization of the enterprise, and outward toward the market and the realm of exchange, perhaps because he found therein both the source of division of labor, in the "propensity in human nature . . . to truck, barter and exchange" and its effective limits.

Another such missed opportunity is when, from the third edition on, Smith discusses 'joint-stock companies'. When considering the internal organisation of such firms Smith raises, but does not develop a theory of, what we would call today, the principal–agent problems that arise from the separation of ownership from control. Perhaps his most famous remark is,

> The directors of such companies, however, being the managers rather of other people's money than of their own, it cannot well be expected, that they should watch over it with the same anxious vigilance with which the partners in a private copartnery frequently watch over their own. Like the stewards of a rich man, they are apt to consider attention to small matters as not for their master's honour, and very easily give themselves a dispensation from having it. Negligence and profusion, therefore, must always prevail, more or less, in the management of the affairs of such a company.
>
> (Smith 1776: Book V, Chapter 1, Part III, 741)

But "[. . .] Smith neither used the modern terms, 'agency' or 'corporate governance', nor developed a general theory – a fact that is often overlooked" (Fleckner 2016: 22).

Blaug (1958: 226) summed up the classical economics approach to the firm by arguing that the classical economists simply "[. . .] had no theory of the firm",[17] and as will be argued later on the neoclassical economists did little better in terms of a genuine theory of the firm. Kenneth Arrow explains,

> In classical theory, from Smith to Mill, fixed coefficients in production are assumed. In such a context, the individual firm plays little role in the general equilibrium of the economy. The scale of any one firm is indeterminate, but the demand conditions determine the scale of the industry and the demand by the industry for inputs. The firm's role is purely passive, and no meaningful boundaries between firms are established.
>
> (Arrow 1971: 68)

He went on to add, with regard to the (general equilibrium) neoclassical model,

> When Walras first gave explicit formulation to the grand vision of general equilibrium, he took over intact the fixed-coefficient assumptions and therewith the passive nature of the firm. In the last quarter of the nineteenth century, J. B. Clark, Wicksteed, Barone, and Walras himself recognized the possibility

> of alternative production activities in the form of the production function. However, so long as constant returns to scale were assumed, the size of the firm remained indeterminate. The firm did have now, even in equilibrium, a somewhat more active role than in earlier theory; it at least had the responsibility of minimizing costs at given output levels.
>
> (Arrow 1971: 68)

This does raise the obvious question as to why economists ignored the firm, as an important economic institution in its own right, for so long.[18] One reason for the neglect of the firm is simply that for a long time economists did not see economic theory as being relevant to business or saw the internal workings of the firm to be outside the competence of economists. Edwin Cannan saw the usefulness of economics as being in politics rather than business, "[t]he practical usefulness of economic theory is not in private business but in politics, and I for one regret the disappearance of the old name 'political economy', in which that truth was recognised" (Cannan 1902: 60). With regard to the relationship between economic theory and business Cannan wrote,

> I do not mean to argue that a knowledge of economic theory will enable a man to conduct his private business with success. Doubtless many of the particular subjects of study which come under the head of economics are useful in the conduct of business, but I doubt if economic theory itself is. [...] economic theory does not tell a man the exact moment to leave off the production of one thing and begin that of another; it does not tell him the precise moment when prices have reached the bottom or the top. It is, perhaps, rather likely to make him expect the inevitable to arrive far sooner than it actually does, and to make him underrate, not the foresight, but the want of foresight of the rest of the world.
>
> (Cannan 1902: 459–60)

Cannan was not alone in making this type of argument, the Cambridge economist Arthur Pigou wrote:

> [...] it is not the business of economists to teach woollen manufacturers how to make and sell wool, or brewers how to make and sell beer, or any other business men how to do their job. If that was what we were out for, we should, I imagine, immediately quit our desks and get somebody – doubtless at a heavy premium, for we should be thoroughly inefficient – to take us into his woollen mill or his brewery.
>
> (Pigou 1922: 463–4)

Lionel Robbins argued similarly, in that[19]

> The technical arts of production are simply to be grouped among the *given* factors influencing the relative scarcity of different economic goods.

> The technique of cotton manufacture [. . .] is no part of the subject-matter of Economics [. . .].
>
> (Robbins 1935: 33)

Foss and Klein (2006: 6–7) argue that there is the possibility of an empirical reason for the firm being overlooked; the relative unimportance of the firm. Until relatively recently firms were simply not a large part of the economy. But they also point out that such an explanation is not wholly convincing. Large firms[20] have existed since before the time of Adam Smith and the classical economists knew this. A more precise, and more defensible, version of the argument would be that the large, vertically integrated and diversified firm was not empirically important until recently. Thus analysing anonymous 'firms'[21] may not have been a bad approximation to the empirical realities of the time. But the evidence presented previously on the size and diversified nature of ancient firms as well as the size of some pre-industrial revolution firms (see Chapter note 20, p. 40) should give us cause for reflection before accepting this conclusion without some reservations.

2.2 Neoclassical

For whatever reason, it is certainly true that it is only in more recent times that the firm has attracted serious attention in terms of its role as an important part of the economic system. Many would date the beginning of a genuine theory of the firm, at its earliest, from either Knight (1921b) or Coase (1937), rather than to either the classical school or the neoclassical revolution.[22]

Before the contributions of Knight and Coase we had discussions of pin factories, but the discussion was about the importance of the division of labour rather than being 'an enquiry into the nature and causes of the firm'.[23] As noted previously, the classical economists[24] followed Adam Smith in neglecting 'micro-microeconomics' in favour of a more 'macro' based approach.

In the period following the classical economists, with the possible exception of Alfred Marshall, few economists wrote anything much on the firm. When reviewing the contribution of the old institutionalists to the theory of the firm Hodgson (2012: 55) writes, "[. . .] we search in vain for a well-defined 'theory of the firm' within the old institutional economics". Carl M. Guelzo argues that one of the leading old institutionalists, John R. Commons, "[. . .] did not construct a rigorous theory of the firm since this was never his purpose" (Guelzo 1976: 45). With reference to the German historical school Le Texier (2013: 80) writes

> [m]embers of the German historical school such as Gustav von Schmoller analysed at length the birth and growth of the business enterprise, but they were more historians than economists. None of these thinkers proposed a theory of the business firm.

When writing about the work of Joseph Schumpeter, Hanappi (2012: 62) says "[a] well-defined theory of the firm thus cannot be found in Schumpeter's oeuvres". As to Austrian economics Per Bylund writes, "[b]ut despite the focus in Austrian economics on [...] "mundane economics", and the fact that "the Austrians [have] so many necessary ingredients for a theory of the firm" [...], there is no Austrian theory of the firm" (Bylund 2011: 191) and "[w]hereas the theory of the firm has been a neglected area of study in mainstream economics, it has been missing from the Austrian economics literature" (Bylund 2011: 191). Hutchison (1953: 308) comments "[t]he Austrian School, with the exception of Auspitz and Lieben, did not concern themselves much with the analysis of markets and firms, except in respect to their general principle of imputation". Hutchison also summarised the early neoclassical contributions to the theory of the firm, and markets, as

> Jevons has little on the firm. [...] Walras's assumptions of perfect competition (maintained virtually throughout) and of fixed technical 'coefficients', limited his contribution to the analysis of firms and markets, [...]. Pareto's contribution to the theory of firms and markets were not rounded off, and of very varying value [...]
>
> (Hutchison 1953: 307)

As has been pointed out by Demsetz (1982, 1988a, 1995), before Knight and Coase – and it could be added for much of the period after them – the fundamental preoccupation of (micro-) economists was with the market and the price system and hence little, or no, attention was paid to either the firm or the consumer as separate, significant, economic entities. Firms (and consumers) existed as handmaidens to the price system.

The interest in the price system, culminating in the (neoclassical) 'perfect competition' model, has its intellectual origins in the eighteenth-century debate between free traders and mercantilists. Butler (2007: 25–6) briefly sums up mercantilism in the following way:[25]

> [...] it measured national wealth in terms of a country's stock of gold and silver. Importing goods from abroad was seen as damaging because it meant that this supposed wealth must be given up to pay for them; exporting goods was seen as good because these precious metals came back. Trade benefited only the seller, not the buyer; and one nation could get richer only if others got poorer. On the basis of this view, a vast edifice of controls was erected in order to prevent the nation's wealth draining away – taxes on imports, subsidies to exporters and protection for domestic industries. [...] Indeed, all commerce was looked upon with suspicion and the culture of protectionism pervaded the domestic economy too. Cities prevented artisans from other towns moving in to ply their trade; manufacturers and merchants petitioned the king for protective monopolies; labour saving devices such as the new stocking-frame were banned as a threat to existing producers.

The extent of government control of the mercantile economy is illustrated by Appleby (2010: 40) with the example of the granting of monopolies in seventeenth-century England,

> King James I found in the granting of monopolies a particularly facile way of increasing his income. As one scholar has reported in the early seventeenth century a typical Englishman lived "in a house built with monopoly bricks ... heated by monopoly coal. His clothes are held up with monopoly belts, monopoly buttons, monopoly pins ... He ate monopoly butter, monopoly currants, monopoly red herrings, monopoly salmon, monopoly lobsters".[26] The holders of monopolies have the exclusive rights to sell these items and charged as much as people would pay for them.

The free trade versus mercantilism debate was, to a large degree, about the proper scope of government in the economy[27] and the model it (eventually) gave rise to reflects this. The question implicitly at the centre of the debate was: Is central planning necessary to avoid the problems of a chaotic economic system? Adam Smith famously answered 'no'.[28] Smith

> [...] realised that social harmony would emerge naturally as human beings struggled to find ways to live and work with each other. Freedom and self-interest need not lead to chaos, but – as if guided by an 'invisible hand' – would produce order and concord. They would also bring about the most efficient possible use of resources. As free people struck bargains with others – solely in order to better their own condition – the nation's land, capital, skills, knowledge, time, enterprise and inventiveness would be drawn automatically and inevitably to the ends and purposes that people valued most highly. Thus, the maintenance of a prospering social order did not require the continued supervision of kings and ministers. It would grow organically as a product of human nature.
>
> (Butler 2007: 27–8)

For Smith competitive markets were the most effective mechanism for coordinating and motivating people to maximise the gains that result from increased specialisation and an expanded division of labour. Well functioning market institutions leave individuals free to pursue self-interested behaviour, but guide their choices by the prices they pay and receive. For economists, the 200 years following Smith involved a search for conditions under which the price system would function well, conditions under which it would not descend into chaos.

The formal (neoclassical) model that arose from this search is one which abstracts completely away from any form of centralised or institutional control in the economy.[29] It is a model, as Harold Demsetz has explained, that is delineated by 'perfect decentralisation' (Demsetz 1982, 1988a).[30] Authority, be it in the form of a government or a firm or a household, plays no role in coordinating resources.[31] The only parameters guiding decision making are those given within the model – tastes and technologies – and those determined impersonally on markets – prices. All parameters are outside the control of any of the economic agents and this effectively deprives all forms of authority a role in resource allocation. This includes, of course, the firm. It does not matter whether it is the general equilibrium version of the neoclassical model, characterised by Walras's tatônnement process, or the partial equilibrium version, characterised by Pigou's equilibrium firm, there is no serious consideration given to the firm as a problem solving institution.[32]

Like so much of neoclassical economics, it was Alfred Marshall who began the developments that resulted in the (partial equilibrium) neoclassical theory of the firm. It was Marshall's notion of the 'representative firm' that began a controversy that led to the development of the now common textbook theory of the firm. For Marshall firms were dynamic, heterogeneous, in disequilibrium; they progressed through a life cycle in much the same way as people. "They began young and vigorous, but after a period of maturity they became old and were displaced by newer more efficient firms" (Backhouse 2002: 179). Marshall gave us the famous metaphor of an industry being like a forest – while it might appear unchanged if considered as a whole, the individual trees that make it up are constantly changing. To reconcile his dynamic view of individual firms with the static view of industries Marshall introduced his (nebulous) idea of a 'representative firm'. The representative firm is "composed of the salient characteristics of all firms in the industry" (Moss 1984a: 308).[33]

> It would need to be in some sense 'representative' both of the cost and of the sales position of other firms within the industry. For this to be true it would need to be 'representative' with respect to its business ability, age, luck, size and its access to net external economies.
>
> (Williams 1978: 102)[34]

Or as D. H. Macgregor put it

> The firm which is to be regarded as our unit is the "representative" firm, the structure which is typical of a period of economic development, which has access to all the normal economies of that period, and is of the size which is suited to their most efficient use. It has had a "fairly long life, and fair success", is "managed with normal ability", while its size takes account of "the class of goods produced, the conditions of marketing them, and the economic environment generally."
>
> (Macgregor 1906: 9)

For Marshall his theory of the firm sought to rationalise his studies of real world firms while the idea of the industry was an abstract concept under the umbrella of which the various producers of goods and services could be grouped to facilitate the analysis of the matter under investigation. The role of the representative firm was to link the dynamic view of the firm with the abstract view of the industry.[35] The representative firm has been seen as a forerunner of the representative agent, the role of which is to stand in for the behaviour of the 'group', meaning the industry for Marshall and the economy for those utilising the representative agent (Blankenburg and Harcourt 2007: 46, Hartley 1996).

Moss (1984a,b) argues that there were three crucial steps in the movement from the Marshallian to the now 'textbook' view of the firm. The first step began with the publication of *Wealth and Welfare* by A. C. Pigou. Pigou utilised a formalisation of Marshall's industrial taxonomy, that is the distinction between constant, increasing and decreasing returns to scale industries, to study the effect of these industries on the 'national dividend'. Pigou applied this taxonomy in *Wealth and Welfare* (published in 1912) and in the first edition of *The Economics of Welfare* (1920) in a wholly abstract manner and this abstract analysis was the target of Clapham's (1922) attack on Marshall and Pigou. Clapham argued that it was not in general possible to assign actual industries to any one of the three categories. If we were to open these conceptual 'boxes', Clapham asked, would we find anything 'real' inside?

Sraffa (1926) also raised two objections to Marshall's theory.[36] Robinson (1971: 19) explains,

> We have already seen that supply-and-demand analysis, despite its status as the textbook introduction to all price situations, if taken literally, really applies only to the special case of pure competition (that being the only case in which the back-ground of the supply curve can be explained). In brief, Sraffa's argument was this: 1) this supply-and-demand, pure-competition package relies excessively on the law of diminishing returns, while at the same time it is blind to the observed fact of increasing returns; 2) the resulting analysis is based on such restrictive assumptions as to have little application to real-life situations.

With regard to increasing returns Sraffa argued that Marshall failed to show that increasing returns to scale are compatible with perfect competition. The problem for the static theory of industry is that a firm that faces a given price and produces under (internal) increasing returns to scale will increase its output without limit. If one firm expands to the point that it captures the whole market, then what are we to make of perfect competition? In today's terminology this is the problem of natural monopoly.[37] Assuming external increasing returns to scale meant reliance on a class of returns that were "seldom to be met with" (Sraffa 1926: 540).

For the case of decreasing returns to scale, Sraffa (1926: 538–9) argued that such returns, and thus rising marginal cost and supply curves, are incompatible with partial equilibrium analysis.[38] First, he noted that for perfect competition we require that it must be possible to draw each of the demand and supply curves in such a manner that both the shape and position of the curves are unaffected by movements along the other curve. But this mutual independence of supply and demand curves cannot be assumed if the production of a given commodity employs a considerable part of an input that is fixed in quantity. For any increase in the production of the commodity, there will be a corresponding increase of the unit price of the fixed factor, which is due to the competition for that input from other goods that utilise it. Thus, the prices of these other goods, be they substitutes or complements, will increase and this will alter the conditions of demand for the original good.

If, on the other hand, the first commodity employs just a small fraction of the available amount of the fixed factor, then any increase in its use will have little effect on the factor's price or the average cost of production. This means that under perfect competition it is difficult to account for either an increasing average cost curve or an increasing marginal cost curve. This in turn implies that upward sloping supply curves are difficult to rationalise under perfect competition. A more modern way of saying this is to note that perfect competition applies to the input markets as well as the output markets, and thus an industry is able to purchase its inputs at the market price which is independent of that industry's output. If all industries expand output, then we get decreasing returns. However, this assumption violates the *ceteris paribus* assumption because the one thing being kept constant is the output of other industries.[39]

Robinson (1971: 20) counters Sraffa's argument by noting two points. First, he notes that in the short-run, at least, a firm's stock of plant and equipment is fixed and this fact is enough to ensure, assuming a sufficient increase in the firm's level of output, higher per-unit costs; that is, diminishing returns. Second, Robinson explains that Sraffa's argument of the long-run amounts to little more than the claim that the long-run pure-competition supply curve is (approximately) flat.

As part of a response to Clapham's claim of empirical irrelevance and Sraffa's claim of logical incoherence, Pigou argued that to carry out comparative static analysis "Marshall's highly complex analytical starting point in a population of heterogeneous disequilibrium firms was, strictly speaking, unnecessary. Pigou insisted on the possibility-and, indeed, desirability-of eliminating this complexity" (Foss 1994a: 1121). Pigou's response is the second of Moss's three steps and, importantly, involved Pigou introducing, as a way to help 'eliminate complexity', the 'equilibrium firm'. In Pigou (1928: 239–40) he describes the equilibrium firm, at some length, as[40]

> Most industries are made up of a number of firms, of which at any moment some are expanding, while others are declining. Marshall, it will be remembered, likens them to trees in a forest. Thus, even when the conditions of demand are constant and the output of an industry as a whole is correspondingly constant, the output of many individual firms will not be constant. The industry as a whole will be in a state of equilibrium; the tendencies to expand and contract on the part of the individual firms will cancel out; but it is certain that many individual firms will not themselves be in equilibrium and possible that none will be. When conditions of demand have changed and the necessary adjustments have been made, the industry as a whole will, we may suppose, once more be in equilibrium, with a different output and, perhaps, a different normal supply price; but, again, many, perhaps all, the firms contained in it, though their tendencies to expand and contract must cancel one another, will, as individuals, be out of equilibrium. This is evidently a state of things the direct study of which would be highly complicated. Fortunately, however, there is a way round. Since, when the output of the industry as a whole is adjusted to any given state of demand, the tendencies to expansion

> and contraction on the part of individual firms cancel out, they may properly be regarded as irrelevant so far as the supply schedule of the industry as a whole is concerned. When the conditions of demand change, the output and the supply price of the industry as a whole must change in exactly the same way as they would do if, both in the original and in the new state of demand, all the firms contained in it were individually in equilibrium. This fact gives warrant for the conception of what I shall call the *equilibrium firm*. It implies that there *can* exist some one firm, which, whenever the industry as a whole is in equilibrium, in the sense that it is producing a regular output y in response to a normal supply price p, will itself also individually be in equilibrium with a regular output x_r. The conditions of the industry are compatible with the existence of such a firm; and the implications about these conditions, which, whether it in fact exists or not, would hold good if it did exist, must be valid. For the purpose of studying these conditions, therefore, it is legitimate to speak of it as actually existing. For any given output, then, of the industry as a whole, the supply price of the industry as a whole must be equal to the price, which, with the then output of the industry as a whole, leaves the equilibrium firm in equilibrium. The industry, therefore, conforms to the law of increasing, constant or decreasing supply prices according as the price which leaves the equilibrium firm in equilibrium increases, remains constant, or decreases with increases in the output of the industry as a whole.

The construct of the equilibrium firm allowed Pigou to utilise marginal and average cost curve diagrams to develop the idea of industries producing under increasing returns, which were characterised by economies of scale that are external to the firm but internal to the industry.

Pigou in his 1928 paper 'An Analysis of Supply' also outlined the conditions for a firm being in equilibrium which, significantly, involves all of the internal economies of scale being exhausted so that all economies had to be external. Pigou maintained that the equilibrium firm produced at its minimum efficient scale so that the output level of the equilibrium firm, for a many-firm industry, would occur where the marginal cost curve cuts the average cost curve (i.e. $p = \frac{F(y)}{y} = F'(y)$) (Pigou 1928: 254).[41]

The last of the three steps was to assume that industries are comprised entirely of equilibrium firms with identical cost curves, and to assume that firms, as production functions,[42] faced household preference (demand) functions. This task was carried out by Robinson (1933) and Chamberlin (1933)[43] in their development of imperfect competition and monopolistic competition, respectively.[44] But as Moss (1984a: 314) points out,

> By assuming that every firm in the industry has an identical cost curve, Robinson and Chamberlin stood Pigou's construction of the equilibrium firm on its head. Where Pigou argued that an equilibrium firm could be derived from the laws of returns obeyed by any particular industry, Robinson and Chamberlin defined the industry on the basis of a population of equilibrium firms.

Thus, by the 1930s the neoclassical approach[45] to the firm had developed.[46] But many economists would argue that the neoclassical model is not a 'theory of the firm' in any meaningful sense.[47] The output side of the standard neoclassical model is a theory of supply or production rather than a true theory of the firm. In neoclassical theory, the firm is a 'black box' which is there to explain how changes in inputs lead to changes in outputs.[48] The firm is a conceptualisation that represents, formally, the actions of the owners of inputs who place their inputs in the highest value uses, and makes sure that production is separated from consumption. The firm produces only for outsiders, there is no on-the-job or internal consumption, no self-sufficiency. In fact there are no managers or employees to indulge in on the job consumption and as production is separated from consumption, no self-sufficiency. Production for outsiders is, according to Demsetz (1995), the definition of a firm in the neoclassical model:

> What is needed is a concept of the firm in which production is exclusively for sale to those formally outside the firm. This requirement defines the firm (for neoclassical theory), but it has little to do with the management of some by others. The firm in neoclassical theory is no more or less than a specialized unit of production, but it can be a one-person unit.
>
> (Demsetz 1995: 9)

As inputs are combined in the optimal fashion by the actions of independent input owners motivated solely by market prices, there is no need for 'management of some by others', there is no role for managers or employees. Also note that as competition assures the absence of profits and losses in (long-run) equilibrium, there is no need to have a residual claimant. This means that, in one sense at least, there are no owners of the firm.[49] As there are no physical assets controlled by the firm, there are no (residual) control rights over these assets to allocate. This implies there are no owners of the firm in the Grossman-Hart-Moore sense.

The neoclassical production function is a way of representing the black box conversion of inputs into outputs but it tells us little about the inner workings of the black box. The production function is independent of the institutional framework of output creation. Thus, it represents the 'firm' without explaining the 'firm'.

That the theory cannot explain the boundaries of the firm has been noted by several authors. Williamson (1993: 4), for example, asks,

> What determines which activities a firm chooses to do for itself and which it procures from others?
>
> A simple answer to that question is that the natural boundaries of the firm are defined by technology—economies of scale, technological non-separabilities, and the like. The firm-as-production function is in this tradition. [. . .] In mundane terms, the issue is that of make-or-buy. What is it that determines which transactions are executed how?

> That posed a deep puzzle for which the firm-as-production function approach had little to contribute.

In a discussion of the neoclassical model with regard to its application to the modelling of global production Antràs (2016: 13–14) adds that,

> [. . .] if firms could foresee all possible future contingencies, and if they could costlessly write contracts that specify in an enforceable manner the course of action to be taken in all of these possible contingencies, then firms would no longer need to worry about "controlling" the workers, the internal divisions, or the supplying firms with whom they interact in production. The complete contract would in fact confer *full* control to the firm regardless of the ownership structure that governs the transactions between all these producers. In other words, and as Coase (1937) anticipated more than seventy-five years ago, firm boundaries are indeterminate in a world of complete contracts.

Hart (1995: 17) criticises the neoclassical model based on three characteristics of the theory. First, he notes that the theory completely ignores incentive problems within the firm. The firm is a perfectly efficient 'black box'. Second, the theory has nothing to say about the internal organisation of the firm. Nothing is said about the hierarchical structure, how decisions are made, who has authority within a firm. Third, the theory tells us nothing about how to pin down the boundaries of the firm. The theory is as much a theory of plant or division size as firm size. As Hart points out,

> To put it in stark terms [. . .] neoclassical theory is consistent with there being one huge firm in the world, with every existing firm [. . .] being a division of this firm. It is also consistent with every plant and division of an existing firm becoming a separate and independent firm.
>
> (Hart 1995: 17)

But while the neoclassical model is certainly consistent with the two interpretations that Hart delineates, Foss (2000) points out that it is also consistent with a third possibility, that there are no firms, since consumers can do it all!

> With perfect and costless contracting, it is hard to see room for anything resembling firms (even one-person firms), since consumers could contract directly with owners of factor services and wouldn't need the services of the intermediaries known as firms.
>
> (Foss 2000: xxiv)

Nearly 30 years before Foss wrote Cyert and Hedrick (1972) had addressed similar points. They argued that in the neoclassical system the firm does not exist, that the theory does not address any of the real world problems that firms face and that there are no organisational problems or any internal decision-making process at all.

> In one sense the controversy over the theory of the firm has arisen over a non-existent entity. The crux of microeconomics is the competitive system. Within the competitive model there is a hypothetical construct called the firm. This construct consists of a single decision criterion and an ability to get information from an external world, called the "market" [8, Cyert and March, 1963, pp. 4–16]. The information received from the market enables the firm to apply its decision criterion, and the competitive system then proceeds to allocate resources and produce output. The market information determines the behavior of the so called firm. None of the problems of real firms can find a home within this special construct. There are no organizational problems nor is there any room for analysis of the internal decision-making process.
>
> (Cyert and Hedrick 1972: 398)

Loasby (2015: 246) makes clear that the neoclassical model of the firm cannot explain why firms exist:

> What was ironically called 'the theory of the firm' could give no theoretical reason for the existence of firms, because it relied entirely on market transactions to explain the prices and quantities of all goods and services. This theory simply required consumers and producers, all conceived as individual agents: in the goods market consumers provided the demand curve and producers the supply curve, and in the labour market the roles were reversed. Demand curves were conceived to be directly derived from individual preferences, which were subjective but well-ordered, and supply curves from costs, which were determined by technology and resources; and preferences, technology and resources were all presumed to be objective data. The intersection of these curves, properly defined, was then sufficient to determine outcomes; there was no need to explore market processes.

Thus within the neoclassical model of the price system, the firm's only role is to allow input owners to convert inputs into outputs in response to market prices. Firms have no internal organisation since they have no need of one, they have no owners since there is nothing to own. Questions about the definition, existence, internal structure and boundaries of the firm are to a large degree meaningless within this framework since firms, by any meaningful definition of that term, do not exist. As Foss, Lando and Thomsen (2000: 632) summarise it:

> The pure analysis of the market institution leaves almost no room for the firm (Debreu 1959). Under the assumption of a perfect set of contingent markets, as well as certain other restrictive assumptions, the model describes how markets may produce efficient outcomes. The question how organizations should be structured does not arise, because market-contracting perfectly

> solves all incentive and coordination issues. By assumption, firm behaviour (profit maximization) is invariant to institutional form (for example, ownership structure). The whole economy can operate efficiently as one great system of markets, in which autonomous agents enter into very elaborate contracts with each other. However, by treating the firm itself as a black box, where internal structure, contracts, etc. disappear from the picture, there are many other issues that the theory cannot address. For example, the theory does not tell us why firms exist.

Despite the fact that by the 1930s the neoclassical approach was the dominant theory of the firm, in its early years the basic tenants of this new orthodoxy were the subject of a number of controversies leading to several protracted debates in both the United Kingdom and the United States.[50] The most famous of these debates were the 'full cost controversy'[51] in the United Kingdom and the related 'marginalist controversy' in the United States (Mongin 1992, 1998). The full cost controversy was started by the publication in 1939 of a paper by R. L. Hall and C. J. Hitch which looked at pricing policies of firms (Hall and Hitch 1939). On the basis of questionnaire data, Hall and Hitch argued that firms set prices in a 'full-cost' way by estimating an average-cost amount at a reference level of output and adding to it a fixed percentage. Full-cost pricing came to be seen as a challenge to the usual marginalist (neoclassical) profit-maximising view of the firm. Long-run profit maximisation would only be achieved if the mark-up bore the correct relationship to the firm's perceived elasticities of demand. The most famous defence of the marginalist theory came from Machlup (1946). Machlup's response, however, was not solely directed towards the full-cost arguments, he also attacked a paper by labour economist R. A. Lester which argued that the theoretical predictions regarding the relationship between wages and employment could not be found in the data (Lester 1946). Lester argued that

> [...] his empirical research raised "grave doubts as to the validity of conventional marginal theory and the assumptions on which it rests" in the following ways: (1) market demand was more important in determining a firm's volume of employment than wage rates; (2) the firm's cost structure was not that suggested by "conventional marginalism" and its capital-labor ratio was not tied to its wage rate structure; and (3) "the practical problems involved in applying marginal analysis to the multi-process operations of a modern plant seem insuperable, and business executives rightly consider marginalism impractical as an operating principle in such manufacturing establishments" [Lester 1946: 81–2].
>
> (Lee 1984: 1114)

Lester's conclusion was that businessman did not adjust their employment levels in relationship to changes in wages and productivity in a manner consistent with the marginalist theory.

At this point it is difficult to separate out the full cost controversy from the Lester initiated marginalist controversy. In reply to both sets of arguments, Machlup

> [. . .] managed to dispute the quality and relevance of the evidence, and at the same time, to claim that data on price-setting were compatible with several of the available models of imperfect competition; he also sketched a general decision-theoretic argument to the effect that "rules of thumb" (the expression in Hall and Hitch) often reflect an underlying optimizing process. Most of the later neoclassical arguments are already in Machlup's proteistic plea. His general conclusion was that the current theory of the firm hardly needed revising even if the allegedly damaging findings were taken at face value.
>
> (Mongin 1992: 341–15)

Effectively these controversies ended when Richard B. Heflebower presented a paper at the Conference on Business Concentration and Price Policy in June 1952 (Heflebower 1955). Heflebower showed that full-cost pricing could be viewed in marginalist terms. He argued that profit maximisation should be understood in a long-run sense and that oligopoly should became the main theoretical focus for economists. He added that the full-cost doctrine did not constitute a well developed body of price theory and that the empirical work on which it was based was "spotty in quality and in its representation of situations" (Heflebower 1955: 391).[52]

Importantly, little changed because of these controversies. As Mongin (1998: 280) notes, for the majority of economists "[. . .] drastic adjustments in the theory of the firm were not needed to resolve the marginalist controversy". Overall,

> Although no contribution to the AER controversy [the marginalist controversy] can be said to be decisive, it can be conjectured that it influenced American economists into thinking that Robinson's and Chamberlin's initial models had to be refined, but that the profit-maximizing framework was flexible enough to accommodate the available evidence.
>
> (Mongin 1998: 279)

And "[i]t is clear from Heflebower's masterly survey that many of the arguments used by supporters of the full-cost principle are in no way inconsistent with orthodox economic theory" (Coase 1955: 393). In other words, these controversies had little impact on mainstream thinking about the theory of the firm.

2.2.1 Summary

It took until the mid-1930s for the neoclassical (textbook) model of the firm to develop. Before then none of the major schools of economic thought dedicated much effort to the modelling of firm level production. The neoclassical model, however, can be interpreted as a model with production but without firms. Given that transaction costs are zero, consumers do not need firms to carry out production.

A number of controversies to do with the marginalist theory arose in the period up until the mid-1950s, but none of these had any lasting effect on the mainstream theory of the firm.

Further challenges to the neoclassical model arose in the 1950s and 1960s from economists who developed the managerial and behavioural theories of the firm.[53]

In terms of the history of the theory of the firm these two sets of models are particularly significant since they represent some of the first attempts to look inside the black box of the neoclassical firm, even if their ultimate impact on mainstream economics has also been limited.

In the next section we will briefly review each of these two approaches to the firm in turn.

2.3 Behavioural and managerial models

In general terms the managerial models share the same basic assumption, they maximise the utility of the firm's managers subject to a profit constraint, while the behavioural theories see the firm as a coalition of self-interested groups, the conflicting demands of which have to be resolved via an ongoing bargaining process within he firm.

2.3.1 Behavioural models

Economists have been developing 'behavioural models' of the firm since the 1950s. In these models it is assumed that there is a separation between ownership and control. Behavioural theorists consider the consequences of conflict between self-interested groups within firms for the way in which firms make decisions on price, output and so on. The emphasis in these models is on the internal relations of the firm and little attention is paid to the external relations between firms.

Although some of the seminal work on the behavioural theories can be traced back to Simon (1955), the theory has largely been developed by Cyert and March, with whose names it has been connected right up to today.[54]

In behavioural theory the company has a multiplicity of different goals. Ultimately, these goals are set by top management via a continual process of bargaining between the groups within the firm. An important point here is that the goals take the form of aspiration levels rather than strict maximisation constraints. Attainment of the aspiration level 'satisfices' the firm: the behavioural firm's behaviour is 'satisficing' in contrast to the maximising behaviour of the traditional firm. The firm seeks levels of profits, sales, rate of growth and so on that are 'satisfactory', not those that are maxima. Satisficing is seen as rational behaviour given the limited information, time and computational skills of the firm's management. The behavioural theory redefines rationality, rationality is now that of 'bounded rationality'.[55]

Cyert and March argue that there are two sources of uncertainty that a firm has to deal with. The first is uncertainty that arises from changes in market conditions; that is, from changes in tastes, products and methods of production. The second is uncertainty arising from competitiors' behaviour. According to the behavioural theory the first form of uncertainty is avoided, as much as it can be, by search activity, by spending on R&D and by concentrating on short-term planning. A difference between the traditional and behavioural theories is the importance given in the behavioural theory to the short-run, at the expense of the long-run. To avoid competitor-originated uncertainty, Cyert and March argue that firms operate within a 'negotiated environment'; that is, firms act collusively with their competitors.

The instruments that the behavioural firm uses in decision-making are the same as those used in the traditional theories. Both theories consider output, price and sales strategy as the major instruments.[56] The difference between the theories lies in the way firms choose the values of these instruments. In the neoclassical theory these values are selected so as to maximise long-run profits. In the behavioural theory the choice is made so that the outcome is the 'satisficing' level of sales, profits, growth and so on.

The behavioural theory also assumes that the firm learns from its experience. In the beginning a firm is not a rational institution in the neoclassical sense of 'global' rationality. In the long run the firm may tend towards global rationality but in the short run there is an important adaptive process of learning. Firms make mistakes, there is trial and error from which the firm learns. In a sense the firm has memory and learns via its past experience. One aspect of the firm neglected by the traditional theory is the allocation of resources within the firm and the decision-making process that leads to that allocation. In the neoclassical theory the firm reacts to its environment, the market, while the behavioural theory assumes that firms have some discretion and do not take the constraints of the market as definite and impossible to change. The important point here is that the behavioural theory looks at the mechanisms for the allocation of resources within the firm, while the neoclassical theory examines the role of the market, or price, mechanism for the allocation of resources between the different sectors of the economy.

The concept of of 'slack' is used by Cyert and March to refer to payments made to groups within an organisation over and above that needed to keep that group in the organisation. Slack is, therefore, the same as 'economic rent' accruing to a factor of production in the traditional theory of the firm. What is significant about the behavioural school is their analysis of the stabilising role of 'slack' on the activities of the firm. Changes in slack payments in periods of good and bad business means that the firm can maintain its aspiration levels despite the changes to its environment.

2.3.2 Managerial models

Another group of models, from outside the mainstream, which have been developed mainly since the 1960s in an effort to overcome some of the shortcomings of the neoclassical model are the managerial models of the firm.[57] These models are also based on the idea that there is a difference between ownership and control of the firm. It is argued that the managers of the firm have taken control of the firm away from the owners. The common theme running through this literature is that the managers of the firm pursue non-profit objectives, generally subject to a performance constraint involving a profit related variable.

One of the earliest and most influential works in the managerial revolution was Berle and Means (1932). It was Berle and Means who famously argued that firms were becoming manager controlled rather than owner controlled, as had been the case in the past. De Scitovsky (1943) was a proto-managerial model of the firm. He modelled an entrepreneur whose utility depends on income and leisure, and who faces an income/leisure trade-off given by the firm's profit function. The entrepreneur maximises his utility at a point involving more leisure, and less profit, than the profit maximising point. More recent work, explicitly developing the managerial approach, can be found in Baumol (1959, 1962), Williamson (1964, 1970) and Marris (1964).[58]

The standard theory of the firm can be interpreted as assuming that the managers of the firm act purely for the good of the owners. The owners can control what the managers do and thus the managers maximise profits. There are no principal–agent problems. Managerial models, on the other hand, start from the twin ideas that ownership and control are separated and that managers, just like other economic agents, act in ways that promote their own interests. But maximising assumptions are still maintained within these models. The obvious question that this gives rise to is: What is maximised?

This question has been addressed by Baumol (1959) in which it is assumed that managers maximise sales subject to a profit constraint and by Baumol (1962) in which he develops a dynamic model in which the firm's objective is to maximise the growth rate of sales. Marris (1964) also assumes growth maximisation, subject to a rate of return constraint. In the Marris model a manager has an incentive to grow a firm past its profit maximising size since the manager's salaries are higher in larger firms.

While it may seem likely that profit maximisation and growth maximisation will led to behavioural differences between the two, work by Robert Solow (Solow 1971) argues that each type of firm would react in qualitatively similar ways to parameter changes, such as changes in factor prices, excise taxes or a profit tax.

Williamson (1964, 1970) assumes a more general managerial utility function. His managerial discretion models let managers make a trade-off between 'slack' and profits. In the static version, slack can be taken either as excessive administrative staff or as managerial emoluments (corporate personal consumption). In the dynamic-stochastic version of Williamson's model, slack comes in the form of internal inefficiency, which has much in common with Leibenstein's (1966) notion of X-inefficiency. Williamson claims that behaviour in his discretionary models is qualitatively different from that under profit, sales or growth maximisation, although Rees (1974), for example, disputes aspects of this claim.

Fritz Machlup famously attempted to repel the managerial and behavioural attacks on the neoclassical model in his 1967 Presidential Address to the American

Economics Association. He first argued that there was confusion as the role of the firm is price theory.

> My charge that there is widespread confusion regarding the purposes of the "theory of the firm" as used in traditional price theory refers to this: The model of the firm in that theory is not, as so many writers believe, designed to serve to explain and predict the behavior of real firms; instead, it is designed to explain and predict changes in observed prices (quoted, paid, received) as effects of particular changes in conditions (wage rates, interest rates, import duties, excise taxes, technology, etc.). In this causal connection the firm is only a theoretical link, a mental construct helping to explain how one gets from the cause to the effect. This is altogether different from explaining the behavior of a firm. As the philosopher of science warns, we ought not to confuse the explanans with the explanandum.
>
> (Machlup 1967: 9)

He then went on to argue that those behavioural and managerial theorists who were attacking the neoclassical model were doing so erroneously since they were working at a different level of analysis relative to that of the neoclassical model. The behavioural and managerial theories are aimed at the level of the individual firm whereas the neoclassical model is aimed at the industry level and thus, Machlup argued, the former are not genuine theoretical rivals to the latter.[59]

Lee (1984: 1122) argues that there is a connection between the behavioural and managerial models of the firm and the 'marginalist controversy' of the 1940s and 1950s. He argues that economists, such as Baumol (1959), Cyert and March (1963) and Marris (1964), were acquainted with and influenced by the marginalist controversy.

While developing models of firm behaviour based on non-profit maximising objectives, these authors showed that an augmented neoclassical framework was compatible and consistent with full cost pricing. Thus, by generalising the neoclassical theory, albeit in different ways, these authors were able to show that it was possible to both make price theory look more realistic and reconcile it with the full cost pricing theory.

But the connection resulted in no real change within the mainstream since, as Mongin (1998: 280) notes, "[...] it would be a mistake to believe that these writers [the behaviourists/managerialists] were representative of the majority of the economics profession".

2.3.3 Summary

The behavioural and managerial theories can be seen as an early attempt to develop a theory of the firm at the level of the individual firm, a theory which, as Oliver Williamson has said of the Cyert and March (1963) book, was an attempt to "pry open what had been a black box, thereupon to examine the business firm in more operationally engaging ways" (Williamson 1996b: 150).[60] But the success of this attempt was limited. Williamson's interaction with people such as Herbert Simon, Richard Cyert and James March while he was at Carnegie-Mellon University did play a role in the development of the transaction cost theory of the firm (Williamson 1996b) but outside of this the behavioural/managerial theories have had little effect on the mainstream economic theories of the firm.[61] In fact the impact of these works may have been greater in management than economics. Argote and Greve (2007: 337), for example, claim that *A Behavioral Theory of the Firm* "continues to be one of the most influential management books of all time".

2.4 Demsetz and the neoclassical model

As noted previously, the neoclassical model held sway in mainstream economics up until the 1970s and even today is still the one model of the 'firm' that every economist knows. In fact, it is likely to be the only model of the firm that they do know. The standard interpretation of the neoclassical model, due to Coase (1937), is one in which firms do not exist, a point explained already. The model is one of zero transaction costs in which agents interact with each other only via the price mechanism and elaborate (complete) contracts. Harold Demsetz is one author who disagrees with this interpretation of the neoclassical model. For him, the 'firm' in the neoclassical model is a specialised production unit, specialised in the sense that it produces only for those outside the firm.

Demsetz (1995: First commentary) argues that the neoclassical model offers both a definition of the firm and a rationalisation for the existence of firms, but he admits that these are mostly implicit. Demsetz starts by noting that the problem that the neoclassical model tackles is to see how the price system works and how it is able to deal with the interdependencies of the modern economy. The theory sets out to do this by envisioning a hypothetical economy within which people must depend on others. Demsetz (1995: 7) explains,

> The construction depends on two characteristics of economic activity: extreme decentralization and extreme interdependency. Extreme decentralization deprives all firms and households of influence over price. So they do not set price; the system does. This aspect of neoclassical theory is well understood. The need for interdependency is not.

The opposite of interdependency is self-sufficiency, by which Demsetz means production for one's own consumption. Robinson Crusoe stranded alone on an island must be self-sufficient; there is no one else to depend on. The neoclassical economy is one in which there is no self-sufficiency so that all people in this hypothetical economy are dependent on all other people in the economy. That is, there is extreme interdependency. Demsetz argues that

> This is accomplished with the aid of two "black boxes": the household and the firm. The household sells its services to others and buys goods from others. It does not self-employ resources to produce goods for its own members; it offers its resources to firms. Firms buy or rent these resources, and they produce goods that are not for consumption by their owners and employees as such, but are for exclusive sale to households. The role of prices in accommodating this high degree of interdependency is of interest, not the manner in which households and firms manage their internal affairs. The contribution made by the household and the firm in this theory is to make the price system deal with extreme interdependency and decentralization. "In-the-household" production and "on-the-job" consumption are ruled out.
> (Demsetz 1995: 8)[62]

The production unit in the neoclassical economy is specialised in the sense that it produces for those outside the firm, so that the firm is not just a black box but is also a specialised black box. There is no discussion of the managing of production. The role of the firm in the neoclassical theory is to separate production from consumption so that there is no self-sufficiency. The coordination of production and consumption is achieved via two factors: first, impersonally determined market prices; and second, personally defined tastes. The neoclassical model lays out the nature of the interactions between these components. Thus, the perfectly competitive firm is one important ingredient in a scenario in which the price system is the only coordination mechanism for harmonising production and consumption.

Demsetz goes on to note that the internal organisation of the firm is not addressed in the neoclassical theory. The firm need not be an organisation at all, a single owner/manager/employee is all that is required. For Demsetz the neoclassical firm is no more or less than a specialised unit of production. The important criterion for the neoclassical firm is that it separates production from consumption with production being exclusively for consumption by those outside the firm.

In the neoclassical world in which everyone possesses perfect information about prices and technologies, each owner of resources can manage their own resources, placing them in their highest value uses in response to the prices that they face. These resource owners can write any contracts needed to coordinate their relationships.

Demsetz then makes the point that this view of the firm is very different from that of either Knight or Coase, or from the modern theory of the firm literature, which follows, in the main, from Coase. In the Coaseian literature markets and firms are seen as substitutes, in that as transaction costs fall, the market is used more and firms do less. In the limit, as transaction costs go to zero the firm ceases to exist and all activities take place via markets. In the Demsetz framework, the relationship between firms and markets is complementary. As transaction costs fall, the costs to specialisation fall as the use of the market becomes cheaper and more specialisation takes place, and thus more firms are created. As transaction costs increase, the use of the market becomes more expensive and thus it is used less, self-sufficiency becomes more common and the number of firms falls.

Demsetz sums up the specialisation theory of the firm as, "The bottom line of specialization theory is that *firms exist because producing for others, as compared to self-sufficiency, is efficient; this efficiency is due to economies of scale, to specialized activity, and to the prevalence of low, not high, transaction costs*" (Demsetz 1995: 11; emphasis in the original).

One interesting implication of the specialisation theory is that it guarantees profit maximisation. Given that firms only produce for sale to those outside the firm, there can be no on-the-job consumption and thus the owner of the firm maximises utility by maximising profits. Given that there can be no utility gained from on-the-job consumption, the owner maximises utility by having the firm maximise profit and then saving or consuming this profit in his role as a consumer.

2.5 Conclusion

For the most part the classical economists utilised a theory of aggregate production, and distribution, not a theory of firm level production or a theory of the firm. Although the neoclassical economists sought to develop a theory of firm level production, their theory can be seen as one without firms. While there was clearly early dissatisfaction with the neoclassical model, it was not until the 1970s that this dissatisfaction reached the point where mainstream economists started to challenge the neoclassical model as the standard theory of the firm.[63] It was only then that the pioneering efforts of Knight (1921b) and Coase (1937) were recognised and developed. It was the work by Oliver Williamson (see, for example, Williamson 1971, 1973, 1975), Alchian and Demsetz (1972) and Jensen and Meckling (1976) that drove the upswing in interest in the firm as a significant economic institution. The 'present' theories of the firm are an attempt to create a theory of the firm. To lay a foundation for our review of the current approaches, we will first survey the founding works on which they are largely based: Knight (1921b) and Coase (1937).

Notes

1 Cho and Ahn (2009: 160) state, "[t]he oldest company in the world is known to be a Japanese construction company, Kongo Gumi, which was founded in 578 and thus existed for 1431 years". However a footnote at this point states "Kongo Gumi went bankrupt in 2006 and was acquired by Takamatsu group, thus depending on the definition of corporate death it may be excluded from a long-lived company" (Cho and Ahn 2009: 160, footnote 2). According to Wikipedia, "[a]s of December 2006, Kongo Gumi continues to operate as a wholly owned subsidiary of Takamatsu" (http://en.wikipedia.org/wiki/Kong_Gumi). Furthermore,

> There are also several other companies which are reported to have existed over 1000 years such as Houshi Ryokan (Japan, Innkeeping, founded in 717), Stiftskeller St. Peter (Austria, restaurant, founded in 803), Chateau de Goulaine

> (France, vineyard, founded in 1000) and Fonderia Pontificia Marinelli (Italy, bell foundry, founded in 1000).
>
> (Cho and Ahn 2009: 160–1)

Depending on one's definition of a firm perhaps the oldest still existing multinational firm is the Roman Catholic Church. Ekelund and Tollison (2011: 1) argue that "[t]he longest-running institution in Western culture and arguably one that has had an enormous influence on Western civilization has been the Roman Catholic Church". Ekelund *et al.* (1996: 17) note that "[t]he formal character of the Catholic Church, the single institution that come to embody Christianity in its official capacity, emerged as a result of the Edict of Milan in A.D. 313". In note 1, page 38, they make the important point that the edict meant that "[. . .] the Church became the recognized legal holder of property".

The first 'modern' company was the Dutch East India Company, which was founded in 1602. Between its founding and 1623 the Dutch East India Company developed the features which would later became the textbook characteristics of modern companies: a permanent capital, legal personhood, separation of ownership and management, limited liability for shareholders and for directors, and tradable shares (Gelderblom, De Jong and Jonker 2013). But see the discussion of *Sreni* on pages 10–11.

For a brief outline of the development of the firm since ancient times see Micklethwait and Wooldridge (2003) and Rosenberg and Birdzell (1986: Chapter 6). For a history of the important developments of the firm in Medieval Europe see Hunt and Murray (1999).

2 The first existence of a firm becomes especially problematic if we consider a farm to be a firm. Farming is an ancient human activity: "The first clear evidence for activities that can be recognized as farming is commonly identified by scholars as at about 12,000 years ago [. . .]" (Barker 2006: 1). Tudge (1998: 3) writes "I want to argue that from at least 40,000 years ago – the late Palaeolithic – people were managing their environments to such an extent that they can properly be called 'proto-farmers' ".

At what historical point did the farm first become a firm? If we accept production for others as an important characteristic of the firm, then farms can be seen (at least partially) as firms from a very early stage. Ofek (2001: Chapter 13) argues that agriculture developed with a symbiotic relationship with exchange/trade. There is a conflict between the fact that we specialise in production but diversify in consumption. This conflict is reconciled by distribution; that is, via exchange/trade. Ridley (2010: 127–30) agues there would be no farming without trade, that trade was a precursor to farming:

> One of the intriguing things about the first farming settlement is that they also seem to be trading towns. [. . .] it is a reasonable guess that one of the pressures to invent agriculture was to feed and profit from wealthy traders – to generate surplus that could be exchanged for obsidian, shells or other more perishable goods. Trade came first.
>
> (Ridley 2010: 127)

Spulber (2009: 103) takes a contrary position when he argues that the early farms where not firms. He writes that

> Farmers, artisans, and merchants from the earliest times to the eighteenth century are precursors to the contemporary firms. What distinguishes these economic actors from firms in that their enterprises tended to be integrated with the personal economic affairs of the entrepreneur. There was no separation between the owner's commercial activities and their personal consumption activities.

For more on Spulber's approach to the firm see the brief discussion on pages 117–120.

3 Importantly, classical Islamic law does not grant standing to companies, it recognises only national persons. For a discussion as to why Islamic law did not develop a concept akin to the company see Kuran (2005).
4 For more on the Old Assyrian trade see Veenhof (2010) and Larsen (2015). For a discussion of business companies in the later, first millennium BC, Babylonian period see Jursa (2010).
5 For more detail on production in ancient Greece see Bresson (2016) and Davies (2007).
6 For a brief discussion of the forms that firms could take in ancient Rome see Hansmann, Kraakman and Squire (2006: 1356–64) and Fleckner (2015).
7 In personal correspondence (November 2008 – used here with permission), Professor Hart said of the 1989 quote

> The language of 1989 is strong, and I'd probably tone it down a bit now. There's been a lot of work in the last twenty years, and some progress. However, we are still not at the point where we have good models of the internal organization of large firms.

8 Stigler (1941: 2–3) writes

> In 1870 there was no *theory* of distribution. Most English economists after Smith devoted separate chapters to rent, wages, and profits, but without important exception such chapters were only descriptive of the returns to the three most important social classes of contemporary England. Rent went to the landowners, wages to the laboring masses, and capitalists secured "profits of stock". This type of analysis may have had its uses in the England of Ricardo and Mill, but its analytical shortcomings are obvious. Extended criticism is unnecessary at this point; the fundamental defect was clearly the failure to develop a theory of the prices of productive services.

9 In terms of the neoclassical theory, the theories considered by Cannan (and Stigler 1941) are 'half a theory'. The neoclassical theory considers 'firms' decisions in both factor and product markets but as Williams (1978: 3) notes

> A study of the historical development of the complete theory of the firm would be redundant. It would be redundant because there already exist standard historical treatments of the firm's decisions in factor markets. [Cannan (1917) and Stigler (1941) are given as an examples of such studies] So the present study relates only to the literature of those decisions of the firm which relate directly to product markets – the pricing and production decisions.

Thus Cannan and Williams each deal with half the components that constitute the neoclassical theory.
10 The first algebraic production function was most likely due to Johann Heinrich von Thünen in his book *The Isolated State* (Humphrey 1997: 63–4). In a letter to Léon Walras, dated 6 January 1877, Hermann Amstein derived the conditions of optimal factor hire from the competitive firm's constrained cost function. He solved a cost-minimization problem in which the production function entered as a constraint (Humphrey 1997: 66–8). Edgeworth (1889) uses a production function when giving the conditions for solving the profit maximisation problem. production functions were common by the early 1890s, see for example, Berry (1891), Johnson (1891) and Wicksteed (1894).
11 " 'Production' and 'distribution' in political economy have always meant the production and distribution of wealth" (Cannan 1917: 1). Chapter 1 of Cannan (1917) surveys the various meanings of 'wealth' utilised in the economic writings of the 1776–1848 period.

12 Two possible (partial) exceptions to this are J.S. Mill's discussion of the advantages and disadvantages of the joint stock company, Mill (1848: Book I, Chapter IX), and Babbage's consideration of the effects of technology and the division of labour, Babbage (1832). O'Brien (1984: 25) argues that these two authors influenced parts of Alfred Marshall's work on the firm. Zouboulakis (2015) also discusses Mill's work.
13 Smith was not the first person to discussion the division of labour and its advantages for production. Such discussions go back (at least) as far as Plato, Aristotle and Xenophon, see Bonar (1893: book 1), Lowry (1987: 68–73) and Robbins (1998: 12–14).
14 For a discussion of the origins of Smith's pin making example see Peaucelle (2006) and Peaucelle and Guthrie (2011).
15 cf. Zouboulakis (2015). Zouboulakis argues that Smith's discussion of the division of labour does offer an elementary explanation for the existence of firms. Fleckner (2016) also discuses Smith's 'theory of the firm'. He argues that the lack of a theory of the firm is one of the weaker points of "An Inquiry into the Nature and Causes of the Wealth of Nations".
16 Robinson (1931) gives a – in economic circles largely forgotten now – 'pre-Coaseian' approach to the firm based around the division of labour. Robinson saw the firm as constituting a more intense division of labour than that utilised across the market, and attempted to identify the 'optimal size' of firms in the market. He argued that firms can grow in terms of both scope and scale through an increased internal division of labour, for management as well as workers. A modern approach which draws, at least, 'inspiration' from this line of thinking is Bylund (2016). For a discussion of Robinson's influence on Coase and, in particular, on his 1937 'Nature of the Firm' paper see Jacobsen (2008).
17 Bowen (1955: 5–6) argues in a similar fashion:

> [...] economists of the classical tradition had usually assumed that the level and distribution of income and the allocation of resources were determined by forces that could be understood without a detailed theory of the firm. [...] Everything else would be settled by the impersonal forces of the market, and there would be no need to consider in detail the decisions and actions of the individual firm.

18 As to why the firm was ignored in Austrian economics Witt (1999: 108) writes,

> The neglect of the firm as the organizational form of an entrepreneurial venture has a tradition in Austrian economics. It may be traced back to a characteristic of the scientific community in the German language countries. There, economic theory (Volkswirtschaftslehre) and business economics (Betriebswirtschaftslehre) were institutionally segregated as early as at the turn of the century to a degree still unknown today in the Anglo Saxon world. As Lachmann once conjectured, Austrian writers therefore considered the organizational form of entrepreneurial activities to be a topic best left to their business economics fellows.

19 Such views were beginning to change, a little, by the mid-1950s, see Chapter note 2, page 6, for an example of such a change in views. Interestingly, however, this interest in the firm is largely made for macroeconomic reasons. It was not an interest in the firm per se.
20 Mokyr (2002: 122–3) summarises manufacturing in the UK before the Industrial Revolution by noting that

> [...] large plants were not entirely unknown before the Industrial Revolution. For instance, Pollard (1968) in his classic work on the rise of the factory, mentions three large British plants, each employing more than 500 employees before 1750. Perhaps the most 'modern' of all industries was silk throwing. The silk mills in

> Derby built by Thomas Lombe in 1718 employed 300 workers and were located in a five-story building. After Lombe's patent expired, large mills patterned after his were built in other places as well. Equally famous was the Crowley ironworks, established in 1682 in Stourbridge in the Midlands (not far from Birmingham), which at its peak employed 800 employees. [...] In textiles, supervised workshops production could be found before 1770 in the Devon woollen industry and in calico printing (Chapman 1974).

The development of factories and firms during the industrial revolution is discussed in Mokyr (2009: Chapter 15). Chartered companies were also well known, as witnessed by Adam Smith's negative assessment of chartered companies in general and the East India Company in particular, contained in the *Wealth of Nations*. Jones and Ville (1996a: 898) note that

> Adam Smith, no friend of chartered companies, argued that this separation of ownership from control contributed to gross administrative inefficiency, inattention to detail, and the pursuit of managerial goals, which raised prices to consumers and reduced returns to shareholders. He believed that only the extraction of monopoly rents ensured the success and continuance of such companies.

See Smith (1776: Book V, Chapter 1, Part e, 731–58). Smith's view of chartered companies is discussed in Kennedy (2010: 143–7) and Fleckner (2016). On the issue of whether the joint-stock chartered trading companies were an efficient institutional response to long-distance trade or were inefficient, rent-seeking monopolists see Carlos and Nicholas (1996), Jones and Ville (1996a,b) and Ogilvie (2011). A general history of the chartered companies is given in Cawston and Keane (1896), Griffiths (1974) and Ekelund and Tollison (1997: Chapters 6 and 7). An important development for the modern large firm, following on from the chartered companies, was the introduction of limited liability. See Copp (2008) for a discussion of the reasons for the introduction of limited liability in the UK. Limited liability protects investors from claims of the company, organisational law also does the converse. The assets of the company are protected from claims by investors. Hansmann and Kraakman (2000a,b) and Hansmann, Kraakman and Squire (2005) emphasise the importance of this 'asset separation' to the development of the firm. Hansmann, Kraakman and Squire (2006) traces the history of the emergence of entity shielding.

21 For a 'real world' approximation to 'anonymous firm' production – that is, fully price-decentralised production – consider the case of rifle manufacture in Birmingham, England in the 1860s,

> Of the 5800 people engaged in this manufacture within the borough's boundaries in 1861 the majority worked within a small district round St Mary's Church. ... The reason for the high degree of localization is not difficult to discover. The manufacture of guns, as of jewellery, was carried on by a large number of makers who specialized on particular processes, and this method of organization involved the frequent transport of parts from one workshop to another.
>
> The master gun-maker-the entrepreneur-seldom possessed a factory or workshop. ... Usually he owned merely a warehouse in the gun quarter, and his function was to acquire semi-finished parts and to give these out to specialized craftsmen, who undertook the assembly and finishing of the gun. He purchased materials from the barrel-makers, lock-makers, sight-stampers, trigger-makers, ramrod-forgers, gun-furniture makers, and, if he were engaged in the military branch, from bayonet-forgers. All of these were independent manufacturers executing the orders of several master gun-makers. ... Once the parts had been purchased from the "material-makers", as they were called, the next task was to

> hand them out to a long succession of "setters-up", each of whom performed a specific operation in connection with the assembly and finishing of the gun. To name only a few, there were those who pre-pared the front sight and lump end of the barrels; the jiggers, who attended to the breech end; the stockers, who let in the barrel and lock and shaped the stock; the barrel-strippers, who prepared the gun for rifling and proof; the hardeners, polishers, borers and riflers, engravers, browners, and finally the lock-freers, who adjusted the working parts.
>
> (Allen (1929: 56–7 and 116–7), quoted in Stigler (1951: 192–3))

Such a method of production could be considered as giving an indication as to now production would take place under a functioning version the neoclassical model of the 'firm'. However it could be argued that this form of production is not neoclassical since it is not clear that the neoclassical separation theorem is satisfied. See Spulber (2009) for a discussion of the separation theorem.

22 O'Brien (1984: 25) takes a contrary position: "[s]erious discussion of the history of the theory of the firm has to start with Alfred Marshall". O'Brien's argument is based, in the main, on Marshall (1920a). O'Brien also argues that developments subsequent to Marshall have resulted in many of Marshall's insights being lost to succeeding generations of economists. We would therefore argue that Marshall has left little in the way of a legacy in terms of the mainstream theory of the firm. In addition to his views on Marshall's work and later developments O'Brien also argues that any "attempt to construct a pre-Marshallian theory from the materials available is likely to be unsuccessful". See, however, Williams (1978) for such an attempt. On the neglect of Marshall's *Industry and Trade* (Marshall 1920a) see also Liebhafsky (1955). The development of the 'theory of the firm' from Marshall to Robinson and Chamberlin is also dealt with in Moss (1984a).

23 When writing about Adam Smith's approach to the firm Williams (1978: 11) says,

> [t]he firm was disembodied and became a unit in which resources congeal in the productive process. When we come to examine the equilibrium/value theory of *The Wealth of Nations* it will be shown that, in that context, the firm is little more than a passive conduit which assists in the movement of resources between alternative activities.

Best (2012: 29) states simply that "Adam Smith did not elaborate a theory of the firm". Fleckner (2016: 8) writes "[n]ot once does he [Adam Smith] speak of a "firm", nor does he develop anything that would resemble a theory of the firm".

24 For discussions of economic thought – including production, the little there is – before the classical economists see, for example, Bonar (1893), Whittaker (1940: Chapter VIII) and Samuels, Biddle and Davis (2003: Chapters 1 to 6).

25 For a detailed discussion of mercantilism see Heckscher (1934), Viner (1937), Beer (1938: Chapter VI), Magnusson (1994, 2003, 2015) and Ekelund and Tollison (1997).

26 The quote given by Appleby is from Hill (1961: 32).

27 Mercantilism requires a dominate state, not just to provide and enforce monopolies but also to regulate and control both domestic and international trade and to direct the economy in general. Beer (1939: 13, footnote 1) lists the characteristics of mercantilism as:

> (i) Conception of money (coin and bullion or treasure) as the essence of wealth. (This conception prevailed from the end of the Middle Ages up to the end of the seventeenth century.) (ii) Regulating foreign trade with a view to bringing in money by the balance of trade. (iii) Making the balance of trade the criterion of national prosperity or decline. (iv) Promotion of manufacture by supplying it with

> cheap raw materials and cheap labour. (v) Protective customs duties on, or prohibition of, import of manufactured commodities. (vi) The view that the economic interests of nations are mutually antagonistic.

Higgs (1897: 16) explains "[t]he Mercantilists seem always to have propounded to themselves the problem, How can Government make this nation prosperous? Nationalism, state-regulation, and particularism are the essence of their policy" while Backhouse (2002: 58) notes "[m]ercantilist policies include the use of state power to build up industry, to obtain and increase the surplus of exports over imports, and to accumulate stocks of precious metals". "In France during this period [mid-1700s] the concept [mercantilism] was utilized in order to describe an economic policy regime characterized by direct state intervention, intended to protect domestic merchants and manufacturers" (Magnusson 2003: 46). When discussing the general economic background to the development of the mercantile chartered companies in England, Griffiths (1974) explains that "[t]he right – and the duty – of the Crown to control the economy was taken for granted and according to Coke 'the royal prerogative had an ancient and special force in the government of trade' " (p. ix) and "[t]he underlying concepts were those of monopolies, collective trading or regulation of trade and the right of the Crown to control the economy" (p. 3). In a comment on Eli Heckscher's view of mercantilism Deepak Lal writes that

> Heckscher had argued that the mercantilist system arose as the Renaissance princes sought to consolidate the weak states they had inherited or acquired from the ruins of the Roman Empire. These were states encompassing numerous feuding and disorderly groups which the new Renaissance princes sought to curb to create a nation. The purpose was to achieve "unification and power", making the "State's purposes decisive in a uniform economic sphere and to make all economic activity subservient to considerations corresponding to the requirements of the State". The mercantilist policies-with their industrial regulations, state-created monopolies, import and export restrictions, price controls-were partly motivated by the objective of granting royal favours in exchange for revenue to meet the chronic fiscal crisis of the state [. . .]. Another objective was to extend the span of government control over the economy to facilitate its integration.
>
> (Lal 2006: 307)

28 According to Smith the government has three duties:

"The first duty of the sovereign, that of protecting the society from the violence and invasion of other independent societies [. . .]" (Smith 1776: 689, Book V, Chapter 1, Part First).

"The second duty of the sovereign, that of protecting, as far as possible, every member of the society from injustice or oppression of every other member of it, or the duty of establishing an exact administration of justice, [. . .]" (Smith 1776: 709, Book V, Chapter 1, Part II).

> The third and last duty of the sovereign or commonwealth is that of erecting and maintaining those publick institutions and those publick works, which, though they may be in the highest degree advantageous to a great society, are, however, of such a nature that the profit could never repay the expense to any individual or small number of individuals, and which it therefore cannot be expected that any individual or small number of individuals should erect or maintain.
>
> (Smith 1776: Book V, Chapter 1, Part III, 723)

For book length discussions of Smith's thought see, for example, Evensky (2005), Kennedy (2005, 2010) and Otteson (2002, 2011).

29 For Adam Smith this would be an abstraction too far. Smith knew of the importance of institutions to the proper functioning of the market economy. Mark Blaug points out that

> [. . .] Smith's faith in the benefits of 'the invisible hand' has absolutely nothing whatever to do with allocative efficiency in circumstances where competition is perfect à la Walras and Pareto; the effort in modern textbooks to enlist Adam Smith in support of what is now known as the 'fundamental theorems of welfare economics' is a historical travesty of major proportions. For one thing, Smith's conception of competition was, as we have seen, a process conception, not an end-state conception. For another society, a decentralised competitive price system was held to be desirable because of its dynamic effects in widening the scope of the market and extending the advantages of the division of labour – in short, because it was a powerful engine for promoting the accumulation of capital and the growth of income.
>
> (Blaug 1997: 60–1)

30 The neoclassical model is often described as one of 'perfect competition' and one reason that the emphasis on the firm diminished as the model developed was that the neoclassical placed a growing emphases on the concept of market competition and thus less emphases was given to the firm. As McNulty (1984: 240) explains

> The 'perfection' of the concept of competition, beginning with the work of A. A. Cournot and ending with that of Frank Knight, which was at the heart of the development of economics as a science during the nineteenth and early-twentieth centuries, led on the one hand to an increasingly rigorous analytical treatment of market processes and on the other hand to an increasingly passive role for the firm.

For Knight

> Perfect competition is conditioned by the existence of a set of assumptions, the most important of which are the following: (1) "a perfect market for productive services [. . .], that is, uniform prices over the whole field" (1921[a], 316); (2) complete rationality and perfect knowledge by free and independent individuals; (3) "perfect mobility in all economic adjustments, no cost involved in movements or changes" (1921[b], 77); (4) "virtually instantaneous and costless" exchange of commodities (1921[b],78); (5) "perfect, continuous, costless intercommunication between all individual members of the society" (1921[b], 78); (6) perfect divisibility of commodities; and (7) "an indefinitely large number of competing organizations, each of the most efficient size" (1921[a], 316).
>
> (Marchionatti 2003: 58)

31 The household in the neoclassical model is as lacking in substance as the firm. Kenneth Boulding made the point that

> This type of analysis [the theory of the firm] is exactly analogous to the analysis of the reactions of a consumer by means of indifference curves. Indeed, a consumer is merely a "firm" whose product is "utility". The indifference curves are analogous to the isoquants, or product contours, the only difference being that they cannot be assigned definite quantities of utility. The utility surface, whose contours form the system of indifference curves, is a "mountain" whose shape we theoretically know, but whose height at any point probably cannot be known; by contrast, we can assume that both shape and height of the production surface are known. The "substitution effect" and the "scale effect" are likewise known in consumption theory, where the scale effect is usually called the "income effect". Thus, a rise in the

> price of a single object of consumption will have a substitution effect tending to reduce the consumption of that object as cheaper alternatives are substituted for it. There will also be an "income effect" tending to reduce all consumption, as the higher price makes the consumer poorer. The effect of a given rise in price, therefore, the elasticity of demand-depends first on the substitutability of the commodity concerned, and, second, on its importance in the total expenditure. This is true either of a consumption good or of a factor of production.
>
> (Boulding 1942: 799)

Fritz Machlup argues that the household is not the subject of study in the theory of the consumer:

> The "household" in price theory is not an object of study; it serves only as a theoretical link between changes in prices and changes in labor services supplied and in consumer goods demanded. The hypothetical reactions of an imaginary decision-maker on the basis of assumed, internally consistent preference functions serve as the simplest and heuristically satisfactory explanation of empirical relationships between changes in prices and changes in quantities. In other words, the household in price theory is not an object of study
>
> (Machlup 1967: 9, footnote 4)

32 About the partial equilibrium approach to the firm Klein (1996: 5) writes,

> In neoclassical economic theory, the firm as such does not exist at all. The "firm" is a production function or production possibilities set, a means of transforming inputs into outputs. Given the available technology, a vector of input prices, and a demand schedule, the firm maximizes money profits subject to the constraint that its production plans must be technologically feasible. That is all there is to it. The firm is modeled as a single actor, facing a series of relatively uncomplicated decisions: what level of output to produce, how much of each factor to hire, and so on. These "decisions", of course, are not really decisions at all; they are trivial mathematical calculations, implicit in the underlying data. In the long run, the firm may also choose an optimal size and output mix, but even these are determined by the characteristics of the production function (economies of scale, scope, and sequence). In short: the firm is a set of cost curves, and the 'theory of the firm' is a calculus problem.

The high water mark for neoclassical general equilibrium approach is arguably Debreu (1959). For Debreu there are no firms, in the normal sense of the word, there are just 'producers', "[...] when one abstracts from legal forms of organization (corporations, sole proprietorships, partnerships, ...) and types of activity (Agriculture, Mining, Construction, Manufacturing, Transportation, Services, ...) one obtains the concept of a producer, i.e., an economic agent whose role is to choose (and carry out) a production plan" (Debreu 1959: 37).

It is also clear from the context that the agent referred to is a person. The only role for the agent is to pick the profit maximising production plan from the set of available plans. Langlois (1981: 5) explains that

> [...] the interesting feature of the general-equilibrium formulation is not so much that it takes as given the mix of market and internal transactions; rather, it is that the assumptions of general-equilibrium theory themselves actually suggest that there need be no internal activity whatsoever. If all commodities are predetermined for all time and the techniques for producing them are given and fully known in all

details, then one could easily conceive of a situation where every separate part of the production process would be in the nature of a market transaction.

33 The following diagram illustrates the properties of the 'representative firm'. In this framework the representative firm is, roughly, the firm which has average total costs equal to the market price. Figure 46.1 is a modified version of the diagram from Macgregor (1949: 44).

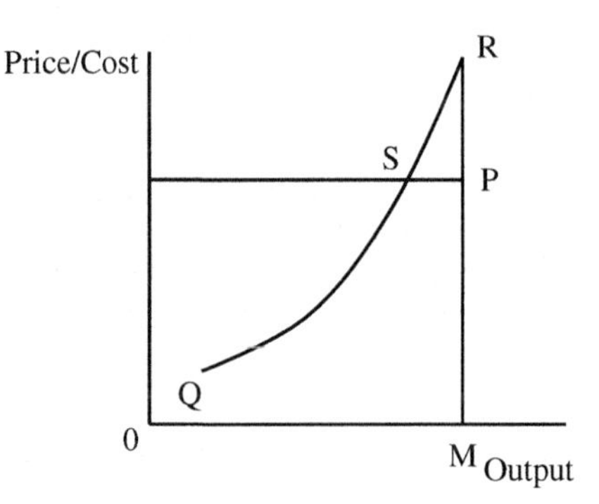

Figure 46.1.

> There is a supply of 0 *M* units and the price is *M P*. The line *Q R* shows the full costs at which different businesses, placed from left to right in the order of their efficiencies, are able to produce. Those between *S* and *R* are, at the moment, high-cost producers, who are not covering their full costs at the standard price *M P*. Some of them will leave the market, others will work their way to a better position in the line *Q R*. Others, now between *Q* and *S*, will, for different causes of lowered efficiency, find themselves between *S* and *R*. All the time, the price-determining cost will be *M P*, and representative conditions will be around *S*.
>
> (Macgregor 1949: 43–4)

Q R is what Marshall called the 'particular expenses curve'. See Appendix 1, page 162, for a brief discussion of this curve.

34 Williams (1978: 101) explains that,

> The representative firm may be used in three ways:
>
> In the first place, its output will alter if and only if the output of the industry alters. Any change in output will be in the same direction for the representative firm as for the industry. So if the industry output is to increase, this must mean that price exceeds the representative firm's unit normal expenses of production.
>
> Second, a firm's long-period supply price (average of normal expenses) includes income forgone by investing capital in this particular enterprise. So when industry output is stable, the representative firm must be earning its opportunity income on capital. This opportunity income is the definition of the normal rate of interest or, if earnings of management are counted in, of profit.
>
> Finally, the representative firm will have a supply curve found by the vertical summation of the supply schedules of the factors it uses, when the factor supply schedules plot the amount of the factor needed to produce a unit of a given quantity of output against the supply price of that quantity of the factor. This exercise does not give any indication of the supply schedules of firms within the industry

in question, but it possibly helps to illustrate the meaning of the costs of particular factors per unit of output.

35 N. Hart (2003: 1140) writes,

> It [the representative firm] was an avenue through which Marshall conjectured a notion of equilibrium at a point in time for the industry as a whole, while at the same time individual firms were in disequilibrium, being subject to an "organic" process of change. The representative firm therefore meets at the junction of Marshall's biological and mechanical notions of opposed forces described in the introductory comments in book 4 of Principles.

36 Sraffa began this assault on Marshall's theory with a paper in Italian, Sraffa (1925). The first few pages of Sraffa's 1926 paper are a summary of the arguments made in the 1925 paper. An English translation of Sraffa (1925) appeared as Sraffa (1998).
37 For an introduction to the theory of natural monopoly see Sharkey (1982).
38 See Robinson (1969: 116–9) and Shackle (1967: 13–21) for more detailed discussion.
39 Shackle (1967: 19) explains,

> If we allow ourselves to speak in modern terms of perfect competition, and mean by this that prices of both product and factors to the individual firm are independent of its output, then the conclusion of Mr Sraffa's argument at this stage is the failure of perfectly competitive assumptions to show any equilibrium of the individual firm. For both the demand curve for its product and the curve relating unit cost to output would be horizontal straight lines. This indictment of the perfectly competitive assumptions is Mr Sraffa's first objective.

40 On the relationship between the Marshall's view of industry equilibrium and firm equilibrium Foss (1994a: 1119) argues, "[. . .] Marshall's concept of industry equilibrium has no room for an equilibrium firm; long run industry equilibrium is a matter of equality between aggregate market demand and supply only. There is no pretension that individual firms are in equilibrium".
41 It was not Pigou alone who expunged Marshall's representative firm from the economic record, Robbins (1928) was his accomplice.

> Marshall's conception of the representative firm became virtually eliminated by Robbins [1928] and Pigou [1928]. Robbins pointed out the unclear analytical status of the representative firm. But more fundamentally, he made clear that (general) equilibrium was not inconsistent with variety among firms.
>
> (Foss 1994a: 1120–1)

In 1954 J. N. Wolfe commented that "[i]t is now more than twenty-five years since Professor Robbins's famous article on the representative firm finally drove that concept from the pages of economic text-books" (Wolfe 1954: 337). But as Quéré (2006) makes clear there was a revival of interest in Marshall's analysis in the 1950s.
42 Moss (1984a: 313) notes that Pigou's analysis of the equilibrium firms gave us the firm as a production function.

> Whatever its relationship to the representative firm, Pigou's introduction of the equilibrium firm gave us the firm as production function. In "An Analysis of Supply", Pigou demonstrated diagrammatically the various possible relationships between marginal and average curves on the assumption, made clear in his algebraic analysis, that factor prices were either unchanged or compensated. All changes in average and marginal costs were due to technological factors alone,

> and since the equilibrium firm was characterized by given average and marginal cost curves which did not shift as a result of any activity of the firm, those technological factors were considered to be entirely exogenous to the firm. Pigou's technique here was analytically equivalent to the derivation of a cost curve from the expansion path of a production function.

43 For a brief but enlightening essay on Chamberlin's work see Robinson (1971).

44 Backhouse (2003: 315) writes that Robinson's *Economics of Imperfect Competition* "[...] virtually created the modern geometry of the theory of the firm, analyzing perfect and imperfect competition, monopoly, monopsony, and even the kinked demand curve (conventionally attributed to Sweezy 1939)".

Shackle (1967: 61–2) writes,

> The two books [Robinson's and Chamberlin's] are very different in scope. Mrs Robinson's central concern is with the effect of supposing the demand for firm's output to be less than perfectly elastic, so that each firm, though only one among a multitude of firms producing substitutes of varying closeness for each other's products, can exploit the essential position, powers and policies of a monopolist. She eschews discussion of those markets where each firm reckons on other firms' active retaliation to its moves, and of expenditure on selling effort. [...] Professor Chamberlin includes selling expenditure in his analysis with a most ingenious formal precision. He also duplicates many arguments about price behaviour in order to point out that the entrepreneur should consider the profit possibilities of all products and choose in the end that output of that product which, with the optimal selling expenditure, yields the biggest total profit. With these ostensibly large extensions of the field, compared with Mrs Robinson's; with different emphases and a chief reliance on different diagrammatic tools; and especially with a personal interpretation of such words as 'supply' and with impalpable distinctions between his own and Mrs Robinson's use of the expressions 'monopoly', 'imperfect competition' and others, Professor Chamberlin is at great pains to insist that the two approaches are essentially different. Almost all other students of the matter have agreed with each other that in describing the structure and mechanism of equilibrium in firms and groups of firms when oligopoly and selling expenditure are absent, the two books present identical theories.

Chamberlin (1937) discuss the differences between monopolistic and imperfect competition.

45 Or the marginalist theory of the firm as it was often referred to at this time. Mongin (1997: 558) notes that marginalist was the commonly used term in the 1940s and 1950s because "the term neo-classical was not yet popular". The term marginalist was still being used in the 1960s, as witnessed by the title of Fritz Machlup's 1967 American Economic Association Presidential Address, 'Theories of the Firm: Marginalist, Behavioral, Managerial' (Machlup 1967).

46 Puu (1970: 230), for example, writes, "[...] the theory of the firm had, in substance, been developed to its present state by 1940".

47 For an example of an approximation to what production could look like in a neoclassical world see Chapter note 21, p. 41.

48 It is a black box in the sense that inputs go in and outputs come out, without any explanation of how one gets turned into the other. The firm is taken as given; no attention is paid to how it came into existence, the nature of its internal organisation, where the boundary between one firm and another is or between a firm and the market; or whether anything would change if two firms merged and called themselves a single firm.

49 Hansmann (1996: 11), for example, states

> A firm's "owners", as the term is conventionally used and as it will be used here, are those persons who share two formal rights: the right to control the firm and the right to appropriate the firm's profits, or residual earnings (that is, the net earnings that remain with the firm after it has made all payments to which it is contractually committed, such as wages, interest payments, and prices for supplies).

He later adds "[n]ot all firms have owners. In non-profit firms, in particular, the persons who have control are barred from receiving residual earnings" (p. 12).

50 In addition to the controversies discussed later on, other disputes occurred throughout the 1940s and 1950s with regard to the applicability of the traditional (marginalist) theory of the firm. See Bodenhorn (1959), Cooper (1949a, 1949b, 1951), Drucker (1958), Earley (1955, 1956), Gordon (1948), Margolis (1958, 1959) and Means (1958), and their references, for some contributions to these debates.

51 Notes on the full cost controversy by G. B. Richardson appear as Appendix 12 of Arena (2011).

52 Earlier Haley (1948: 13) had also questioned the conclusions given the nature of the survey data these studies utilised,

> Those responsible for the studies have relied so heavily upon the answers of their respondents alone, however, that it probably would be unwise to give too much weight to their conclusions until these studies have been supplemented by further research in the behavior and motivation of entrepreneurs with respect to price policy.

53 A good intermediate level discussion of these models is given in Sections E and F of Koutsoyiannis (1979).

54 The major reference for the behavioural model of the firm is Cyert and March (1963). For a review of Cyert and March, after 50 years, from the perspective of organisational economics see Gibbons (2013).

55 "This refers to behavior that is intendedly rational but only limitedly so; it is a condition of limited cognitive competence to receive, store, retrieve, and process information" (Williamson 1996a: 377).

56 Sales strategy here includes all activities of non-price competition, such as, advertising, salesmanship, service, quality and so on

57 For a full treatment of dynamic models of the managerial firm see Ekman (1978).

58 Alchian (1965a) gives a brief critique of the Marris (1964) and Williamson (1964) models.

59 A related 'level of analysis' attack has been made on the 'present' theories of the firm, as has been noted by Foss and Klein (2008: 429): "[...] the critics are protesting the application of concepts designed for analysis of *markets exchange* to the study of firm organization". That is, concepts appropriate at the market level are not appropriate at the firm level.

60 For retrospective look at *A Behavioral Theory of the Firm* after 45 years see Augier and March (2008).

61 If you look at the standard microeconomics textbooks, both undergraduate and graduate, it is difficult to find a discussion of either behavioural or managerial models.

Koutsoyiannis (1979: section E and section F) is one of the few (even relatively recent) undergraduate microeconomics textbooks that gives serious attention to these models, and it is now more than 30 years old. Undergraduate textbooks on the theory of the firm from the 1970s, such as Hawkins (1973: chapter 5), Crew (1975: Chapter 5) and Sawyer (1979: Chapter 7 and Chapter 8), did offer some discussion of these theories but there is little in the way of more recent consideration of them.

62 This separation between the household and firm is also noted by Hicks (1946: 79): "[...] the enterprise (the conversion of factors into products) may be regarded as a separate economic unit, detached from the private account of the entrepreneur. It acquires factors, and sells products; its aim is to maximize the difference between their value".

Spulber (2009: 125) calls this separation of the firm's objectives and the consumer's objectives the 'neoclassical separation theorem', which he says makes three assertions: "(1) firms maximise profits, (2) firms generate gains from trade compared to autarky, and (3) firm decisions are separate from consumer decisions".

For expanded discussion see Spulber (2009: 127–32). For Spulber the firm "is defined to be a transaction institution whose objectives differ from those of its owners" (Spulber 2009: 63). For more on Spulber's approach to the firm see the subsection beginning on page 117.

The importance of this separation is noted by Mas-Colell *et al.* (1995: 153) when they observe "[i]f prices may depend on the production of the firm, the objective of the owners may depend on their tastes as consumers". This implies that the objective of profits maximisation by the firm may be lost.

63 As Aghion and Holden (2011: 181) note,

> Until the 1970s, the dominant theory of the firm was the neoclassical theory: namely, there are economies of scale (or scope) which justify that production activities up to some efficient scale (or up to efficient variety) be concentrated within one firm rather than scattered across multiple producers.

3 The founding works

The contemporary mainstream theory of the firm is largely based on two works. The majority of mainstream theories draw on Coase's 1937 paper 'The Nature of the Firm' but the influence of Frank Knight's 1921 book 'Risk, Uncertainty and Profit' is growing. When looking back over the history of economics, Demsetz (1988a: 141) praises these two works as the only publications that have had a significant effect on economist's view of the firm in nearly 200 years:

> From the birth of modern economics in 1776–1970, a span of almost 200 years, only two works seem to have been written about the theory of the firm that have altered the perspectives of the profession – Knight's *Risk, Uncertainty, and Profit* (1921) and Coase's "The Nature of the Firm" (1937).[1]

Here we give brief overviews of each of these works.

3.1 Knight – *Risk, uncertainty and profit*

Demsetz (1988b: 244) has provocatively argued that "[...] it can be said without hesitation that Knight launched the modern theory of the firm in 1921". However the primary motivation of Knight (1921b) was not to examine the organisation of the firm or explain the existence of the firm, it was to explain the existence of profit. The theory of the firm was a by-product of his explanation of profit. Although as Foss (2000: xix) notes "[...] the connection between his theory of profits and his theory of the firm is not entirely clear".

The standard view of Knight's rationale for the existence of the firm, see for example Demsetz (1995: 2–4), does not depend on profit but on risk or, more accurately, risk distribution. The entrepreneur forms a firm as a way of specialising in risk-taking. Employees receive a stipulated income and the entrepreneur takes the residual income of the firm and, thereby, bears most of the risk associated with uncertainty about the future. The advantage of the firm, according to the standard view, is that there are gains to be made from this distribution of risk between the entrepreneur and the firm's employees. The profit and loss consequences of fluctuations in the business outcomes can be better absorbed by the entrepreneur than the employees. The entrepreneur contracts to pay a fixed wage to workers, thereby protecting them from the fluctuations in business outcomes. Knight sees this as efficient since the entrepreneur is less averse to bearing risk. Presumably, risk is not handled as well without firms.

Another view is offered by Boudreaux and Holcombe (1989).[2] They see Knight's theory of the firm as stemming from the role of the entrepreneur as the person who decides what to produce or whether or not to introduce a new production process in a world of Knightian uncertainty. For Knight, the goods and services to be produced are not given, as in the neoclassical theory, thus entrepreneurs must make a decision as to which goods to produce. Given that the entrepreneurs face a world of uncertainty, such decisions must be made on the basis of 'intuitive judgement'. The need for 'judgement' is due to the entrepreneur having to deal with uncertainty resulting from the fact that prices of the outputs are unknown when the decisions about production are made. This price uncertainty is the result of changing consumer desires and the uncertainty as to the reactions of competitors. Entrepreneurs differ from non-entrepreneurs in that entrepreneurs receive the return from 'judgement'; that is, entrepreneurs receive the residual (positive or negative) left after the costs incurred at the time the production decision was made are subtracted from the revenues.

For Boudreaux and Holcombe "[t]he distinguishing characteristic of the Knightian entrepreneur [. . .] is that he makes decisions under uncertainty about how resources will be allocated" (Boudreaux and Holcombe 1989: 152). The Knightian firm's primary function is, in Boudreaux and Holcombe's view, entrepreneurial, decisions must be made without the guidance of market prices since the market doesn't exist yet. Entrepreneurial activity is necessary for the development of markets. New goods create new markets. For Knight, the products to be produced is a decision made within the firm. The entrepreneur is the person in the firm who makes such decisions. Thus for Boudreaux and Holcombe the Knightian theory of the firm is driven by a theory of the entrepreneur, this they claim differentiates the Knightian theory from that of Coase, who they argue puts forward a theory of management that leaves no room for genuine entrepreneurship. For Boudreaux and Holcombe, the Knightian firm exists in order to facilitate decision making in a world of true uncertainty, that is, to facilitate true entrepreneurial decision making.[3] Presumably, such decision making is not as efficient without firms.

Barzel (1987) and McManus (1975) put forward moral hazard explanations for the Knightian firm. The firm arises here "[. . .] because, for certain kinds of risks, the functions of risk taking and management are inseparable [. . .] due to the prohibitively high costs of enforcing constraints that would induce one individual, the manager, to maximize the wealth of another, the risk-taker" (McManus 1975: 348). As previously noted in the distribution of risk story, firms are one way of specialising in risk-taking. Knight was aware of contractual and insurance arrangements as alternatives to the firm as ways of specialising in risk-taking but thought that, because of the moral hazard problems, they were particularly costly to enforce in the case of risks of enterprise and, hence, the need for the creation of a firm. Presumably, monitoring the manager is easier for the risk-taker in a firm that it is over the market.

An alternative view is given by Langlois and Cosgel (1993). Here it is argued that Knight's theory of organisation has things in common with the more recent incomplete contracts approach to the firm.[4] Langlois and Cosgel summarise their view of Knight's theory of organisation as

> Because of the non-mechanical nature of economic life, novel possibilities are always emerging, and these cannot be easily categorized in an intersubjective way as repeatable instances. To deal with this "uncertainty", one must rely on judgment. Such judgment will be one of the skills in which people specialize, yielding the usual Smith economies. Moreover, some will specialize in the judgment of other people's judgment. As the literature since Coase [1937] suggests, however, a theory of specialization is not by itself a theory of organization, since, in the absence of transaction costs, there is no reason why the division of labor could not be undertaken through markets rather than within a firm. Knight's answer is that the function of judgment is ultimately non-contractible.
>
> (Langlois and Cosgel 1993: 462)

The non-contractibility of judgement leads to the entrepreneur's skills not being tradable on markets, thus the advantages of specialisation and the division of labour cannot be realised over the market and, hence, the need for the firm.[5] The optimal organisational structure that results from this has the entrepreneur as the residual claimant, and he hires the other agents for a fixed payment. Langlois and Cosgel argue that incompleteness results in the entrepreneur owning the other assets in the firm on the assumption that the entrepreneur's participation is the most important to the resulting joint product. If we compare this case with that of the standard risk distribution case that was previously noted, we see that the residual claimant does not so much insure the other agents, as in the risk redistribution story, rather it is simply that, due to the non-contractibility, the optimal arrangement is for the entrepreneur to receive the residual and the other agent to receive a fixed payment.

Thus, if one wished to write Whig History,[6] Knight's theory of the firm would be a forerunner not of the theory of moral hazard and asymmetric information but of the incomplete contracts approach to vertical integration. Langlois and Cosgel contend that Knight saw the causes of incompleteness in the lack of knowledge of the categories of action and the consequent need for judgement. For Knight incompleteness of contract was ultimately a matter of uncertainty.

3.2 Coase – 'The nature of the firm'

Coase opens the paper by pointing out that there has been, in economics, a failure to clearly state the assumptions on which theories are built. He notes that two questions can be asked of a set of assumptions: Are they tractable? and Do they correspond with the real world? Coase argues that it is important to have a clear definition of the word 'firm' since much economic analysis starts with the individual firm rather than the industry and it is important to know the difference between the theoretic firm and the real world firm. The aim of Coase's paper was to provide a definition of the firm that

> [...] is not only realistic in that it corresponds to what is meant by a firm in the real world, but is tractable by two of the most powerful instruments of economic analysis developed by Marshall, the idea of the margin and that of substitution, together giving the idea of substitution at the margin.
>
> (Coase 1937: 386–7)

Coase begins his search for a definition of the firm by pointing out that the standard treatment of the economic system is one where the price mechanism provides all of the coordination of resources required. Resource allocation is dependent directly on the price mechanism. But in the firm, Coase notes, the price system does not allocate resources, authority does. The use of authority to supersede the price mechanism is, in Coase's view, the distinguishing mark of the firm. He then asks: If all of the coordination can be done by the price mechanism, why then is the firm, with its coordination by authority, necessary?

In Section II, Coase states the the task ahead is to explain why a firm would emerge in a specialised exchange economy. He first points out that it could emerge if it was desired for its own sake. It could arise if some people preferred working under the direction of others or if some people wished to control others. Firms may also arise if customers preferred goods produced in this way to goods produced by other institutional arrangements. However, Coase points out that these motivations cannot explain all of the firms that we see, hence there must be other factors involved.

The, now, most famous 'other factor' is that there are costs to using the price mechanism. To quote Coase (1937: 390–2):

> The most obvious cost of "organising" production through the price mechanism is that of discovering what the relevant prices are. [...] The costs of negotiating and concluding a separate contract for each exchange transaction which takes place on a market must also be taken into account. [...] It is true that contracts are not eliminated when there is a firm but they are greatly reduced. [...] There are, however, other disadvantages-or costs-of using the price mechanism. It may be desired to make a long-term contract for the supply of some article or service. [...] Now, owing to the difficulty of forecasting, the longer the period of the contract is for the supply of the commodity or service, the less possible, and indeed, the less desirable it is for the person purchasing to specify what the other contracting party is expected to do. [...] When the direction of resources (within the limits of the contract) becomes dependent on the buyer in this way, that relationship which I term a "firm" may be obtained. A firm is likely therefore to emerge in those cases where a very short term contract would be unsatisfactory. [...] We may sum up this section of the argument by saying that the operation of a market costs something and by forming an organisation and allowing some authority (an

"entrepreneur") to direct the resources, certain marketing costs are saved. The entrepreneur has to carry out his function at less cost, taking into account the fact that he may get factors of production at a lower price than the market transactions which he supersedes, because it is always possible to revert to the open market if he fails to do this.

Coase also notes that the different treatment of in-house and market transactions by government and regulatory bodies could also explain why some firms exist. Having explained why a firm could exist, Coase goes on to note that a firm consists of the relationships that are brought into existence when the control of resources is dependent on an entrepreneur.

An advantage of this approach, claims Coase, is that it is possible to give a meaning to a firm becoming larger or smaller. A firm becomes larger when a transaction that could be carried out in the market is instead organised by the entrepreneur. The firm, therefore, becomes smaller when the entrepreneur gives up organising such a transaction.

Next Coase considers the question as to why, if by creating a firm, the costs of production can be reduced, are there are any market transactions at all? "Why is not all production carried on by one big firm?" (Coase 1937: 394). The answer according to Coase is, first, that as a firm gets bigger there may be decreasing returns to entrepreneurial activity. That is, the cost of an additional transaction being organised within the firm may rise. Second, as the number of transactions which are organised in-house increases, the entrepreneur may fail to place the factors of production in the uses where their value is maximised. This means that the entrepreneur fails to make the best use of the available factors of production. Finally, the supply price of one or more of inputs to production may increase because the 'other advantages' of a small firm are greater than those of a large firm.[7] As a result of these factors a firm will grow to the point where the costs of organising an additional transaction within the firm become equal to either the costs of carrying out the same transaction via the market or the cost of organising the transaction in another firm (Coase 1937: 395).

At this point Coase summaries the argument so far by noting that if we hold all other things equal a firm will tend to become larger when: 1) the costs of implementing a transaction in the firm are lower and such costs rise more slowly; 2) the probability that mistakes will be made by the firm's management is smaller, and the rate of increase in such errors is lower, as more transactions are carried out within the firm; and 3) making a firm larger decreases the cost of any factors of production for that firm, or least growing the firm reduces the rate of increase in the costs of the factors of production Coase (1937: 396–7).

An additional reason why efficiency will decrease as the firm grows larger is that as more transactions are controlled by an entrepreneur, these transactions are likely to be either different in kind or different in place. Mistakes in decision making are more likely as there is an increase in the spatial distribution of transactions, in the dissimilarity of the transaction and in the probability of changes in prices relevant to production. Changes which lessen the spatial distribution between transactions will lead to an increase in the size of the firm, as will improvements in managerial technique.

The ideas of 'combination' and 'integration' can be given precise meaning using the analysis presented previously. Combination happens when transactions normally undertaken by two or more entrepreneurs are undertaken by one and this turns into integration when the transaction was previously carried out in the market. Firms can grow via either or both of these two ways.

In the last section of the paper Coase asks whether the concept of the firm that he has developed is realistic and manageable? As to realism, he contends that the best way to see what constitutes a firm in practice is to look at the legal relationship between the master and servant, or employer and employee.[8] The essentials of the employer and employee relationship are given by Coase as follows:

> 1 The servant must be under the duty of rendering personal services to the master or to others on behalf of the master, otherwise the contract is a contract for sale of goods or the like.
> 2 The master must have the right to control the servant's work, either personally or by another servant or agent. It is this right of control or interference, of being entitled to tell the servant when to work (within the hours of service) and when not to work, and what work to do and how to do it (within the terms of such service) which is the dominant characteristic in this relation and marks off the servant from an independent contractor, or from one employed merely to give to his employer the fruits of his labour. In the latter case, the contractor or performer is not under the employer's control in doing the work or effecting the service; he has to shape and manage his work so as to give the result he has contracted to effect.
>
> (Coase 1937: 403–4)

It is noted by Coase that what distinguishes an agent from an employee is not the presence or absence of a fixed wage or the payment only of commission, but rather the freedom with which an agent may carry out his or her employment. Coase argues that it is the fact of direction that is the essence of the legal concept of the employer and employee relationship just as it was in the economic concept of the firm he developed. He concludes that his definition is therefore realistic. The question is then asked: Is it manageable? Again the answer is yes, the principle of marginalism works smoothly. The next questions are: Does it pay to organise an additional transaction under a given entrepreneur? And, should the transaction be undertaken by this firm or some other firm or in the market? At the margin the cost of undertaking the transaction in any given firm will equal the cost to either another firm or in the market.

For some economists "Coase's questions about why firms and markets coexist are brilliant, but his answers are less satisfactory" (Hart 2008: 405). Hart (2008) refers to what are normally called transaction costs as 'haggling costs'. He criticises the Coaseian approach for three reasons: (i) it has proved difficult to formalise or operationalise haggling costs.[9] (ii) Coase's costs of using the firm are unconvincing.[10] Why cannot an overstretched manager just hire another manager to help him out? (iii) Hart thinks that it optimistic and unrealistic to suppose that placing a transaction inside a firm eliminates all haggling costs.

The modern approach to the theory of the firm (see Chapter 4) has been developed to deal with issues like those raised by Hart and when compared to the approach of Coase (1937) a number of differences become apparent. For example, there is no notion of morally hazardous behaviour or of differential attitudes to risk in Coase but these ideas are prominent in the post-1970 theories. The reason for the importance of incompleteness of contracts is also different in Coase than it is in the current theories. For Coase incomplete contracts are important because they allow flexibility in future decision making given that we have little knowledge today on which to base decisions about tomorrow's actions. An employment contract, for example, is incomplete because the employer does not know today what tasks he will want the employee to carry out tomorrow and thus the future tasks cannot be specified in the contract. Within limits the employer has the flexibility to be able to decide on the task tomorrow. In the current theories incompleteness is important because in conjunction with relation-specific investments and opportunistic/morally hazardous behaviour it helps specific the patterns of ownership of, for example, the physical assets that a firm utilises. Such ownership effects the incentives that the various contracting parties face. Foss (1996d: 88) argues for another understanding of incompleteness:

> [...] incompleteness may be of distinct value because it allows the firm to engage in organizational learning. In other words, contractual incompleteness is an instrument of adaptation. For example, it allows the firm to adapt to partly unanticipated learning which the firm itself generates and of course also to outside developments. That such an instrument is necessary follows from the basic epistemological impossibility theorem, formulated by Knight (1921[b]: 318): future learning and knowledge cannot be fully anticipated, for if it could, it would be present knowledge and not future knowledge.

Foss claims that this interpretation moves Coase closer to Knight.

> As I have interpreted Knight and Coase's alternative theories, they both center on knowledge and on the need for adaptation in a hard-to-predict world, rather than on incentives, property rights and transaction costs. In Knight's theory, it is idiosyncratic knowledge-namely entrepreneurial judgment-that cannot be traded. In Coase's theory, incomplete contracts are important because they allow us to wait and acquire more knowledge. This suggests that we should look for modern counterparts to Coase and Knight's analyses in those contemporary theories of the firm that are primarily concerned with the knowledge dimensions of firms.
>
> (Foss 1996: 88)

Garrouste and Saussier (2008: 26) criticise Coase for using a definition of a firm which is too vague. It is difficult to give a precise meaning to Coase's notion that a firm is a place where coordination via authority replaces coordination by price since such authority relationships can be found on markets as well. In so far as Coase deals with the internal structure of a firm he reduces it to authority and command but this only scratches the surface of the true complexity of the internal organisation of the modern firm. Garrouste and Saussier also argue that the relationships between firms and markets are only weakly analysed. Finally, they claim that the refutability of the approach taken by Coase has been questioned on the basis that it is impossible to accurately measure the transaction costs for alternative contractual arrangements, meaning that the ex post rationalisation of almost any contractual choice is possible.

Cowen and Parker (1997: 44) suggest that from a contracts point of view firms do not differ sharply from markets. While Coase distinguished precisely between intra-firm and inter-firm transactions, with the former taking more of a 'command' view of the firm, the contracts approach to the firm allows for the possibility that intra-firm transactions can be market like. Jensen and Meckling (1976: 310–11) go so far as to say,

> The private corporation or firm is simply one form of legal fiction which serves as a nexus for contracting relationships and which is also characterized by the existence of divisible residual claims on the assets and cash flows of the organization which can generally be sold without permission of the other contracting individuals. [. . .] Viewed this way, it makes little or no sense to try to distinguish those things which are "inside" the firm (or any other organization) from those things that are "outside" of it. There is in a very real sense only a multitude of complex relationships (i.e., contracts) between the legal fiction (the firm) and the owners of labor, material and capital inputs and the consumers of output.

Thus, from this viewpoint[11] Coase was wrong to emphasise the differences between firms and markets.

Another issue raised about Coase's work is the role of the entrepreneur. Foss and Klein (2005: 64) argue that Coase's position with regard to the entrepreneur is ambiguous. On the one hand his entrepreneur is a Robbinsian maximiser whose job is to decide how to organise transactions within the firm and to make the make-or-buy decision. But on the other hand, Coase also sees the entrepreneur as a speculating and coordinating agent. His approach to the employment contract appeals to unpredictability and the need for qualitative coordination in a world of uncertainty. Here there is the possibility of genuine entrepreneurial activity.

There is also the related issue as to what the role of the entrepreneur is with regard to the creation of firms. While Coase's approach explains why there are firms, it does not address the process that brings them about.

Demsetz (1988a) argues that a more complete theory of the firm must give greater weight to information costs than is given in Coase (1937). The form that an economic organisation will take will depend, in Demsetz's view, on the fact that knowledge is costly to produce, maintain, and use. In all such aspects there are economies to be achieved through specialisation. Firms are, in part, repositories of specialised inputs required to make use of knowledge that is specific to that firm or industry. Steel firms, for example, specialise in different stocks of knowledge and equipment than do firms involved in investment banking or firms producing chemical products, and even within a given industry firms will utilise different sets of knowledge and equipment. Coase (1937) does not clearly articulate such a view.

The 'Nature of the Firm' uses the employer-employee relationship as the archetype of the firm.[12] This emphasis on the employment contract has been questioned by economists including Coase himself. He writes that this concentration "[...] gives an incomplete picture of the nature of the firm. But more important, I believe it misdirects out attention" (Coase 1988a: 37). The misdirection comes about because the emphasis on the employment relationship leads to a concentration on firms as purchasers of inputs rather than an emphasis on the main activity of the firm, the running of a business. This has de-emphasised the major point of 'The Nature of the Firm' which Coase sees as the comparison of the costs of coordinating the activities of factors of production within a given firm with the costs of achieving the same outcome by the use of market transactions or by the use of another firm.[13]

3.3 Conclusion

It is normally the work of Knight and Coase that is credited with providing the foundations for the development, starting around 1970, of the current theories of the firm. Knight's work can be seen as, depending on interpretation, arguing that a firm is needed to facilitate risk redistribution, or because of the need for intuitive judgement in a world of uncertainty, or as a catalyst for moral hazard and asymmetric information theory, or as a catalyst for incomplete contract theory. So while many authors argue for Knight as a founder of the modern approaches to the firm, they cannot agree on why. One feature common to many of the Knightian based theories, however, is an emphasis on the role of the entrepreneur in the formation of firms.

The importance of Coase (1937) stems from the fact that it was the starting point for much of the contractual literature on the firm, and the theory of economic organisations more generally, insomuch as it is in this paper that we see the main questions underlying the modern theory of the firm being raised together for the first time. Coase sets out to "discover why a firm emerges at all in a specialized exchange" – a question about the existence of the firm; he also sets out to "study the forces which determine the size of the firm" – an issue to do with the boundaries of the firm; and he inquires into the reasons for "diminishing returns to management" – issues to do with the internal organisation of the firm. It was the efforts to answer these questions that initiated the change from seeing the theory of the firm as just part of price theory to seeing it as an important topic in its own right. Coase also provides one of the main building blocks for answering these issues, the 'costs of using the price mechanism' or transaction costs.

But as Coase notes "[t]he article was not an instant success" (Coase 1988a: 23). In fact it took nearly 40 years for it to become an overnight success. Before 1970 the paper was, in Coase's own words, "an article much cited and little used" (Coase 1972: 63). Coase argues that this changed both with the publication of 'The Problem of Social Cost' (Coase 1960) which helped rekindle interest in 'The Nature of the Firm' via the greater appreciation of transaction costs it brought about and with the writings of Oliver Williamson who incorporated transaction costs into the analysis of the distinction between hierarchy and markets (Coase 1988b: 34–5).

Interestingly, in the modern approach to the theory of the firm there is no obvious purely Knightian research programme in the same way that there is a Coasian programme. Despite this, it can be argued that the post-1970 literature combines crucial elements from both Knight and Coase, although it is Coase's influence that is seen as dominate (Foss 1996).

It is to the post-1970 literature we now turn.

Notes

1 With regard to this quote Jacobsen (2015b: 2) has written,

> Demsetz seemingly overlooked Alfred Marshall's *Principles* and *Industry and Trade* especially given the august influence of Marshall on Coase particularly as transmitted by the works of his disciples D.H. Macgregor, Dennis Robertson, Austin Robinson, Gerald Shove, and Joan Robinson to Coase beginning with the conception of 'Nature of the Firm' (Jacobsen 2013, 2015[a]).

2 See Foss (1993) for criticism of Boudreaux and Holcombe.

3 Foss (1993: 273) conceptualises this as "[...] the firm and vertical integration exist because entrepreneurs cannot communicate – without exorbitant information costs – their idiosyncratic 'versions' (innovations) to owners of assets necessary for realizing this vision; therefore, they integrate such activities". This inability to communicate with assets owners means that it is difficult to hire assets on the market and thus the need for entrepreneurs to supply the needed assets themselves by forming a firm.

4 See Grossman and Hart (1986, 1987), Hart and Moore (1990) and Hart (1995).

5 Foss and Foss (2006: 54–5) note that "[...] there is no market for judgement that entrepreneurs rely on, and therefore exercising judgment requires the person with judgment to start a firm".

6 The term 'Whig history' was coined in Butterfield (1931) and is often applied, in a pejorative sense, to mean that the past is seen as the inexorable march of progress towards enlightenment. The expression is also found in the history of science where it means historiography which concentrates on the successful chain of theories and experiments that led to present-day science, while ignoring failed theories and dead ends. Here it just means that the incomplete contracts approach to the firm is seen as an inevitable outcome of the development of the theory of the firm. Notions of incompleteness of contract are read back into the thoughts and ideas of pasteconomists.

7 This point is explained by Coase in footnote 1, p. 395, which reads:

> For a discussion of the variation of the supply price of factors of production to firms of varying size, see E. A. G. Robinson, *The Structure of Competitive Industry*. It is sometimes said that the supply price of organising ability increases as the size of the firm increases because men prefer to be the heads of small independent businesses rather than the heads of departments in a large business. See Jones, *The Trust Problem* (p. 531), and Macgregor, *Industrial Combination* (p. 63). This is a common argument of those who advocate Rationalisation. It is said that larger units would be more efficient, but owing to the individualistic spirit of the smaller entrepreneurs, they prefer to remain independent, apparently in spite of the higher income which their increased efficiency under Rationalisation makes possible.

8 In footnote 3, p. 403, Coase explains that the legal concept of employer and employee and the economic concept of a firm are not identical. He notes that the firm may imply control over another person's property in addition to their labour. But the identity of these two concepts is sufficiently close for an examination of the legal concept to be of value in appraising the worth of the economic concept.

9 For example Oliver Williamson writes,

> Transaction costs are appropriately made the centerpiece of analysis but these are not operationalized in a fashion which permits one to assess the efficacy of completing transactions as between firms and markets in a systematic way.
>
> (Williamson 1975: 3)

10 As an example Richard Langlois argues,

> [. . .] his [Coase's] "theory" of the costs of internal administration amounts to little more than a claim that there are inevitably decreasing returns to the managerial function (for reasons largely unspecified) and perhaps to other factors of production as well.
>
> (Langlois 2013: 248)

11 This is referred to as the 'nexus of contracts' view.

12 For a more detailed discussion of Coase's approach to the employment relationship see Foss, Foss and Klein (2016) and Freeland (2016).

13 For a more severe criticism of Coase that sees 'The Nature of the Firm' as a defence of socialist economic planning, see Bylund (2014a).

4 The 'present'

After a long delay the theory of the firm started to gather momentum in the 1970s, driven mainly by a belayed surge of interest[1] in the ideas of Ronald Coase.[2] The 'present' of the theory of the firm will be discussed in this chapter under three main headings. The first section considers the post-1970 theory of the firm literature per se while the second section scrutinises the relationship between the three most prominent of the modern sets of theories: the reference point, property rights and transaction cost approaches to the firm. The third section looks at the theory of privatisation. Roughly, as presented here, the contemporary theory of the firm focuses on questions to do with the existence, internal organisation and boundaries of the firm while the theoretical privatisation literature looks at issues to do with the boundary between state and private firms.

4.1 The post-1970 theories of the firm

4.1.1 Mainstream theories

Foss, Lando and Thomsen (2000: 634) offer a useful classification, which we follow here, of the mainstream post-1970 economics literature on the theory of the firm. They partition the theory into two general groups:

1 Principal–agent type models, where agents can write comprehensive contracts characterised by ex ante incentive alignment under the constraints imposed by the presence of asymmetric information.[3]
2 Incomplete contracts models, which are based on the idea that it is costly to write contracts and thus contracts will have holes or inefficient provisions; therefore, there is a need for ex post governance.[4]

This division can be seen as resulting from the breaking of two different assumptions embedded in the general equilibrium (Arrow-Debreu) version of the neoclassical model.[5] The first group corresponds to the breaking of the assumption that there are no asymmetries of information between parties and thus no principal–agent problems, of either the adverse selection or moral hazard kind. The second grouping results from breaking the assumption that agents can foresee all future contingencies and can costlessly contract on all such eventualities. We discuss each group in turn.

4.1.1.1 Principal–agent type models

Within this classification Foss, Lando and Thomsen (2000: 636–8) identify three sub-groups: (1) the nexus of contracts view; (2) the firm as a solution to moral hazard in teams approach; and (3) the firms as an incentive system view.

4.1.1.1.1 THE NEXUS OF CONTRACTS VIEW

The nexus of contracts view was developed in papers by Alchian and Demsetz (1972), Jensen and Meckling (1976), Barzel (1997), Fama (1980) and Cheung (1983). The important innovation here was the recognition that it is difficult to draw a line between firms and markets, firms are seen as a special type of market contracting. What distinguishes firms from other forms of market contracting is the continuity of the relationship between input owners.

Most famously, in the Alchian and Demsetz version of this approach it is argued that the authority relationship between the employer and employee is in no way the defining characteristic of a firm.[6] In this approach there is no essential difference between an employment contract – such as, having an employee produce some good – and, say, a spot contract – such as, buying the good from a 'grocer' – or obtaining the good via a supply contract with an independent contractor. They are all contractual relationships. The employer has no more authority over an employee than a customer has over his grocer. 'Firing', of either the employee or grocer, is the ultimate punishment that either the employer or customer can use in cases of 'disobedience'. Alchian and Demsetz argue that, in economic terms, the customer 'firing' his grocer is no different from the employer firing his employee. In both cases one party stops dealing with the other, terminating the 'contract' between them. In this approach the firm is seen as little more than a nexus of contracts, special in its legal standing and characterised by the long term nature of the relationship between the input owners. Under this interpretation it is not generally useful to talk about firms as distinctive entities, a nexus of contracts could be called more firm-like if, for example, the residual claimants belong to a concentrated group but the term 'firm' has little meaning beyond this.

Roberts (2004: 104) responds to this line of argument:

> While there are several objections to this argument, we focus on one. It is that, when a customer "fires" a butcher, the butcher keeps the inventory, tools, shop, and other customers she had previously. When an employee leaves a firm, in contrast, she is typically denied access to the firm's resources. The employee cannot conduct business using the firm's name; she cannot use its machines or patents; and she probably has limited access to the people and networks in the firm, certainly for commercial purposes and perhaps even socially.

Another counter argument follows from Coase (1937), as described previously, and Simon (1951), as described later. Both authors emphasise 'fiat'; the idea that employers can, within bounds, control an employee's activities by directive. Employment contracts are open-ended, they are incomplete in that not all situations are covered by the contract and employers, and employees do not fill the gaps by negotiating over which task is to be carried out at any given time, as would happen with an independent contractor: the employer simply instructs the employee as to what is to be done. Oliver Williamson, see below, argues that the legal distinction between the manner of dispute resolution within versus between firms demonstrates a critical difference between employment and market contracts.

4.1.1.1.2 THE FIRM AS A SOLUTION TO MORAL HAZARD IN TEAMS APPROACH

The second grouping, the 'firm as a solution to moral hazard in teams approach', was developed by Alchian and Demsetz (1972) and Holmström (1982). Alchian and Demsetz (1972) extend their discussion, outlined previously, by noting that the firm is more than just a special legal arrangement, it is also characterised by team production. The problem that arises here is that with team production, the marginal products of the individual members of the team are hard to measure. This means that free-rider behaviour is now possible since team production can act as a cover for shirking. The Alchian and Demsetz solution is to give the right to hire and fire the members of the team to a monitor who observes the employees and their marginal products. To ensure that the efficient amount of monitoring takes place, the monitor is given the rights to the residual income of the team.[7]

Holmström (1982) looks at the incentive problems of teams and identifies possible solutions.[8] Holmström assumes that the members of the team each take actions which are unobservable to the monitor but the overall result of the combined actions is observable. What Holmström shows is that it is only under very restrictive assumptions that the monitor can ensure that efficient effort levels will be provided by each team member. The monitor can do this by designing a sophisticated incentive scheme. But Holmström shows that given unobservable effort levels, the requirements for the incentive scheme to be a Nash equilibrium, to balance the budget and to be Pareto optimal, cannot be met together.[9] More specifically, a budget-balancing incentive scheme cannot reconcile the Nash equilibrium requirement and Pareto optimality because each team member will equalise the costs and benefits of extra effort; that is, if the team revenue is increased by the efforts of a single member, then that member should receive that revenue to ensure that they are properly motivated. But as the monitor only knows that team revenue has increased and not the effort levels of each individual member, then all members of the team would have to each receive the extra revenue to ensure that the hard working member is rewarded for his or her efforts. But this will, obviously, violate the balanced budget condition. This suggests that there is an advantage, in terms of incentives, in the team not having to balance their budget.[10]

Clearly the role of the 'monitor' in the Alchian and Demsetz model is very different to their role in the Holmström model. For Alchian and Demsetz, the monitor oversees the behaviour of the team members, in the Holmström model, the monitor injects the capital needed so that the team members do not have to balance their budget.

Given that Holmström's paper has acted as a catalyst for much of the formal moral hazard in teams literature, we will look at a more analytical, but still straightforward, discussion of the Holmström model which is due to Border (2004). Border starts by noting that Holmström's problem is to find a scheme to compensate members of a team where the individual effort levels of each team member cannot be observed by the other members, only the total output of the team is known.

We start by assuming that there are $n > 1$ team members. Each member i chooses an action or effort level $a_i \in \Re_+$. The team's output x depends on the effort of each individual, so that

$$x : \Re^n_+ \rightarrow \Re_+.$$

It will be assumed that x is continuous, strictly increasing (and the strictly bit will matter – see the proof to Theorem 68.1), concave and differentiable.

As far as the members of the team are concerned, each of them cares only about his effort level and his monetary compensation. It will be assumed, for simplicity, that each team member has a quasi-linear utility function:

$$u_i(m_i, a_i) = m_i - v_i(a_i),$$

where m_i denotes the members monetary compensation and a_i is effort. The value $v_i(a_i)$ can be interpreted as giving the minimum compensation needed to induce member i to exert the effort level a_i. It will assumed that each v_i is continuous, strictly increasing, convex, and differentiable.

An allocation is an ordered list

$$(m, a) = ((m_1, \ldots, m_n), (a_1, \ldots, a_n))$$

that satisfies the condition

$$\sum_{i=1}^{n} m_i \leq x(a_1, \ldots, a_n). \qquad (65.1)$$

Condition (65.1) can be interpreted as saying that the team's compensation is derived from the team's output.

An allocation is said to be efficient if there is no other allocation that gives every member greater utility. Border now states, and proves, the proposition that an allocation is efficient if and only if it maximises the total surplus.

PROPOSITION 65.1 (Border 2004: 2, Proposition 1) Due to the quasi-linearity of utility, the allocation $(m^\star, a^\star)$ is efficient if and only if $a^\star = (a_1^\star, \ldots, a_n^\star)$ maximizes the total surplus

$$S(a) = x(a) - \sum_{i=1}^{n} v_i(a_i) \tag{66.1}$$

and the total reward is fully distributed:

$$\sum_{i=1}^{n} m_i^\star = x(a^\star). \tag{66.2}$$

Border's proof proceeds in two steps.

Proof. Step 1: 'if'. Assume that $(m^\star, a^\star)$ maximises (66.1) and satisfies (66.2). Then for any other allocation (m', a') we have

$$\left[\sum_{i=1}^{n} m_i' - v_i(a_i')\right] \leq \left[x(a') - \sum_{i=1}^{n} v_i(a_i')\right] \leq \left[x(a^\star) - \sum_{i=1}^{n} v_i(a_i^\star)\right]$$
$$= \left[\sum_{i=1}^{n} m_i^\star - v_i(a_i^\star)\right]$$

which implies that we cannot have $u_i(m_i', a_i') = m_i' - v_i(a_i') > m_i^\star - v_i(a_i^\star) = u_i(m_i^\star, a_i^\star)$ for each i. In other words, $(m_i^\star, a_i^\star)$ is efficient.

Step 2: 'only if'. Assume by way of contraposition that either $a^\star$ does not maximize (66.1) or violates (66.2). That is, there is some a' (possibly $a' = a^\star$) satisfying

$$x(a') - \sum_{i=1}^{n} v_i(a_i') > \sum_{i=1}^{n} m_i^\star - \sum_{i=1}^{n} v_i(a_i^\star),$$

Math aside: First assume that (66.1) does not hold but that (66.2) does. Then there exists an a' such that

$$x(a') - \sum_{i=1}^{n} v_i(a_i') > x(a^\star) - \sum_{i=1}^{n} v_i(a_i^\star) = \sum_{i=1}^{n} m_i^\star - \sum_{i=1}^{n} v_i(a_i^\star),$$

Next assume that (66.1) does hold but that (66.2) does not. Then for $a' = a^\star$

$$x(a') - \sum_{i=1}^{n} v_i(a_i') = x(a^\star) - \sum_{i=1}^{n} v_i(a_i^\star) > \sum_{i=1}^{n} m_i^\star - \sum_{i=1}^{n} v_i(a_i^\star),$$

since $\sum_{i=1}^{n} m_i^\star < x(a^\star)$.

so define

$$c = x(a') - \sum_{i=1}^{n}(m_i^\star - v_i(a_i^\star) + v_i(a_i')) > 0.$$

Setting $m_i' = m_i^\star - v_i(a_i^\star) + v_i(a_i') + \frac{c}{n}$ gives $u_i(m_i', a_i') = m_i' - v_i(a_i') > m_i^\star - v_i(a_i^\star) = u_i(m_i^\star, a_i^\star)$ for each i, and $\sum_{i=1}^{n} m_i' = x(a')$. That is, $(m^\star, a^\star)$ is not efficient. ■

Math aside: To see the effects of the conditions for the existence of a strictly positive surplus maximiser noted below consider them in light of the following diagram,

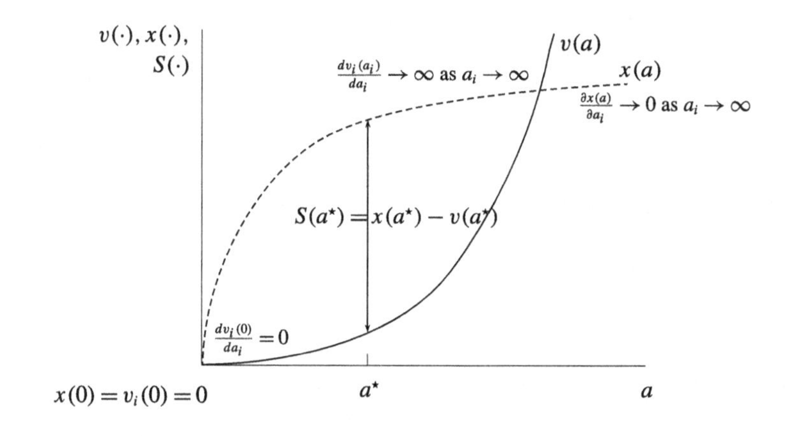

where $a^\star$ is the surplus maximising level of a.

Next, another important assumption is added, which is a 'non triviality assumption'. It is assumed that a surplus maximiser, $a^\star \gg 0$, exists and that the surplus obtained is positive; that is, $x(a^\star) - \sum_{i=1}^{n} v_i(a_i^\star) > 0$. The following conditions are sufficient to ensure that if a maximiser, $a^\star$, exists then it must be such that $a_i^\star > 0$: (1) $x(0) = 0$; (2) $v_i(0) = 0$ and (3) $\frac{dv_i(0)}{da_i} = 0$ for all i. In addition to ensure the existence of a maximiser the following conditions are sufficient: (1) $\frac{dv_i(a_i)}{da_i} \to \infty$ as $a_i \to \infty$, for all i; and (2) $\frac{\partial x(a)}{\partial a_i} \to 0$ as $a_i \to \infty$ for all i.

Now we look at the incentives that a member of the team faces via their compensation package. Given that only team output is observable, compensation must depend on total output and not individual output. Let a sharing rule be a function such that

$$s : \Re_+ \to \Re^n$$

and s satisfies the balanced budget condition:

$$\sum_{i=1}^{n} s_i(x) = x \quad \text{for all } x \in \Re_+. \tag{68.1}$$

These two conditions just mean that $s_i(x)$ is member $i's$ compensation when total output is x and that total compensation equals total output so that output is divided among the team members. Note that $s_i(x)$ could be negative, which would amounts to fining member i.

A sharing rule defines a game among the team members where the strategies are the effort levels and the pay-off functions are given by

$$\pi_i(a_1, \ldots, a_n) = s_i(x(a_1, \ldots, a_n)) - v_i(a_i).$$

An ordered strategy list, $\bar{a} = (\bar{a}_1, \ldots, \bar{a}_n)$, is a Nash equilibrium if for every member i and every effort level a_i

$$s_i(x(\bar{a})) - v_i(\bar{a}) \geq s_i(x(\bar{a}_{-i}, a_i)) - v_i(a_i)$$

where $(\bar{a}_{-i}, a_i) = (\bar{a}_1, \ldots, \bar{a}_{i-1}, a_i, \bar{a}_{i+1}, \ldots, \bar{a}_n)$. This means that no member of the team can unilaterally deviate from $\bar{a}$ and get a larger pay-off. If we have such a Nash equilibrium, then we say that the sharing rule s implements the effort vector $\bar{a}$.

Next Border looks at the trade off between incentives and efficiency. He states the following theorem.

THEOREM 68.1 (Border 2004: 3, Theorem 3) Under the assumptions we have made, if $a^\star \gg 0$ maximizes surplus (66.1), then there is no sharing rule satisfying budget balance (68.1), for which $a^\star$ is an equilibrium.

Border's proof begins by giving an intuitive outline followed by the detailed argument.

Proof. The basic intuition is:
If s implements $a^\star$, then any member i must be deterred from cutting his effort from $a_i^\star$ by a loss in compensation. So consider a reduction in member $i's$ effort by Δa_i that reduces output by ε. His compensation must fall more than his utility gain $v_i(a_i^\star) - v_i(a_i^\star - \Delta a_i)$. But here is the key: since effort is not observable, we do not know who shirked, so everyone's compensation must be cut, and by enough to deter each and everyone of them. That is, total compensation must fall by at least $\sum_{j=1}^{n} v_j(a_j^\star) - v_j(a_j^\star - \Delta a_i)$. Now we ask, how much does output fall when only person i shirks? The answer is approximately $\frac{\partial x(a^\star)}{\partial a_i} \Delta a_i$. How much must compensation fall? By approximately $\sum_{j=1}^{n} \frac{dv(a_j^\star)}{da_j} \Delta a_i$. But here is the rub, since $a^\star$ maximizes surplus, the first-order conditions imply $\frac{\partial x(a^\star)}{\partial a_j} = \frac{dv(a_j^\star)}{da_j}$. Now think of the person i who gains least by deviating by Δa_i . The total compensation must fall at least n times as much as for that individual. But now the budget balance condition kicks in. Total compensation falls only by the reduction in total reward,

which is approximately proportional to the agent's individual utility gain, not n times as much. Which means that the fall in compensation is not enough to provide the correct incentives for all team members to act efficiently.

The detailed argument is:
For convenience set $x^\star = x^\star(a^\star)$. Since x is continuous and strictly increasing, and $a^\star \gg 0$, for every $\varepsilon > 0$ small enough,

> *Math aside:* For each j, we know that $x(x^\star) - x(a^\star_{-j}, 0) > 0$, so setting $m = \min_j x(a^\star) - (a^\star_{-j}, 0)$, we have $m > 0$. Any ε satisfying $0 < \varepsilon < m$ is small enough.

by the Intermediate Value Theorem,

> *Math aside:* The intermediate value theorem states: Let f be a continuous function on the closed interval $[a, b]$. Let $\alpha = f(a)$ and $\beta = f(b)$. Let γ be an intermediate number between α and β, that is $\alpha < \gamma < \beta$ or $\alpha > \gamma > \beta$ depending on which of α or β is the larger. Then there exists a number c such that $a < c < b$ and such that $f(c) = \gamma$.

for each j there is some $a_j(\varepsilon)$ satisfying

$$0 < a_j(\varepsilon) < a_j^\star$$

and

$$x(a^\star_{-j}, a_j(\varepsilon)) = x^\star - \varepsilon.$$

Note that it is important that the right-hand side is independent of j.

If $a^\star$ is an equilibrium, then by definition, for each j, it cannot pay member j to switch from $a^\star$ to $a_j(\varepsilon)$, so

$$s_j(x(a^\star)) - v_j(a_j^\star) \geq s_j(x(a^\star_{-j}, a_j(\varepsilon))) - v_j(a_j(\varepsilon))$$

or

$$s_j(x(a^\star)) - s_j(x(a^\star_{-j}, a_j(\varepsilon))) \geq v_j(a_j^\star) - v_j(a_j(\varepsilon))$$

or using the fact that $x(a^\star_{-j}, a_j(\varepsilon)) = x^\star - \varepsilon$, independent of j, we have

$$s_j(x(a^\star)) - s_j(x^\star - \varepsilon) \geq v_j(a_j^\star) - v_j(a_j(\varepsilon)). \tag{69.1}$$

Summing over j gives

$$\sum_{j=1}^{n} s_j(x(a^\star)) - \sum_{j=1}^{n} s_j(x^\star - \varepsilon) \geq \sum_{j=1}^{n} v_j(a_j^\star) - v_j(a_j(\varepsilon))$$

so using the balanced budget condition $\left(\sum_{j=1}^{n} s_j(x) = x\right)$

$$x^{\star} - (x^{\star} - \varepsilon) \geq \sum_{j=1}^{n} v_j(a_j^{\star}) - v_j(a_j(\varepsilon)).$$

Now let i be an/the member for whom the gain in utility (reduction in disutility) from changing his effort level is the smallest; that is,

$$v_i(a_i^{\star}) - v_i(a_i(\varepsilon)) \leq v_j(a_j^{\star}) - v_j(a_j(\varepsilon)) \quad \text{for all } j.$$

Summing over j gives

$$n(v_i(a_i^{\star}) - v_i(a_i(\varepsilon))) \leq \sum_{j=1}^{n} v_j(a_j^{\star}) - v_j(a_j(\varepsilon)) \leq x^{\star} - (x^{\star} - \varepsilon)$$

$$\Rightarrow x^{\star} - (x^{\star} - \varepsilon) \geq n(v_i(a_i^{\star}) - v_i(a_i(\varepsilon))) > 0. \tag{70.1}$$

(Note that i may depend on ε but the notion used here does not reflect this.)

Using Taylor's Theorem

Math aside: Young's Form of Taylor's Theorem: Let $f : (\alpha, \beta) \rightarrow \Re$ be $n-1$ times continuously differentiable on (α, β) and assume that f has an nth derivative at the point x in (α, β). For any v such that $x + v$ belongs to (α, β),

$$f(x+v) = f(x) + \sum_{i=1}^{n} \frac{f^k(x)}{k!} v^k + \frac{r(v)}{n!} v^n$$

where the remainder term $r(v)$ satisfies

$$\lim_{v \to 0} r(v) = 0.$$

Here we have $f(\cdot) = v(\cdot), k = 1, x + v = x_i(\varepsilon), v = (a_i(\varepsilon) - a_i^{\star}) < 0$ and $x = a_i^{\star}$. Substituting in to the previous formula we get

$$v_i(a_i(\varepsilon)) = v_i(a_i^{\star}) + \frac{\frac{dv_i(a_i^{\star})}{da_i}}{1!}(a_i(\varepsilon) - a_i^{\star}) + \hat{r}_i(\varepsilon)$$

$$\Rightarrow -\frac{dv_i(a_i^{\star})}{da_i}(a_i(\varepsilon) - a_i^{\star}) - \hat{r}_i(\varepsilon) = v_i(a_i^{\star}) - v_i(a_i(\varepsilon))$$

$$\Rightarrow v_i(a_i^{\star}) - v_i(a_i(\varepsilon)) = \frac{dv_i(a_i^{\star})}{da_i}(a_i^{\star} - a_i(\varepsilon)) - \hat{r}_i(\varepsilon).$$

(or the definition of a derivative) we get

$$v_i(a_i^\star) - v_i(a_i(\varepsilon)) = \frac{dv_i(a_i^\star)}{da_i}(a_i^\star - a_i(\varepsilon)) - \hat{r}_i(\varepsilon) \tag{71.1}$$

$$\text{where} \quad \frac{\hat{r}_i(\varepsilon)}{(a^\star - a_i(\varepsilon))} \to 0 \quad \text{as } \varepsilon \to 0.$$

Similarly,

$$x(a_i^\star) - x(a_{-i}^\star, a_i(\varepsilon)) = \frac{\partial x(a^\star)}{\partial a_i}(a_i^\star - a_i(\varepsilon)) - \tilde{r}_i(\varepsilon) \tag{71.2}$$

$$\text{where} \quad \frac{\tilde{r}_i(\varepsilon)}{(a^\star - a_i(\varepsilon))} \to 0 \quad \text{as } \varepsilon \to 0.$$

Math aside: Here we have $f(\cdot) = v(\cdot), k = 1, x + v = x(a_{-i}^\star, a_i(\varepsilon)), v = (a_i(\varepsilon) - a_i^\star) < 0$ and $x = a^\star$. Substituting in to the previous formula we get

$$x(a_{-i}^\star, a_i(\varepsilon)) = x(a_i^\star) + \frac{\frac{\partial x(a^\star)}{\partial a_i}}{1!}(a_i(\varepsilon) - a_i^\star) + \tilde{r}_i(\varepsilon)$$

$$\Rightarrow -\frac{\partial x(a^\star)}{\partial a_i}(a_i(\varepsilon) - a_i^\star) - \tilde{r}_i(\varepsilon) = x(a_i^\star) - x(a_{-i}^\star, a_i(\varepsilon))$$

$$\Rightarrow x(a_i^\star) - x(a_{-i}^\star, a_i(\varepsilon)) = \frac{\partial x(a^\star)}{\partial a_i}(a_i^\star - a_i(\varepsilon)) - \tilde{r}_i(\varepsilon).$$

Since $a^\star$ maximises total surplus, it is the solution to the problem:

$$\max_a S(a) = x(a) - \sum_{i=1}^{n} v_i(a_i) \tag{71.3}$$

which means it satisfies the first-order conditions

$$\frac{\partial x(a^\star)}{\partial a_i} = \frac{dv_i(a_i^\star)}{da_i} \quad i = 1, \ldots, n. \tag{71.4}$$

This means we can rewrite (71.2). Remember that $x^\star - \varepsilon = x(a_{-i}^\star, a_i(\varepsilon))$ so that

$$x^\star - x(a_{-i}^\star, a_i(\varepsilon)) = x^\star - (x^\star - \varepsilon) = \frac{\partial x(a^\star)}{\partial a_i}(a_i^\star - a_i(\varepsilon)) - \tilde{r}_i(\varepsilon)$$

which means

$$\frac{\partial x(a^\star)}{\partial a_i}(a_i^\star - a_i(\varepsilon)) - \tilde{r}_i(\varepsilon) = x^\star - (x^\star - \varepsilon)$$

$$\geq n(v_i(a_i^\star) - v_i(a_i(\varepsilon))) \text{ (using 70.1)}$$

$$= n\left(\frac{\partial x(a^\star)}{\partial a_i}(a_i^\star - a_i(\varepsilon)) - \hat{r}_i(\varepsilon)\right) \text{ (using 71.1 and 71.4)}$$

Dividing by $a_i^\star - a_i(\varepsilon)$ and gathering the remainders gives

$$\frac{\partial x(a^\star)}{\partial a_i} \geq n\frac{\partial x(a^\star)}{\partial a_i} + \frac{\tilde{r}_i(\varepsilon) - n\hat{r}_i(\varepsilon)}{a_i^\star - a_i(\varepsilon)}.$$

Letting $\varepsilon \to 0$ gives

$$\frac{\partial x(a^\star)}{\partial a_i} = n\left(\frac{\partial x(a^\star)}{\partial a_i}\right) \quad \text{(utilising Equations (71.1) and (71.2)).}$$

Math aside: Now there is a caveat here: Remember that i in (70.1) depends on ε, so as $\varepsilon \to 0$, the index i may change. Nevertheless, since there are only n choices for i, some index i must occur infinitely often, so for such an index the previous equation must hold.

But this equation can only hold if $n = 1$ or $\frac{\partial x(a^\star)}{\partial a_i} = 0$. However $n > 1$ by assumption and x is strictly increasing and concave so $\frac{\partial x(a^\star)}{\partial a_i} \neq 0$. Thus, the equation cannot hold, this is a contradiction.

Such a contradiction proves that no sharing rule (even a non-differentiable rule)[11] can implement the efficient effort vector, $a^\star$. ■

But what if we are willing to work with the weaker balanced budget condition $\sum_{i=1}^n s_i(x) \leq x$ for all $x \in \Re_+$? That is, what if we are willing to throw money away? If we are, then there are many sharing rules that implement $a^\star$. Border gives a typical example:

Choose $b_i, i = 1, \ldots, n$, to satisfy

$$b_i > v_i(a^\star)$$

and

$$\sum_{i=1}^n b_i < x(a^\star)$$

and define

$$s_i(x) = \begin{cases} b_i & \text{if } x \geq x(a^\star) \\ 0 & \text{otherwise.} \end{cases} \tag{72.1}$$

This rule, s, implements $a^{\star}$. It is interesting to note that s is not even continuous, let alone differentiable everywhere and that unless $a = 0$, the team always produces more than its members receive in compensation.

4.1.1.1.3 THE FIRMS AS AN INCENTIVE SYSTEM VIEW

The third subgroup is the 'firms as an incentive system view'. This approach to the theory of the firm was developed by Holmström and Milgrom (1991, 1994), Holmström and Tirole (1989) and Holmström (1999) and has been described by Gibbons (2005: 206) as an "accidental theory of the firm". The reason for Gibbons's description is that the focus of these papers was not on the make-or-buy problem of the transaction cost or Grossman-Hart-Moore approaches but rather on a multi-task, multi-instrument principal–agent problem and its application to the firm was an 'accidental' outcome of this endeavour. In this view the firm is characterised by a number of factors: (1) the employees do not own the non-human assets of the firm; (2) the employees are subject to a 'low-powered incentive scheme' (see the following); and (3) the employer has authority over the employee.

Holmström and Milgrom (1991) make two observations. First, they note that there are a number of ways that an employee can spend their time, many of which can be of value to an employer. But if these multiple activities compete for the worker's attention, then the incentives offered for each of the activities must be comparable. Otherwise, the employee will put most effort into those things that are most well compensated and put less effort into the others activities. The second observation relates to the provision of strong incentives to a risk-averse employee. Providing strong financial incentives is costly because it loads extra risk into the worker's pay. In addition, the cost is greater the more difficult it is to measure performance. This means that, other things being equal, tasks where performance is hard to measure should not be given as intense incentives as ones that are more accurately observed. But having low-powered incentives means that the employer needs to be able to exercise authority over the use of the employee's time, since the employee will not have the proper incentives to be productive.

This logic suggests that, conversely, an independent contractor should face the opposite combination of instruments. The choice between having an employee or using an independent contractor depends on the ability of the principal to measure each dimension of the agent's contribution. Thus, in the Holmström and Milgrom approach, measurability of performance is one important determinant of the boundaries of the firm. In addition their approach incorporates the importance of the allocation of property rights to the physical assets in determining incentives via determination of bargaining positions as is the case with the Williamson and Grossman-Hart-Moore approaches, both of which are discussed later on.

To analyse the application of this theory to the firm we will take advantage of Gibbons (2005: 210–12) 'stick-figure rendition' of the theory. In the simple Gibbons model there is a technology of production which is a linear combination of the Agent's actions: $y = f_1 a_1 + f_2 a_2 + \varepsilon$ where the $a_i s$ are actions chosen by the Agent and ε is a noise term. Evaluation of performance by the Agent is based upon the indicator p which is a different linear combination of the Agent's actions: $p = g_1 a_1 + g_2 a_2 + \phi$, where ϕ is another noise term. Gibbons assumes that both parties are risk-neutral, ω is the total compensation paid by the Principal to the Agent and $c(a_1, a_2)$ represents the Agent's cost function. Gibbons makes the assumption that,

$$c(a_1, a_2) = \frac{1}{2}a_1^2 + \frac{1}{2}a_2^2.$$

In addition Gibbons assumes that the Principal and the Agent sign a linear contract, $\omega = s + bp$, based upon the performance indicator p.

To provide a theory of the firm, this model has to be extended to include physical capital, a machine, which is used by the Agent during the production of y. Post-production this capital has a value determined by a third linear combination of the Agent's actions: $v = h_1 a_1 + h_2 a_2 + \xi$ where ξ is a third noise term.

The choice variables in the model are, therefore, the Agent's actions $a_i, i = 1, 2$, and b the slope of the optimal contract. As a point of comparison, note that the first-best actions of the Agent are those which maximise the expected total surplus; that is, they will maximise the expected value of the sum of the Principal's pay-off, $y - \omega$, the Agent's pay-off, $\omega - c(a_1, a_2)$ and the value of the physical asset, v:

$$\begin{aligned} TS^{FB} &= E(y - \omega + \omega - c(a_1, a_2) + v) \\ &= E(y + v) - c(a_1, a_2) \\ &= E(f_1 a_1 + f_2 a_2 + \varepsilon + h_1 a_1 + h_2 a_2 + \xi) - c(a_1, a_2) \\ &= f_1 a_1 + f_2 a_2 + h_1 a_1 + h_2 a_2 - c(a_1, a_2) \quad \text{(assuming } E(\varepsilon) = E(\xi) = 0) \\ &= f_1 a_1 + f_2 a_2 + h_1 a_1 + h_2 a_2 - \frac{1}{2}a_1^2 - \frac{1}{2}a_2^2 \end{aligned}$$

and, therefore, $a_1^{FB} = f_1 + h_1$ and $a_2^{FB} = f_2 + h_2$.

Note TS^{FB} is independent of the value of b.

Math aside:

$$\begin{aligned} &\frac{\partial TS^{FB}}{\partial a_i} = 0 \\ &\Rightarrow f_i + h_i - a_i = 0 \\ &\qquad \Rightarrow a_i^{FB} = f_i + h_i. \end{aligned}$$

If the Principal owns the machine, then the Agent is an employee of his firm and the Principal's pay-off is $y + v - \omega$, while the Agent's pay-off is $\omega - c$. In this case the Agent's optimal actions maximise

$$\begin{aligned} E(\omega) - c(a_1, a_2) &= E(s + bp) - \frac{1}{2}a_1^2 - \frac{1}{2}a_2^2 \\ &= E(s + b(g_1 a_1 + g_2 a_2 + \phi)) - \frac{1}{2}a_1^2 - \frac{1}{2}a_2^2 \\ &= s + bg_1 a_1 + bg_2 a_2 - \frac{1}{2}a_1^2 - \frac{1}{2}a_2^2 \quad \text{assuming } E(\phi) = 0. \end{aligned}$$

The optimal actions are, therefore, $a^{\star}_{1E}(b) = bg_1$ and $a^{\star}_{2E}(b) = bg_2$.

Math aside:

$$\begin{aligned} &\frac{\partial E(\omega) - c(a_1, a_2)}{\partial a_i} = 0 \\ &\Rightarrow bg_i - a_i = 0 \\ &\quad \Rightarrow a^{\star}_i(b) = bg_i. \end{aligned}$$

The efficient contract slope, $b^{\star}_E$, maximises the expected total surplus, $E(y + v) - C(a_1, a_2)$ or

$$TS_E(b) = (f_1 + h_1)a^{\star}_{1E}(b) + (f_2 + h_2)a^{\star}_{2E}(b) - \frac{1}{2}a^{\star}_{1E}(b)^2 - \frac{1}{2}a^{\star}_{2E}(b)^2.$$

Alternatively the machine can be owned by the Agent. Gibbons interprets this case as the Agent being an independent contractor. In this situation the pay-offs for the Principal will be $y - w$ and for the Agent they are $w + v - c$. The optimal actions for the Agent will therefore be, $a^{\star}_{1C}(b) = g_1 b + h_1$ and $a^{\star}_{2C}(b) = g_2 b + h_2$.

Math aside:

$$\begin{aligned} E(\omega + v) - c(a_1, a_2) &= E(s + b(g_1 a_1 + g_2 a_2 + \phi) + h_1 a_1 + h_2 a_2 + \xi) \\ &\quad - \frac{1}{2}a_1^2 - \frac{1}{2}a_2^2 \\ &= s + bg_1 a_1 + bg_2 a_2 + h_1 a_1 + h_2 a_2 \\ &\quad - \frac{1}{2}a_1^2 - \frac{1}{2}a_2^2 \quad \text{assuming } E(\phi) = E(\xi) = 0. \end{aligned}$$

The first-order conditions are, therefore, of the form, $bg_i + h_i - a_i = 0$ which gives $a^{\star}_{iC}(b) = g_i b + h_i$, $i = 1, 2$.

For this case the efficient slope, $b_C^\star$, will maximise the expected total surplus of

$$TS_C(b) = (f_1 + h_1)a_{1C}^\star(b) + (f_2 + h_2)a_{2C}^\star(b) - \frac{1}{2}a_{1C}^\star(b)^2 - \frac{1}{2}a_{2C}^\star(b)^2.$$

Gibbons (2005: 211) summaries the analysis so far as

> [...] having the Agent own the asset causes the Agent to respond to a given contract slope (b) differently than when the Agent does not own the asset [i.e. $a_{iE}^\star(b) \neq a_{iC}^\star(b)$], so the make-or-buy problem amounts to determining which of the Agent's best-response functions – that of the employee, $(a_{1E}^\star(b), a_{2E}^\star(b))$, or that of the independent contractor, $(a_{1C}^\star(b), a_{2C}^\star(b))$ – allows the parties to achieve greater total surplus.

The discussion so far has relied on an unspecified assumption; that the value of the asset is not contractible and, therefore, the owner of the asset receives its value. Since the asset's value is not contractible, putting ownership in the hands of the Agent provides him with incentives that cannot be replicated via a contract. But providing the Agent with the incentive to increase the value of the asset may or may not help the Principal control the Agent's incentives via contract. That is, if the Agent owns the asset then he has two sources of incentives: the asset's post-production value and contracted for performance. Without ownership he concentrates solely on the contracted for performance. Integration would be efficient – that is, having the Principal own the asset is efficient – when having the Agent do so hurts the Principal's efforts to create incentives via contract.

4.1.1.2 *Incomplete contracts models*

In the incomplete contracting theories group Foss, Lando and Thomsen (2000: 638–43) identify five subgroups: (1) the authority view; (2) the firm as a governance mechanism; (3) the firm as an ownership unit; (4) relational (or implicit) contracts; and (5) the firm as a communication-hierarchy. In the next subsection we will add a sixth group, 'the reference point approach'. As noted in the next section, the theory of privatisation also relies on the incomplete contracts framework to explain why ownership makes a difference to the performance of firms.

4.1.1.2.1 THE AUTHORITY VIEW

In the authority view, the firm is seen as being defined as an employment relation. This view is one example where an approach to the firm founded in the pre-1970 period – this approach is most closely associated with Coase (1937) and Simon (1951) – is still being developed in the current mainstream. As was explained in more detail in Chapter 3, for Coase a firm will arise when it is cheaper to carry out a transaction in a firm than it is to do so over the market. Given that it costs something to enter into a market contract – that is, there are transaction costs – firms will emerge to carry out what would otherwise be a market transaction when it is cheaper for the firm to handle that transaction. The size of the firm (the boundaries of the firm) will be determined when the cost of organising a transaction within the firm equals the cost of using the market. Coase notes that within the firm contracts are not eliminated but are greatly reduced and the nature of the contract changes. When a factor of production is employed within the firm the contract controlling it is incomplete. The factor (or its owner) agrees, for remuneration, to obey the directions of the manager of the firm, within certain limits. In the last section of Coase (1937), it is noted that the relationship that constitutes the firm corresponds closely to the legal concept of the relationship between the employer and employee. Coase explains that 'direction' is the essence of the legal concept of the employment relationship, just as it is for the concept of the firm that he developed.

It is often suggested that the first formal model of an incomplete contracting problem was Simon (1951),[12] but, more importantly for our purposes, this paper is also a contribution to the theory of the firm, and thus we start our more detailed discussion of incomplete contracting models with a look at this seminal contribution.[13] For Simon (1951) the issue is a comparison of an employment contract against a contract between two autonomous agents. A contract between autonomous agents specifies an action to be taken in the future along with its price while an employment contract specifies a set of acceptable instructions that the employee has to accept if asked to carry them out by the employer. The advantage of the employment contract is its flexibility, the employer does not have to pre-commit to an action and can adapt the choice of action to the state of the world that occurs.

Simon opens his paper by pointing out that in standard economic theory employees (i.e. those people who contract to exchange their services for a wage) enter into the system in two sharply distinct roles. Initially, they are owners of their own labour, which is a factor of production, which they sell for a definite price. Having done so, they become completely passive factors of production employed by the entrepreneur in such a way as to maximise his profit. Next Simon notes that this approach to the employment contract and to the management of labour involves a very high order of abstraction. He argues that it abstracts away the most obvious peculiarities of the employment contract, those which distinguish it from other kinds of contracts; and it ignores the most significant features of the administrative process, i.e., the process of actually managing the factors of production, including labour. Simon states that the aim of his paper is to put forward a theory of the employment relationship that reintroduces some of the more important of these empirical realities into the economic model.

Simon asks: what is the nature of the authority relationship between an employer and an employee? This relationship, which is created by the employment contract, plays a central role in Simon's theory.

Simon's notion is to denote the employer, or 'boss', B and the 'worker' or employee W. The collection of actions taken by the worker on the job is called his *behaviour*. The set of all possible behaviour patterns of W is considered and we will let x designate an element of this set. A particular x might then represent a given set of tasks, performed at a particular rate of working, a particular level of accuracy, and so on.

Authority, in Simon's, view is exercised by B over W if W permits B to select x. In other words, W accepts authority when his behaviour is determined by B's decision. In general, W will accept authority only if x_0, the x chosen by B, is restricted to some given subset (W's 'area of acceptance') of all of the possible values.

Simon states that W enters into an employment contract with B when W agrees to accept the authority of B and B agrees to pay W a stated wage, denoted by w. Here Simon notes the difference between this contractual form and that of a sales contract. In the sales contract, each party to the contract promises a specific consideration in return for the consideration promised by the other. The buyer (like B) promises to pay a stated amount of money; but the seller (unlike W) promises in return a specified quantity of a completely specified commodity. Also, the seller is not interested in how the commodity is used after it is sold, unlike the worker who is interested in how the entrepreneur will use him in the future (i.e. what x will be chosen by B).

An attempt is made to answer two questions: (1) Why is W willing to sign a blank check by giving B authority over his behaviour? (2) Given that both parties behave rationally, under what circumstances will a sales contract be signed and when will an employment contract be signed?

The suggestion is then made by Simon that two conjectures, if true, offer possible answers to these questions.

1. W will be willing to sign an employment contract with B only if he is indifferent to the x that is selected by B, out of the areas of acceptance. Or, if W is compensated in some way for the possibility that B will choose an x that is not desired by W; that is, B will ask that W undertake an unpleasant task.
2. It will be to B's advantage to offer W additional compensation for agreeing to an employment contract if B is unable to predict with certainty, at the time the contract is agreed to, which behaviour x will be the optimum one. That is, B will pay for the privilege of postponing the selection of x until after the contract is signed.

Simon assumes that W and B are each trying to maximise their respective *satisfaction functions*. Each person's satisfaction will depend upon:

(a) the particular x that is chosen – the $F_i(\cdot)$ function can be thought of as the 'pay-off', positive or negative, for each party from x being chosen[14] and

(b) the particular wage w that is received or paid.

It is also assumed that these two components of satisfaction enter the satisfaction function additively:

$$S_1 = F_1(x) - a_1 w \qquad (78.1)$$

$$S_2 = F_2(x) + a_2 w \qquad (78.2)$$

where S_1 and S_2 are the satisfactions of B and W, respectively, and $w > 0$ is the waged paid by B to W.

Each party's opportunity cost of agreeing to a contract can be used to define the zero point of his satisfaction function. In other words, if B does not contract with W, then $S_1 = S_2 = 0$. For the circumstances relevant here, it is reasonable to assume $F_1(x) \geq 0$, $F_2(x) \leq 0$, $a_1 > 0$, $a_2 > 0$ for the relevant range of x.

As we have $S_1 = S_2 = 0$ if no agreement can be reached between B and W, it will be assumed that if an agreement is reached then $S_1 \geq 0$, $S_2 \geq 0$. If an x and w can be found satisfying these two equations, then the system is said to be *viable*. The conditions for a viable system can be rewritten as:

$$F_1(x) \geq a_1 w \tag{79.1}$$

$$-F_2(x) \leq a_2 w. \tag{79.2}$$

Equations (79.1) and (79.2) imply that

$$a_2 F_1(x) \geq a_2 a_1 w \geq -a_1 F_2(x). \tag{79.3}$$

Conversely, if for some x, $a_2 F_1(x) \geq -a_1 F_2(x)$, then it is always possible to find a $w \geq 0$ such that (79.3) holds. Thus (79.3) is a necessary and sufficient condition for the system to be viable.

So far the only thing imposed on an agreement between B and W is that it should satisfy the viability condition. This amounts to saying that the agreement is advantageous for both parties.

Simon notes that, in general, if there is any agreement then it will not be unique. That is, if there exists a viable agreement then there will be a region in the (x, w)-space satisfying (79.3) and it will only be in rare cases that this region will be a single point.

In Figure 79.1, the set of x's has been represented by a scalar; F_1 and F_2 are continuous in x, and reach extrema at $x = x_1$ and $x = x_2$, respectively. The grey hatched area is the region of viability.

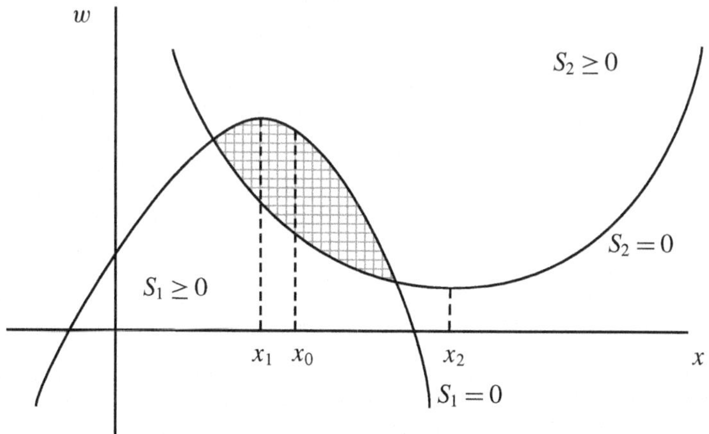

Figure 79.1.

Source: Simon 1951: Figure 1, p. 296.

Simon now considers a stronger notion of rationality. The requirement here is that when one agreement (a point in $\{x, w\}$) yields the satisfactions (S_1, S_2) and a second agreement the satisfactions (S_1', S_2') to B and W, respectively, then the first agreement will be preferred to the second if $S_1 \geq S_1'$ and $S_2 \geq S_2'$ with at least one of the two inequalities being a strict one.

If this requirement holds, then we say that the second solution is an 'inferior' one. The subset of solutions that are not inferior to any solutions is called the set of preferred solutions.

A function, $T(x, w)$, is now defined by Simon:

$$T(x, w) = a_2 S_1(x, w) + a_1 S_2(x, w) = a_2 F_1(x) + a_1 F_2(x) = T(x). \qquad (80.1)$$

THEOREM 80.1 (Simon 1951: 297, Theorem) The set of preferred solutions is the set $\{x, w\}$ for which $T(x)$ assumes its greatest value.

Proof. See Appendix 2, page 165.

The argument Simon has used thus far suggests that the rational procedure for B and W is to first determine a preferred x and then to bargain over the size of w so to fix S_1 and S_2. The result of this type of procedure would be a sales contract of the kind where W agrees to perform a specific, determinate act x_0 for which he would be paid a price w_0.

Now Simon assumes that $F_1(x)$ and $F_2(x)$, the satisfactions associated with x for B and W, respectively, are not known with certainty when B and W must negotiate an agreement. All we know is that W is to undertake some activity for B at some point in the future. The issue here is that at the time B and W make their agreement, it is not known what activity will be optimal. Under such circumstances Simon argues there are two ways in which the parties could proceed:

1 From a knowledge of the probability distributions functions of $F_1(x)$ and $F_2(x)$, for each x, they estimate what x would be optimal in the sense of maximising the expected value of, say, $T(x)$. They could then contract for W to perform this specified x for a specified wage, w. This is essentially the sales contract procedure with mathematical expectations substituted for certain outcomes.
2 B and W could agree on a wage, w, to be paid by B to W and in addition upon a procedure to be followed at a later date when the actual values for all x of $F_1(x)$ and $F_2(x)$ are known, for selecting a specific x. Of the many conceivable procedures for selecting x, the simplest is for W to allow B to select x from some specified set X; that is, for W to accept B's authority. Given that w is fixed, B would, we assume, select the x from X which maximises $F_1(x)$. But this kind of arrangement is what has previously been defined as an employment contract.

At the time when contract negotiations are carried out, F_1 and F_2 have a known joint probability density function for each element x:

$$p(F_1, F_2; x) dF_1 dF_2.$$

Defining the expectation operator, $\mathcal{E}$, in the usual manner, we have for fixed x:

$$\mathcal{E}[T(x)] = \mathcal{E}[a_2 F_1(x) + a_1 F_2(x)] = a_2 \mathcal{E}[F_1(x)] + a_1 \mathcal{E}[F_2(x)]. \tag{81.1}$$

ALTERNATIVE 1: Sales contract.

Assume that at the time of contract negotiations B and W agree on a particular x that will maximise $\mathcal{E}[T(x)]$ and agree on a w that divides the total satisfaction between them. The measure of the advantage of this procedure is given by $\max_x \mathcal{E}[T(x)]$.

ALTERNATIVE 2: Employment contract.

Here it is assumed that at the time of the negotiations B and W agree upon a set X from which B will choose x and upon a wage w that divides the total satisfaction between them. In a later time period, when $F_1(x)$ and $F_2(x)$ become known with certainty, B will choose x as to maximise $F_1(x)$; that is B chooses $\max_{x \, in \, X} F_1(x)$. The advantage from this procedure is given by

$$T_X = \mathcal{E}[a_2 F_1(x_m) + a_1 F_2(x_m)] \tag{81.2}$$

where x_m is the x in X which maximises $F_1(x)$.

Simon now points out that the concept of preferred solutions can be generalised with the preferred set, X, being a set for which T_X assumes its maximum value. Theorem 80.1 can be extended to show that if B and W agree upon an X which is not preferred, then the expected satisfactions of both can be increased by substituting a preferred X and adjusting w appropriately.

The idea of a preferred set provides a rational theory for the determination of the range of authority of B over W; that is, W's areas of acceptance. Moreover the sale contract can be seen as a special case in which X contains a single element. Hence, the difference between $\max T_X$ for all sets and $\max T_X$ for single-element sets provides a measure of the advantage of an employment contract over a sales contract for specified distribution functions of $F_1(x)$, $F_2(x)$.

Here Simon uses an example as an illustration of the theory. In this example W's behaviour choice is restricted to two elements, x_a and x_b. If W's behaviour pattern is x_a then B and W will receive the satisfactions $S_1(x_a, w)$ and $S_2(x_a, w)$, respectively, where

$$S_1 = F_1(x_a) - a_1 w \tag{81.3}$$

$$S_2 = F_2(x_a) + a_2 w. \tag{81.4}$$

Let us assume that at the time of contracting, $F_1(x_a)$ and $F_1(x_b)$ have a joint probability density function given by

$$p(F_1(x_a), F_1(x_b)) dF_1(x_a) dF_1(x_b). \tag{81.5}$$

Also assume that $F_2(x_a)$ and $F_2(x_b)$ have known fixed values:

$$F_2(x_a) = \alpha, \quad F_2(x_b) = \beta. \tag{81.6}$$

If B and W are to sign a sales contract, then they will need to choose between x_a and x_b. Based on our previous assumptions of rationality, they will choose x_a if and only if:

$$\begin{aligned}\mathcal{E}[T(x_a)] &= \left[a_2 \int_{-\infty}^{\infty}\int_{-\infty}^{\infty} F_1(x_a)p(F_1(x_a), F_1(x_b))dF_1(x_a)dF_1(x_b)\right] + a_1\alpha \\ &\geq \left[a_2 \int_{-\infty}^{\infty}\int_{-\infty}^{\infty} F_1(x_b)p(F_1(x_a), F_1(x_b))dF_1(x_a)dF_1(x_b)\right] + a_1\beta \\ &= \mathcal{E}[T(x_b)]. \end{aligned} \tag{82.1}$$

Assume that (82.1) does hold. Simon asks the question, Will the parties gain anything further by entering into an employment contract instead of using a sales contract? This question amounts to asking if there is any advantage to giving B the right to choose between x_a and x_b when $F(x_a)$ and $F(x_b)$ become known with certainty. To answer this question Simon compares $\mathcal{E}[T(x_a)]$ (Equation (82.1)) with T_X (Equation (81.2)), where X consists of the set x_a and x_b.

We know

$$\begin{aligned}\mathcal{E}\left\{\max_{x\in X} F_1(x)\right\} &= \int_{F_1(x_a)=-\infty}^{\infty}\int_{F_1(x_b)=F_1(x_a)}^{\infty} F_1(x_b)p(F_1(x_a), F_1(x_b))dF_1(x_b)dF_1(x_a) \\ &+ \int_{F_1(x_b)=-\infty}^{\infty}\int_{F_1(x_a)=F_1(x_b)}^{\infty} F_1(x_a)p(F_1(x_a), F_1(x_b))dF_1(x_a)dF_1(x_b)\end{aligned} \tag{82.2}$$

where $p(F_1(x_a), F_1(x_b))$ is the joint probability density function of $F_1(x_a)$ and $F_1(x_b)$. This means that

$$\begin{aligned}T_X &= \int_{F_1(x_a)=-\infty}^{\infty}\int_{F_1(x_b)=F_1(x_a)}^{\infty} (a_2F_1(x_b) + a_1\beta)p(F_1(x_a), F_1(x_b))dF_1(x_b)dF_1(x_a) \\ &+ \int_{F_1(x_b)=-\infty}^{\infty}\int_{F_1(x_a)=F_1(x_b)}^{\infty} (a_2F_1(x_a) + a_1\alpha)p(F_1(x_a), F_1(x_b))dF_1(x_a)dF_1(x_b)\end{aligned} \tag{82.3}$$

and to choose between an employment contract and a sales contract Simon notes that the sign of $T_X - \mathcal{E}[T(x_a)]$ (see Appendix 2, page 166, for the derivation of $T_X - \mathcal{E}[T(x_a)]$) must be determined where

$$\begin{aligned}T_X - \mathcal{E}[T(x_a)] &= \int_{F_1(x_a)=-\infty}^{\infty}\int_{F_1(x_b)=F_1(x_a)}^{\infty} (a_2(F_1(x_b) - F_1(x_a)) + a_1(\beta - \alpha)) \\ &\cdot p(F_1(x_a), F_1(x_b))dF_1(x_b)dF_1(x_a).\end{aligned} \tag{82.4}$$

Given that we know that $(F_1(x_b) - F_1(x_a)) \geq 0$ in the region of integration, we can conclude that the employment contract is preferable to the sales contract with $x = x_a$, if $\beta > \alpha$ (i.e. if W prefers x_b to x_a) and even if $(\beta - \alpha) < 0$ but not too

Math aside:

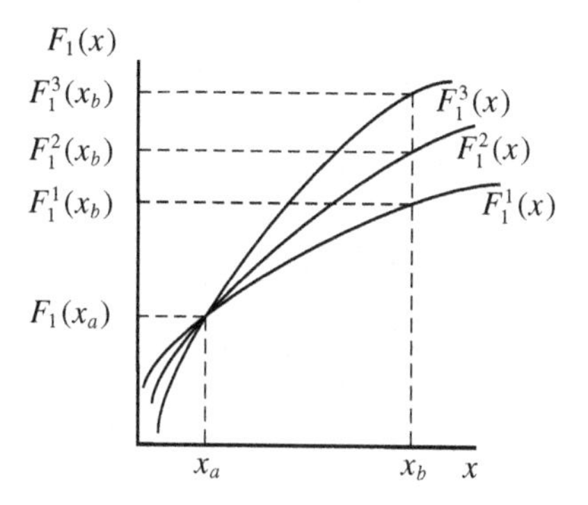

Figure 83.1.

To understand the joint probability density function

$$p(F_1(x_a), F_1(x_b))dF_1(x_a)dF_1(x_b),$$

first consider Figure 83.1. Let us assume that $F_1(x)$ can take three different functional forms, $F_1^1(x)$, $F_1^2(x)$ or $F_1^3(x)$. The probabilities for each of these forms are P_1^1, P_1^2 and P_1^3, respectively, where $\sum_{i=1}^{3} P_1^i = 1$. We can arbitrarily fix x at x_a and assume that all three of the functions pass through the point $(x_a, F_1(x_a))$. But the values of x_b for each of the three functional forms are different and they occur with probabilities P_1^1, P_1^2 and P_1^3, respectively. Thus, for a given x_a – and hence $F_1(x_a)$ – we get a probability distribution over the value of $F_1(x_b)$: $F_1^1(x_b)$ occurs with probability P_1^1, $F_1^2(x_b)$ occurs with probability P_1^2 and $F_1^3(x_b)$ with probability P_1^3. This gives us the conditional probability for each value of $F_1(x_b)$ assuming a given value of $F_1(x_a)$. To obtain the joint distribution $P(F_1(x_a), F_1(x_b))$ we multiply the conditional probability, $P(F_1^i(x_b)|F_1(x_a)) = P_1^i$, by the marginal probability, $P(F_1(x_a))$. Each $P_1^i * P(F_1(x_a))$ result gives us one of the black dots in Figure 83.2. As we increase the range of values of $F_1(x_a)$ and $F_1(x_b)$ considered, to $(-\infty, +\infty)$, the black dots merge to form a the probability surface giving the joint probability distribution, $P(F_1(x_a), F_1(x_b))$.

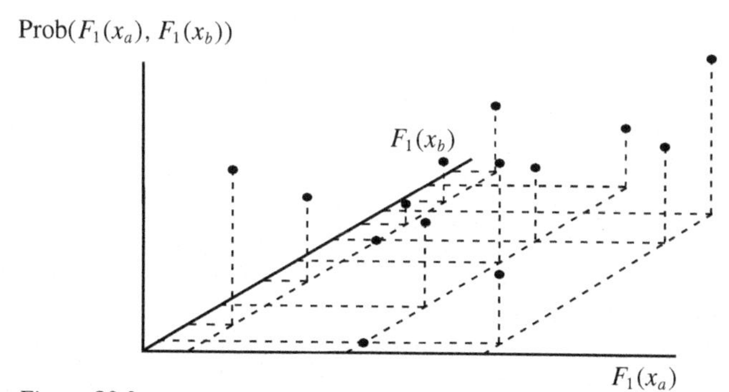

Figure 83.2.

negative. Since $(F_1(x_b) - F_1(x_a)) \geq 0$, B prefers x_b to x_a and if W also prefers x_b to x_a then the employment contract is preferred to the sales contract since the sales contract results in x_a while the employment contract puts positive probability on getting x_b, the preferred outcome.

Simon now considers a special case of Equation (82.4) in which W is indifferent between x_a and x_b; that is, $\alpha = \beta$, and $F_1(x_a)$ and $F_1(x_b)$ are independently normally distributed:

$$P(F_1(x_a), F_1(x_b)) = \frac{1}{2\pi\sigma_a\sigma_b} \exp\left\{-\frac{1}{2}\left[\left(\frac{F_1(x_a) - A}{\sigma_a}\right)^2 + \left(\frac{F_1(x_b) - B}{\sigma_b}\right)^2\right]\right\} \tag{84.1}$$

where A and B are the means and σ_a and σ_b the standard deviations of $F_1(x_a)$ and $F_1(x_b)$, respectively. Given (84.1), Equation (82.4) can be written as

$$T_X - \mathcal{E}[T(x_a)] = \frac{a_2}{2\pi\sigma_a\sigma_b} \int_{F_1(x_a)=-\infty}^{\infty} \int_{F_1(x_b)=F_1(x_a)}^{\infty} (F_1(x_b) - F_1(x_a)) \times \exp\left\{-\frac{1}{2}\left[\left(\frac{F_1(x_a) - A}{\sigma_a}\right)^2 + \left(\frac{F_1(x_b) - B}{\sigma_b}\right)^2\right]\right\} dF_1(x_b)dF_1(x_a). \tag{84.2}$$

The situation described by Equation (84.2) is pictured in Figure 85.1. Here is it assumed that $A = 0$ and $B < 0$. The ellipses about the point $(0, B)$ are the contours of the probability function and the region of integration is above, to the left, of the line $F(x_a) = F_1(x_b)$.

Math aside: Remember that the bivariate normal distribution can be represented as a bell-shaped surface $z = f(x, y)$, as in the following diagram. Any plane parallel to the xy plane which cuts the surface will intersect it in an elliptic curve.

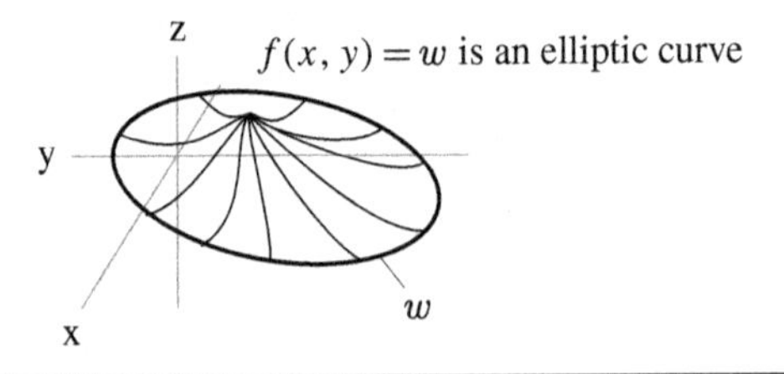

From Figure 85.1 it should be clear that $T_X - \mathcal{E}[T(x_a)]$ will increase if there is an increase in σ_a or σ_b and with a decrease in the absolute value of B. An increase in σ_a or σ_b increases the size of the ellipses and a decrease in the absolute vale of B moves $(0, B)$, the largest value of $T_X - \mathcal{E}[T(x_a)]$, towards the origin and thus the region of integration. This tells us that an increase in the uncertainty of either $F_1(x_a)$ or $F_1(x_b)$ when the contract is made will increase the advantage of the employment contract over the sales contract, while a decrease in average disadvantage of x_b as compared to x_a will have the same result.

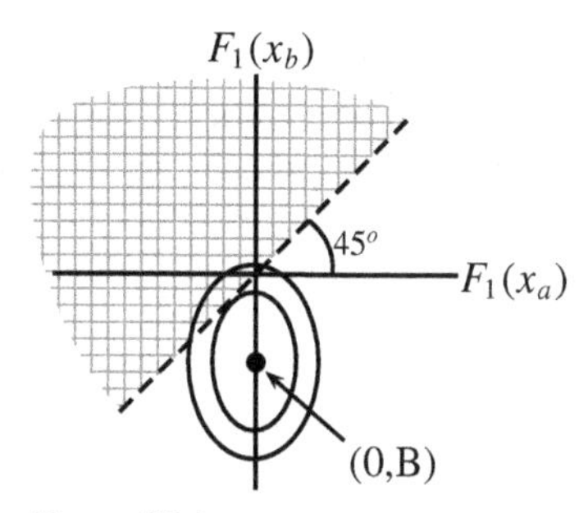

Figure 85.1.

Source: Simon 1951: Figure 2, p. 301.

Simon now notes that it is clear that these results will hold, qualitatively, even when $F_1(x_a)$ and $F_1(x_b)$ are not independently distributed, or when the distribution is not exactly normal. Thus, it is concluded that both the conjectures set forth at the end of second section prove to be correct.

Next Simon argues that one objection to his analysis needs to be raised and disposed of. He has assumed so far, that in the employment contract, that B, when $F_1(x_a)$ and $F_1(x_b)$ become known will choose the larger of the two. Why does B not choose the larger of $(a_1 F_1(x_a) + a_2\alpha)$ or $(a_1 F_1(x_b) + a_2\beta)$? If he did, then this the employment contract would always be preferred to the sales contract. This would maximise the sum of the satisfactions. w could be used to split this satisfaction between B and W to their mutual advantage. In this situation there would be no advantage to limiting X.

The problem with such an agreement is that once B and W have agreed on a w, there is no way for W to enforce the understanding that B will choose x on the basis of maximising $(a_1 F_1(\cdot) + a_2 F_2(\cdot))$ rather than $F_1(\cdot)$. Moreover it is to B's short-run advantage to maximise $F_1(\cdot)$ rather than $(a_1 F_1(\cdot) + a_2 F_2(\cdot))$ once w is determined. In other words, the worker has no assurance that the employer will consider anything other than his own profit when deciding on what action he will ask the worker to carry out.

Simon then argues that if the worker had a responsible expectation that the employer would take account of his satisfactions, then the worker would presumably be willing to work for a smaller wage than if he thought these satisfactions were going to be ignored in the employer's exercise of authority and only profitability to the employer taken into account. On the other hand, unless the worker is thereby induced to work for a lower wage, the employer has no incentive to use his authority in any other way than to maximise $F_1(\cdot)$. Hence, we might expect the employer to maximise $(a_1 F_1(\cdot) + a_2 F_2(\cdot))$ only if he thought that by so doing he could persuade the worker, in subsequent renewals of the employment contract, to accept a wage sufficiently smaller to compensate him for this. Otherwise, the employer would rationally maximise $F_1(\cdot)$. The interpretation that Simon gives to this is that the maximising $F_1(\cdot)$ behaviour represents 'short-run' rationality, whereas the maximising $(a_1 F_1(\cdot) + a_2 F_2(\cdot))$ behaviour represents 'long-run' rationality when a relationship of confidence between employer and worker can be attained. The fact that the former rule leads to solutions that are preferable to those of the latter shows that it 'pays' the employer to establish this relationship.

In this discussion, the situation that was considered was limited to having only two behaviour alternatives available for W. This analysis can be interpreted as answering the following question:

> Suppose that B and W have already agreed to enter into an employment contract, with B to choose x from some subset, X_a that does not include x_b. Is it now advantageous to the parties to enlarge W's area of acceptance to include x_b?

Simon interprets x_a to mean the element of X_a which maximises $F_1(x)$ for x in X_a. Assume that the joint probability distribution $p[F_1(x_1), F_1(x_2), \ldots]$ for $x_1, x_2 \ldots$ in X_a is known and, therefore, we can calculate the probability distribution of $F_a = F_1(x_a)$. This is, in fact, the distribution of the maximum of a sample where each element of the sample is drawn from a different population. Placing this interpretation of the F_a that enters (82.4), we see that it will be advantageous to enlarge X_a to include x_b iff

$$T_{(X_a + X_b)} \geq T_{X_a}. \qquad (86.1)$$

Simon notes that any actual employment contract specifies more than the wage to be paid by B to W and the authority relationship. When the employer will not exercise his authority is often spelled out in great detail; for example, hours of work, nature of duties (in general or specifically) and so forth. For a relationship which endures over time, all sorts of informal understandings grow up in addition to formal agreements that are made when the contract is periodically renegotiated. Given the involvement of labour unions in negotiations, many of these contract terms are spelled out specifically and in detail in the union agreement. Simon deals with this fact by recognising that authority is accepted within limits, but such limits can be introduced in a different manner.

So to extend the model in this direction, Simon assumes that the behaviour of the worker, or group of workers, is specified not by a single, x, element but by a sequence of such elements $(x, y, z, \ldots)$. In addition, assume that each of these determines a separate component in the satisfaction functions and that these components enter additively:

$$S_1 = f_{1x}(x) + f_{1y}(y) + \cdots - aw \qquad (86.2)$$

and similarly for S_2.

The parties now enter into a contract in which some of the elements, say $x, \cdots$, are specified as terms in the contract; a second set of elements, say, $y, \cdots$, is subject to the authority of the employer; and a third set of elements, say, $z, \cdots$, is left to the discretion of the workers. Analogously to the assumptions made previously, Simon assumes that if the element y is subject to the authority of B, then he will fix it so as to maximise $f_{1y}(y)$, while if z is left to the discretion of W, then he will fix it so that $f_{2z}(z)$ is maximised. It is now possible to derive inequalities analogous to (82.4) that will show which of the elements should fall into each of these three categories.

Reviewing the previous results, it is clear that the conditions making it advantageous to (1) stipulate the value of a particular variable in the contract are

(a) sharp conflict of interest with respect to the optimum value of the element (f_1 high when f_2 low and vice versa);

(b) little uncertainty as to the optimum values of the element (σ_{f_1} and σ_{f_2} are small).

The conditions making it advantageous to (2) give B authority over an element or (3) to leave it to the workers' discretion are just the opposite of those noted previously. Moreover, (2) will be preferable to (3) if B's sensitivity to departures from optimality turn out to be greater than those of W.

A number of limitations of Simon's paper have been noted. First, Simon's comparison of the two contracts is only in terms of ex post efficiency. There is no consideration of ex ante investment or ex post renegotiation by Simon.[15] A criticism, made by Alchian and Demsetz (1972), of the master-servant relation implicit in the employment relationship is that there is no difference between the relationship between an employer and his employee and the relationship of a customer with his grocer. In other words, there is no difference between a 'sales' and 'an employment relation' contract as seen by Simon. But as has been noted previously – see page 63 – this argument itself has been criticised. But perhaps the most serious limitation of the model lies in the assumption of rational utility-maximising behaviour by the players.

Wernerfelt (1997) uses a more modern approach that builds on Simon's ideas. Wernerfelt portrays governance mechanisms as game forms chosen by rational agents to regulate their relations. He compares three alternative game forms for situations where a buyer needs a sequence of human asset services: (1) the hierarchy game form; (2) the price list game form; and (3) the negotiation-as-needed game form.[16] An employee is defined as someone who sells his services in a specific game form characterised by the absence of bargaining over adaptations to changing circumstances. The firm is seen as consisting of the buyer of human asset services, along with a set of sellers, provided that the human services are traded in the 'employment relationship' or 'hierarchy' game form. The hierarchy game form is defined as the situation in which the parties engage in once-and-for all wage negotiation, the manager describes desired services sequentially, and either party may terminate the relationship at will. In this model, the boundaries of the firm are given by the set of agents employed by the buyer. Whether one uses the employment relationship or an alternative game form depends on the nature of the expected adaptations. If many diverse and frequent adjustments are needed, the employment relationship involves lower adjustment costs than any of the other governance structures. The price list game form is better when the list of possible adjustments is small and the negotiation-as-needed game form is better when adjustments are needed infrequently.

In a more recent paper, Wernerfelt (2015), Wernerfelt asks why, in different circumstances, are all of firms (an employment relationship), contracts and markets used as trading mechanisms? He notes that we do not have a theory that can explain the use of each of these mechanisms within a unified framework. His proposed theory is based upon the interaction of four factors: the advantages of specialisation, workers' costs of switching between entrepreneurs, the size of entrepreneurs, and the frequency with which entrepreneur's requirements change.

Most importantly, for our purposes the employment contract (a firm) occurs when the entrepreneur has many, frequently changing needs, it is costly for workers to switch from one entrepreneur to another, and the advantages of specialisation are small. Wernerfelt (2015: 351) illustrates the effects of specialisation, switching costs and adjustment frequency with the example of the maintenance of a medium-sized apartment building,

> The owner [of the building] will typically have an employee-the superintendent-to perform minor repairs ('the toilet leaks'). The building generates a steady flow of small problems that tend to be urgent, and the superintendent can solve each of them pretty well. On the other hand, certain minor renovations, such as those having to do with electricity ('install LED light bulbs in public spaces'), are normally done through the market. The jobs are often larger, specialists can do them better, and the building does not need a full time electrician. Major renovations, for which advance planning reduces the need for in-process changes, are typically governed by a bilateral contract subject to occasional, though typically costly, renegotiations.
>
> The same example can illustrate the effects of size. A landlord who owns just one or two units will typically go to the market even for minor repairs because these units do not generate enough work to support a superintendent. On the other hand, very large landlords, such as universities, typically use specialist employees (their 'own' electricians) for both repairs and minor renovations.

4.1.1.2.2 THE FIRM AS A GOVERNANCE MECHANISM

The 'firm as a governance mechanism' approach is most commonly associated with the work of Oliver Williamson (see, for example, Williamson 1971, 1973, 1975, 1979, 1985, 1996a). Williamson's work is based on the twin notions of bounded rationality, which results in contractual incompleteness, and opportunism, thought of as 'self-interest with guile'. An upshot of these ideas is that contractual agreements need various kinds of safeguards built into them. For example, contractual agreements could involve 'hostages'; that is, one party may post a bond with the other. The contractual arrangements and their associated safeguards are referred to as 'governance structures' by Williamson. The basic idea is that transactions can be assigned to governance structures on the basis of their transaction properties.

Gibbons (2005: Sections 1.1, 1.4, 2.2, and 3) argues that Williamson's works can be read as suggesting two elemental theories of the firm – rent-seeking and adaptation. In the rent-seeking theory of the firm integration can be the efficient governance structure because integration can put a stop to socially destructive haggling over 'appropriable quasi-rents' (or AQRs). Williamson argues that within firms conflicts are settled by fiat, which can be a more efficient way to handle such issues than haggling. The basic logic is that, in the presence of AQRs, non-integration cannot avoid inefficient haggling because even though the haggling is jointly and socially unproductive, it is a source of private pecuniary gain, and thus integration, which brings with it dispute-resolution by fiat – and thus less haggling – can be more efficient. Also note the result that the larger the AQRs are, the more likely is integration; presumably because the socially unproductive haggling is either more likely or more costly (or both) when the AQRs are larger.

In Gibbon's adaptation version of Williamson's theory of the firm, integration can be the optimal governance structure for transactions that require adaptive, sequential decision-making in situations where uncertainty is resolved over time. To formulate an adaptation theory, a setting – in which uncertainty is endemic – must be created such that neither ex ante contracts nor ex post renegotiation can achieve post-uncertainty first-best adaptation. A second-best solution may be to concentrate authority in the hands of a 'boss' who makes decisions – albeit self interested decisions – after the resolution of any uncertainty. Thus, for the adaptation (and the rent-seeking) theory the emphasis is on authority and control, where the 'boss' makes any necessary decisions. This is in contrast to the 'firm as a solution to moral hazard in teams approach' which concentrates on incentives and thereby ignores control and the 'firm as an ownership unit' approach which blends the two but it does mean that the adaptation theory shares similarities with 'the authority view' discussed previously.[17] Williamson argues that it is only when there is a need to make unforeseen adaptations that the market versus internal organisation question become an interesting issue.

Within the rent seeking framework it is often argued that AQRs arise because of relationship specific investments and asset specificity. Assets are specific to a transaction when they have high value within the context of a particular transaction but little value outside it. This leads to the possibility of (ex post) opportunism. In so far as contracts are incomplete, as uncertainty unfolds and unanticipated events occur, the contract will need to be renegotiated and if one party has made a sunk investment via the development of assets specific to the relationship then the other party could attempt to opportunistically appropriate an undue part of the pay-offs to this investment by threatening to withdraw from the relationship. Significantly Gibbon sees the adaptation interpretation as being independent of these hold-up type issues, which makes the adaptation view a non-standard interpretation of Williamson's work.

Williamson can be seen as proposing that both asset specificity and adaptation are necessary if a theory of the firm is to be realistic.

While Williamson's work has explained why there are benefits to integration, Aghion *et al.* (2014b: i2) argues it still leaves at least two important questions unanswered: (1) how does integration succeed in eliminating ex post opportunism? and (2) what are the costs of integration? The Grossman-Hart-Moore approach to the firm, which will be described later in this chapter, offers a model that addresses these questions.

Tadelis and Williamson (2013: 170–9) offer a simple formal model of transaction cost economies (TCE). Their model considers two modes of governance: market and hierarchy and asks: When does each mode enjoy an advantage over the other? The basic features of the Tadelis and Williamson model are: (1) exchange takes place between successive (technologically separable) stages of production; (2) spot markets aside, all contracts are incomplete to varying degrees; (3) the critical attributes of transactions are asset specificity and contractual incompleteness (disturbances), where the former is responsible for bilateral dependency and the latter creates a need for adaptation; (4) if the parties are independent and if a disturbance occurs for which the contract is not adequate, then adaptation is accomplished by renegotiation and/or court ordering; and (5) efficiency is served by aligning transactions with governance structures in a way that economizes on transaction costs.

Two points about the formal model, which analyses a relationship between a buyer and a seller of an intermediate good, are worth noting at this point. First, adaptation costs are incurred only by the buyer. Second, it is assumed, for simplicity, that asset specificity is treated as a probability of finding an alternative seller without incurring adaptation costs, rather than as an actual loss in surplus if the seller is replaced. More detail on these points will follow.

Tadelis and Williamson consider a transaction between a buyer and a seller where the buyer obtains a value v, > 0, if he procures a good (or service) from the seller and incorporates that good into his own output. The transaction is characterised by both asset specificity and contractual incompleteness.

Asset specificity is modelled by $\sigma \in [0, 1]$, where higher values of σ represent higher degrees of asset specificity. Tadelis and Williamson interpret σ as the probability that the seller cannot be replaced when disruptions in supply occur and adaptation costs are therefore incurred. $(1 - \sigma)$ is the probability that another supplier will perform any necessary adaptations and adaptation costs will be avoided. Note that when σ is higher, the expected loss from having to switch suppliers will be larger, making the fundamental transformation more severe.[18]

Next, the probability that renegotiation of the contract will be required due to some significant disruption is modelled as $\rho \in [0, 1]$. Should disruption occur, then enforcement of the ex ante design of the contract will not result in the value v being obtained. Achieving v will then require ex post adaptation, at some additional cost. ρ is interpreted as a measure of the contractual incompleteness of the transaction and is assumed to be exogenous.

As previously noted, two forms of governance are considered. The first being the market and the second hierarchy. Transaction cost economics associates two basic properties with the market: (1) high-powered cost incentives and (2) retention of controls rights by each party. Hierarchy, on the other hand, is identified with low-powered cost incentives and the parties relinquishing control to a third party. In their model Tadelis and Williamson formally define market versus hierarchy along only one of these dimensions: the allocation of administrate control over production and adaptation processes, and they assume that the strength of incentives is endogenously derived.

Market governance, denoted M, is defined to be the situation in which each of the parties retains autonomy over its own production process decisions and the supplier is expected to provide a product in line with conditions as specified in the contract. Importantly any adaptation of the ex ante design that becomes necessary due to disturbances has to be negotiated between the two autonomous parties. For simplicity, it is assumed that adaptation will only be required with receipt to the seller's production process.

Hierarchy, denoted H, is defined to be the situation in which each party forgoes their administrative control in favour of a third party, called the interface coordinator. This is to say that routine tasks are carried out as planned but should a disruption occur any necessary decisions are made by the interface controller who has unified ownership and thus control over production and adaptation stages for both the buyer and the seller. The notion of hierarchy Tadelis and Williamson use is different from that of the Property Rights Theory (PRT) associated with Grossman-Hart-Moore in that Tadelis and Williamson assign responsibility for implementing routines to the managers at each stage and only assign responsibility for coordinated adaptations arising from disturbances to the interface coordinator. Tadelis and Williamson (2013: 172) write,

> TCE identifies this interface coordinator as often being a third party whose incentives are aligned with total profit maximization. That is, instead of a preexisting buyer and supplier, the transaction is a de novo investment whose governance needs to be determined. Efficiency considerations will determine whether the transaction is integrated (controlled by an interface coordinator) or not integrated (controlled by the contract and mutually agreed-upon adaptations). PRT, in contrast, identifies integration with the situation in which one of the two parties becomes the owner of all productive assets and controls the decisions related to their use. The predictions of PRT are as much about which of the two parties maintains control as about when unified ownership is called for.

In addition to the allocation of administrative control, the interfirm contract (or intrafirm compensation scheme) must also include a compensation mechanism which is utilised by the buyer (or interface coordinator) to determine payment to the supplier. This scheme will, of course, affect the incentives that the seller has to reduce costs. Let c denote the seller's production cost which includes items such as materials, lost opportunities, labour costs etc faced by the seller. Attention is restricted to linear compensation schemes of the form $F + (1 - z)c$ where F is a fixed component and $(1-z) \in [0, 1]$ a share of production costs. Thus, a supplier who incurs a cost c receives a payment of $F + (1-z)c$ where $z \in [0, 1]$ is the share of production costs borne by the seller. An important interpretation of z is as a measure of the 'strength' of the cost reduction incentives the supplier faces. For example, when $z = 1$ and $F > 0$ the seller is paid a fixed-price payment and bears all of the production costs. This seems to be the standard for market transactions and provides the seller with strong incentives to reduce production costs. On the other hand, a cost-plus contract would be one where $F > 0$ and $z = 0$ so that the seller bears none of the production costs and just receives a fixed payment. This seems more like what we find in hierarchical structures and, importantly, it provides little, or no, incentive to engage in cost reductions. Note that the F in the two situations will be different. In the current model both F and z are chosen endogenously.

The seller's production costs are given by the function $c(e, G) = \bar{c} - Ge$ where $e \geq 0$ is the intensity of effort expended by the seller and $G \in \{M, H\}$ denotes the mode of governance where $M > H > 0$ (think of M and H as being 'numbers'). This last requirement just means that for a given level of effort $Me > He$ and thus $c(e, M) < c(e, H)$. This amounts to saying that more effort reduces production costs, and effort is more effective in reducing production costs under market governance than under hierarchy. The opportunity cost of effort e to the seller is $y(e)$ where $y'(e) > 0$, $y''(e) > 0$ and $y'''(e) \leq 0$. To ensure an interior solution to the seller's optimisation problem it is assumed that $y'(0) = 0$. It is also assumed that contracting on e is impossible.

Should a disruption occur, then additional costly adaptations must be made in order to secure the value υ.

> Adaptation costs can have at least two sources. The first involves activities that were wasted and redone, or modifying initially planned production processes that fit the original design. These adaptation costs stem from contractual incompleteness and could have been spared if a complete contract and accurate design were in place. The second source of adaptation costs results from haggling, rent seeking, and other renegotiation costs that parties expend to get a better deal, which are a pure dead-weight loss.
>
> (Tadelis and Williamson 2013: 174)

These two costs are combined to give total adaptation costs denoted $k(z, G) > 0$.

These adaptation costs are incurred if and only if two events occur. First, obviously, a disruption must occur, an event which happens with probability ρ, which measures the incompleteness of the contract. But it must also be the case that a new supplier, from the competitive market, cannot step in and supply the modified good. This occurs with probability σ, the measure of specificity. Tadelis and Williamson assume, for simplicity, that any adaptation costs are borne by the buyer alone. It is also assumed that $\upsilon - k(z, G) > 0$ meaning that the adaptation costs are worth incurring ex post, to gain υ. Thus the expected gross benefit from the transaction is $\upsilon - \rho\sigma k(z, G) > 0$ and the expected adaptation costs are increasing in both ρ and σ.

Next Tadelis and Williamson make three assumptions concerning the nature of adaptation costs:

ASSUMPTION 93.1 (Tadelis and Williamson 2013: 175, Assumption 1) Adaptation costs are lower in hierarchy: $k(z, M) > k(z, H)$ for $0 \leq z \leq 1$.

This says that adaptation costs are greater under market governance than hierarchy.

ASSUMPTION 93.2 (Tadelis and Williamson 2013: 175, Assumption 2) Adaptation costs are lower when cost incentives are weaker: $\frac{\partial k(z,G)}{\partial z} > 0$.

This simply states that adaptation costs are increasing in seller cost reduction incentives.

ASSUMPTION 93.3 (Tadelis and Williamson 2013: 176, Assumption 3) Reducing adaptation costs by weakening incentives is more effective under hierarchy: $\frac{\partial k(z,H)}{\partial z} > \frac{\partial k(z,M)}{\partial z} > 0$.

This can be seen as saying that the slope of the hierarchy function is greater than that of the market function.

If we take, as an example, the two functions $k(z, H)$ and $k(z, M)$ to be affine, then these three assumptions mean that the two function can be represented as:

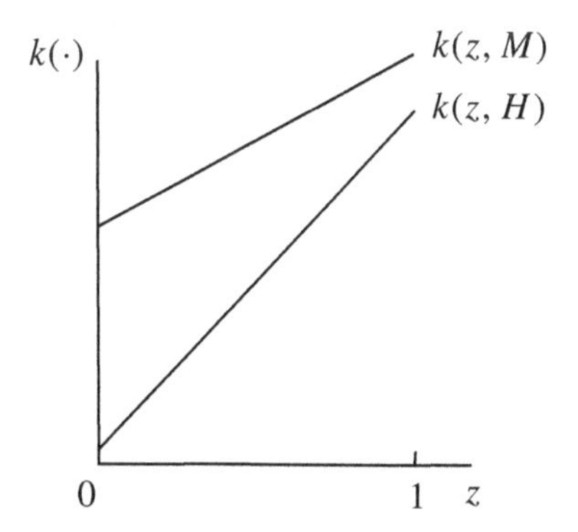

The implication of assumptions 93.1–93.3 is that market governance reduces production costs but increases adaptation costs. Hierarchy, as you may expect, works in the opposite way. There seems an obvious solution to this trade-off between these costs, let the seller control decisions to do with production of the original design and have the interface coordinator control adaptation retain decisions. This type of 'selective intervention'[19] is ruled out by Assumption 93.4.

ASSUMPTION 93.4 (Tadelis and Williamson 2013: 176, Assumption 4) Administrative control is allocated over both production and adaptation, and the two processes cannot be separated to allow for selective intervention.

Now Tadelis and Williamson turn to analysing the endogenous determination of governance and incentives. First, the objective of the seller is studied.

$$\max_{e \geq 0} u_S(e; z, G) = F - z(\bar{c} - Ge) - y(e).$$

Math aside: Remember that a seller who incurs a production cost c is paid $F+(1-z)c$, and $c=\bar{c}-Ge$. The seller's pay-off is equal to the payment he receives less production and effort costs, that is

$$\begin{aligned} u_S(e;z,G) &= F+(1-z)c-c-y(e) \\ &= F+c-zc-c-y(e) \\ &= F-zc-y(e) \\ &= F-z(\bar{c}-Ge)-y(e). \end{aligned}$$

Next Tadelis and Williamson state Lemma 94.1.

LEMMA 94.1 (Tadelis and Williamson 2013: 177, Lemma 1) Given the pair (z,G), the seller's optimal choice $e_G(z)$ is increasing in z, $e^G(0)=0$ for $G\in\{M,H\}$, and $e^M(z)>e^H(z)$ for any $z\in(0,1]$. Furthermore, $\frac{de^M(z)}{dz}>\frac{e^H(z)}{dz}$ for any $z\in[0,1]$.

The proof to the lemma is provided in the appendix to Tadelis and Williamson's chapter.

Proof. The first-order condition, $zG-y'(e^G(z))=0$,

Math aside:

$$\text{Solving} \quad \max_{e\geq 0} u_S(e;z,G)=F-z(\bar{c}-Ge)-y(e)$$

$$\text{gives} \quad \frac{\partial u_S(e;z,G)}{\partial e}=zG-y'(e)=0$$

$$\Rightarrow y'(e^G(z))=zG$$

to the seller's problem can be represented by the following diagram.

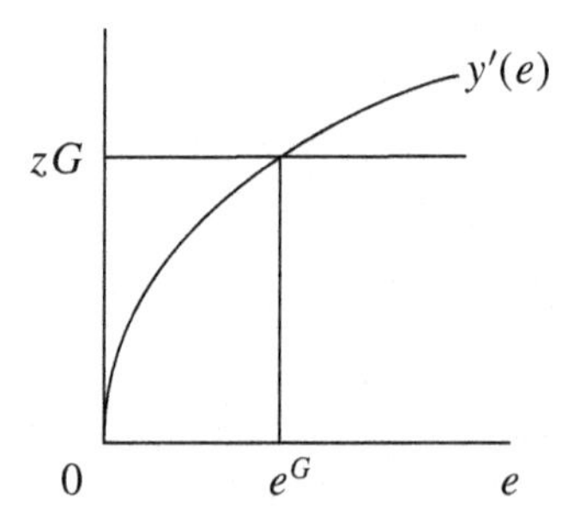

Given that $y'(0)=0$ and $y(e)$ is convex, $y'(e)$ must start at the origin and be an increasing function of e. (The condition $y'''(e)<0$ means $y'(e)$ is concave.) This means that it must intersect the zG line and do so only once. Note that if $z=0$ then $zG=0$ and thus $y'(e^G(0))=0$ which implies $e^G(0)=0$ as $y'(0)=0$. As $M>H>0$

it follows – $zM > zH \Rightarrow y'(e^M(z)) > y'(e^H(z)) \Rightarrow e^M(z) > e^H(z) > 0$ as $y'(e)$ is increasing – that $e^M(z) > e^H(z) > 0$ for all $z \in (0, 1]$. See the following diagram.

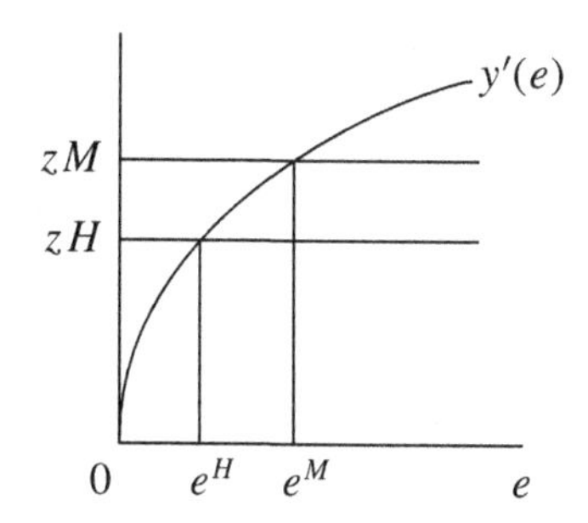

Now take the derivative of the first-order condition with respect to z. The first-order condition is

$$\frac{\partial u_S(e; z, G)}{\partial e} = zG - y'(e^G(z))$$

and so

$$\begin{aligned}\frac{\partial^2 u_S(e; z, G)}{\partial e \partial z} &= G - y''(e^G(z))\frac{de^G(z)}{dz} = 0 \\ &\Rightarrow y''(e^G(z))\frac{de^G(z)}{dz} = G \\ &\Rightarrow \frac{de^G(z)}{dz} = \frac{G}{y''(e^G(z))}.\end{aligned}$$

Because $M > H > 0$ the numerator in the right-hand side of the previous equation is greater in the M case than the H case and $y'''(e) \leq 0$ tells us that $y''(e)$ is a decreasing function of e and thus $e^M(z) \geq e^H(z)$ implies that $y''(e^M(z)) \leq y''(e^H(z))$ which makes the denominator in the H case at least as large as in the M case. The combination of these conditions on the numerator and the denominator mean that $\frac{de^M(z)}{dz} > \frac{de^H(z)}{dz}$. ■

Given the optimal response of the seller, surplus maximisation requires the choice of G and z to maximise the objective function, $S(z, G; \rho, \sigma)$, as given next.

$$\max_{\substack{G \in \{H, M\} \\ z \in [0,1]}} S(z, G; \rho, \sigma) = \underbrace{v}_{\substack{\text{Value} \\ \text{to} \\ \text{buyer}}} - \overbrace{\underbrace{(\bar{c} - Ge^G(z))}_{\text{Production costs}} - \underbrace{y(e^G(z))}_{\text{Compensation}} - \underbrace{\sigma \rho k(z, G)}_{\substack{\text{Expected} \\ \text{adaptation costs}}}}^{\text{Total transaction costs}}$$

Math aside: The buyer's utility is given by

$$reu_B(z, G; \rho) = \underbrace{v}_{\substack{\text{Value}\\\text{to}\\\text{buyer}}} \underbrace{-F-(1-z)c-}_{\substack{\text{Payment to}\\\text{the seller}}} \underbrace{\sigma\rho k(z, G)}_{\substack{\text{Expected}\\\text{adaptation costs}\\\text{to the buyer}}}$$

Social surplus is given by

$$\begin{aligned} S(\cdot) &= u_S + u_B \\ &= [F - zc - y(e)] + [v - F - (1-z)c - \sigma\rho k(z, G)] \\ &= F - F - zc + zc - c - y(e) - \sigma\rho k(z, G) + v \\ &= v - c - y(e) - \sigma\rho k(z, G) \\ &= v - (\bar{c} - Ge) - y(e) - \sigma\rho k(z, G) \quad \text{given that } c = \bar{c} - Ge. \end{aligned}$$

$e^G(z)$ has been substituted in the objective function in place of e to take into account the seller's incentive compatibility constraint. This is just to make sure it is in the seller's best interests to provide the assumed level of effort.

Solving this maximisation problem results in Tadelis and Williamson's central result.

PROPOSITION 96.1 (Tadelis and Williamson 2013: 177, Proposition 1) When asset specificity increases (higher σ), or when contracts are more incomplete (higher ρ), the relative benefits of hierarchy over markets increase. Furthermore, optimal incentives become weaker.

The proof comes from the appendix to Tadelis and Williamson (2013).

Proof. The proposition states that as σ or ρ increase, both solutions $z^\star(\sigma, \rho)$ and $G^\star(\sigma, \rho)$ will (weakly) decrease. Decreasing $z^\star$ implies that the 'strength' of cost saving incentives for the seller are decreasing while decreasing $G^\star$ implies a change from M to H. It, therefore, suffices to prove that the objective function of maximising total surplus exhibits decreasing differences. In particular we need to show that $\frac{\partial^2 S}{\partial z \partial \rho} < 0$ and $\frac{\partial^2 S}{\partial z \partial \sigma} < 0$ and that $\frac{\partial S}{\partial \rho}$ and $\frac{\partial S}{\partial \sigma}$ are decreasing in G and that $\frac{\partial S}{\partial z}$ is increasing in G. (See Appendix 3, page 172, for a very brief discussion of some of the relevant aspects of monotone comparative statics and why the conditions given here are what they are.) First note that

$$\frac{\partial S}{\partial z} = G\frac{\partial e^G(z)}{\partial z} - y'(e^G(z))\frac{\partial e^G(z)}{\partial z} - \sigma\rho\frac{\partial k(z, G)}{\partial z}$$

and, therefore,

$$\frac{\partial^2 S}{\partial z \partial \rho} = -\sigma\frac{\partial k(z, G)}{\partial z} < 0$$

and

$$\frac{\partial^2 S}{\partial z \partial \sigma} = -\rho \frac{\partial k(z, G)}{\partial z} < 0.$$

These last two inequalities hold since σ and ρ are probabilities and from Assumption 93.2 we have that $\frac{\partial k(z,G)}{\partial z} > 0$.

Next we need to show that $\frac{\partial S}{\partial \rho}$ is decreasing in G. To do so it is sufficient to show that $\left.\frac{\partial S}{\partial \rho}\right|_{G=M} - \left.\frac{\partial S}{\partial \rho}\right|_{G=H} < 0$ since $M > H$. Using the expression for $S(z, G; \rho, \sigma)$ given previously we see that

$$\left.\frac{\partial S}{\partial \rho}\right|_{G=M} - \left.\frac{\partial S}{\partial \rho}\right|_{G=H} = -\sigma k(z, M) + \sigma k(z, H) < 0, \quad \text{due to Assumption 93.1.}$$

To show that $\frac{\partial S}{\partial \sigma}$ is decreasing in G we just follow the same procedure to obtain

$$\left.\frac{\partial S}{\partial \sigma}\right|_{G=M} - \left.\frac{\partial S}{\partial \sigma}\right|_{G=H} = -\rho k(z, M) + \rho k(z, H) < 0, \quad \text{due to Assumption 93.1.}$$

Last we need to show that $\frac{\partial S}{\partial z}$ is increasing in G. For this we must show that $\left.\frac{\partial S}{\partial z}\right|_{G=M} - \left.\frac{\partial S}{\partial z}\right|_{G=H} > 0$ where $M > H$.

Utilising the expression for $\frac{\partial S}{\partial z}$ derived previously we get that

$$[M - y'(e^M(z))]\frac{\partial e^M(z)}{\partial z} - [H - y'(e^H(z))]\frac{\partial e^H(z)}{\partial z} + \sigma\rho\left(\frac{\partial k(z, H)}{\partial z} - \frac{\partial k(z, M)}{\partial z}\right) > 0.$$

Assumption 93.3, tells us that the term $\sigma\rho\left(\frac{\partial k(z,H)}{\partial z} - \frac{\partial k(z,M)}{\partial z}\right)$ is positive so we are left with showing that

$$[M - y'(e^M(z))]\frac{\partial e^M(z)}{\partial z} - [H - y'(e^H(z))]\frac{\partial e^H(z)}{\partial z} > 0.$$

From the first-order conditions of the seller's maximisation problem we know that $y'(e^M(z)) = zM$ and $y'(e^H(z)) = zH$. Substituting these expressions into the directly previous inequality gives

$$(1 - z)M\frac{\partial e^M(z)}{\partial z} - (1 - z)H\frac{\partial e^H(z)}{\partial z} > 0.$$

This is true because $M > H$ and from Lemma 94.1 we know that $\frac{\partial e^M(z)}{\partial z} > \frac{\partial e^H(z)}{\partial z}$.■

What we can conclude from the results presented so far is that as contractual incompleteness, ρ, increases, total transaction costs increase for both markets and hierarchies. Importantly, however, the market transaction costs are increasing faster than those for hierarchies, resulting in hierarchies being better for a larger range of specificity, σ, a point made by Proposition 96.1. In the model ρ and σ are multiplied implying that contractual incompleteness and asset specificity are complements. This tells us that an increase in adaptation costs resulting from contractual incompleteness is larger when asset specificity is higher.

4.1.1.2.3 THE FIRM AS AN OWNERSHIP UNIT

What Foss, Lando and Thomsen refer to as the 'firm as an ownership unit' approach to the firm is more commonly called the property rights theory or incomplete contracts theory of the firm. Early contributions to this approach include Grossman and Hart (1986, 1987), Hart and Moore (1990) and Hart (1995) (denoted GHM from now on).[20] The central idea in the property rights approach is that as contracts are incomplete the allocation of control rights[21] affects the incentives that people face, and thus their behaviour and the allocation of resources. This theory defines ownership of an asset as the possession of the *residual* control rights over that asset.[22] A firm is defined as a collection of jointly-owned (non-human) assets. This means, for example, that the distinction between an independent contractor and an employee turns on who owns the non-human assets with which the agent works. An independent contractor owns his own 'tools' while an employee does not.

But, how and why does ownership matter? The answer is that in a world of incomplete contracts, ownership (i.e. having residual control rights) can serve as a source of power. Given that incomplete contracts contain gaps (or ambiguities) the question arises of who gets to make decisions in these non-contracted for situations? For the property rights theory, it is the owner. This matters since if there are two separate firms, A and B say, then the management of each firm can make decisions for their firm in the uncontracted for situations. If, on the other hand, A was to take over B then A's management could make decisions for both A and B in the uncontracted for cases. To see the implications of this imagine that B supplies A with an input for A's production process. If A and B are separate firms then B's management could threaten to withdraw both its assets and its own labour if the firms cannot, say, agree on the terms for an increase in the supply of the input. If A owns B then B can only threaten to withhold its labour. The latter threat is normally weaker than the former. Such differences in power will effect the distribution of surplus generated by the relationship between A and B. If the firms are separate, then A may have to pay a lot to induce B to supply the increased level of inputs whereas if A owns B, then it can enforce the supply at a much lower cost since B's management has a reduced threat, and thus, bargaining power.

Determining the boundaries of the firm requires us to balance the advantages of integration against its disadvantages. The benefit of integration is that the acquiring firm's, A above, incentives to make relationship-specific investments is stronger because it now has greater residual control rights and thus can command a larger share of the *ex post* surplus created by such investments. The disadvantage of integration is that the incentives of the acquired firm, B, to make relationship-specific investments is reduced since they now have fewer residual controls rights and thus are able to capture less of the *ex post* surplus that their investments creates. To put this in employee/independent contractor terms, the optimal size of a firm trades off the fact that hiring an employee means hiring someone who lacks optimal incentives since they risk being held up by the firm because they can be fired, and thereby separated from the assets they need to be productive, versus using an independent contractor who could hold-up the firm by threatening to quit the relationship and taking his assets with him.

An implication of this is that if a non-contractible, specific to a particular set of assets, investment is undertaken then a non-owner risks being held-up by the owner. Thus, the property rights theory would say that whoever makes the most important, non-contractible, asset-specific investment should be the owner of the asset.

A simple, more formal, version of the GHM approach, based on incompleteness due to both a lack of foresight and verifiability of actions to third parties, is presented in a model by Tirole (1988: 31–3).[23] The Tirole model is a simplified version of the model presented in Grossman and Hart (1986). The time line is given in Figure 99.1.

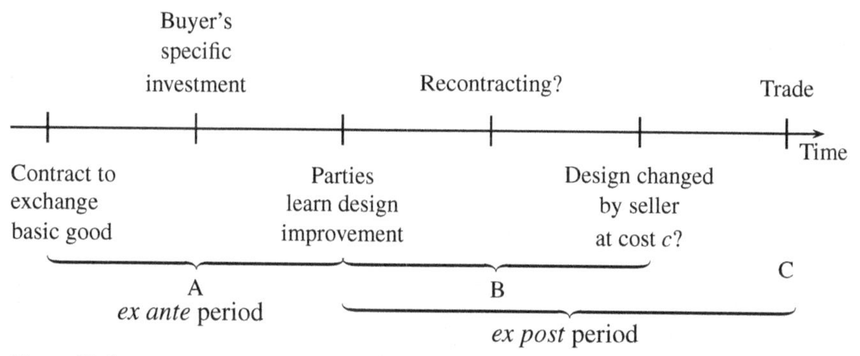

Figure 99.1.

Here we see that there is a Buyer and a Seller who agree – at time A – to trade – at time C – a basic design of some commodity. These parties know that at time B the opportunity to improve the good's quality may arise but at time A they do not know what the quality improvement will be. This means that at time A the parties cannot make their contract contingent on a design change at time B. At time B, however, they learn about the quality change and can at this point contract on it. To implement the quality change costs the Seller a non-contractible amount $c > 0$. It will be assumed that the cost c is independent of the nature of the improvement. The probability, π, that the improvement comes about can be increased by the Buyer making a relationship-specific investment in period A. The cost of the Buyer's specific investment is $I = \frac{\pi^2}{2}$. The Buyer's valuation of the improvement in time B is $\tilde{v}$ which can take on just two values: either $\tilde{v} = v > c$ – so the improvement should be implemented – occurring with probability π or $\tilde{v} = 0$ – so the improvement should not be implemented – occurring with probability $(1-\pi)$. These values for $\tilde{v}$ and the cost c are known to both the Buyer and Seller at time A but cannot be contracted on. The Seller can observe the Buyer's investment and thus its level is known to both parties at time B. However, such investments cannot be contracted on. Note that v and c are *extra* valuation and costs; that is, beyond the values corresponding to the basic design. Trade takes place at time C. Finally, it is assumed the both parties are risk-neutral.

For purposes of comparison, we will first determine the first-best outcome; that is, the outcome that maximises the expected additional joint profit of the two firms with no consideration given to the distribution of the surplus.[24] Obviously the quality improvement should be made if and only if the buyer's valuation is v. Denote the expected additional joint surplus

$$E(\Delta S) = \pi(v-c) + (1-\pi)(0-0) - \frac{\pi^2}{2}. \tag{100.1}$$

The optimal level of π is determined by

$$\max_{\pi} E(\Delta S)$$

which results in the first-order condition,

$$\begin{aligned}\frac{\partial E(\Delta S)}{\partial \pi} &= (v-c) - \pi = 0\\ &\Rightarrow \pi^{\star} = v - c \quad (>0).\end{aligned}$$

The optimal level of investment in time A is, therefore,

$$\begin{aligned}I^{\star} &= \frac{\pi^{\star 2}}{2}\\ &= \frac{(v-c)^2}{2}\end{aligned} \tag{100.2}$$

and thus the maximum joint profits are

$$\begin{aligned}\Delta S^{\star} &= \pi(v-c) - \frac{\pi^2}{2} \qquad \Delta S \equiv E(\Delta S)\\ &= (v-c)(v-c) - \frac{(v-c)^2}{2}\\ &= \frac{(v-c)^2}{2} > 0.\end{aligned}$$

This gives the first-best optimum.

But in general we cannot achieve the first-best. We will consider three second-best cases (three ownership structures). From now on we assume that the firms act as self-interested organisations and that the quality improvement, although unable to be contracted upon at time A, becomes known at time B and thus can be contracted for.

It is worth remembering that the cost c is incurred by the Seller while the valuation v and investment I are related to the Buyer. Also, both parties know that should a situation where $v > c$ occur then the improvement will be implemented.

Case I: Separate firms and thus both firms can block any change in design.

The Buyer and the Seller are non-integrated but they can bargain in period B over whether or not to make the quality improvement. If they fail to agree, then the improvement is not implemented because it cannot be specified in the contract.

It will be assumed that any extra surplus generated by carrying out the design modification are allocated via the Nash-bargaining solution. In this, simple, case this means that any additional profits will be split 50–50. Anticipating this, the Buyer maximises his ex ante expected profits:

$$\max_{\pi} \Delta S_B = \frac{1}{2}[\pi(v-c)] - \frac{\pi^2}{2}.$$

The first-order condition is

$$\frac{\partial \Delta S_B}{\partial \pi} = \frac{1}{2}(v-c) - \pi = 0$$

$$\Rightarrow \pi^{**} = \frac{1}{2}(v-c)$$

which results in specific investments of

$$\begin{aligned} I^{**} &= \frac{\pi^2}{2} \\ &= \frac{1}{2}\left(\frac{1}{2}(v-c)\right)^2 \\ &= \frac{(v-c)^2}{8} \qquad < I^{*}. \end{aligned}$$

Clearly the Buyer 'underinvests' when compared to the first-best case. The Buyer's expected pay-off is

$$\begin{aligned} \Delta S_B^{**} &= \frac{1}{2}[\pi(v-c)] - \frac{\pi^2}{2} \\ &= \frac{1}{2}\left[\left(\frac{1}{2}(v-c)\right)(v-c)\right] - \frac{\left(\frac{1}{2}(v-c)\right)^2}{2} \\ &= \frac{1}{4}(v-c)^2 - \frac{1}{8}(v-c)^2 \\ &= \frac{1}{8}(v-c)^2 \end{aligned}$$

while the Seller's pay-off (his half of the Nash bargaining solution) is

$$\begin{aligned}\Delta S_S^{\star\star} &= \frac{1}{2}[\pi(v-c)] \\ &= \frac{1}{2}\left[\frac{1}{2}(v-c)(v-c)\right] \\ &= \frac{1}{4}(v-c)^2.\end{aligned}$$

This results in an expected joint surplus of

$$\begin{aligned}\Delta S^{\star\star} &= \Delta S_B^{\star\star} + \Delta S_S^{\star\star} \\ &= \frac{1}{8}(v-c)^2 + \frac{1}{4}(v-c)^2 \\ &= \frac{3}{8}(v-c)^2 \quad < \Delta S^{\star}\end{aligned}$$

which means the surplus is less than the social optimum.

Case II: Seller ownership, which means the Seller can carry out (or not carry out) the design change by fiat.

The two firms integrate and the Seller has the right to decide whether or not the quality improvement is made. If the value of the improvement is v, then both parties want the design change to take place and thus there will be no renegotiation. If the value of the improvement is zero, then the Seller will not make the improvement since by not doing so he avoids the cost c. This means that the Buyer will reason as in Case I, which results in the same results as Case I. There will be under investment by the Buyer and the total surplus will be less than the social optimum.

Case III: Buyer ownership, which means the Buyer can carry out (or not carry out) the design change by fiat.

Again, the two firms integrate but this time the Buyer has the right to decide on the implementation of the quality improvement, without compensation being paid to the Seller. For this right he pays the Seller a sum at date A. Importantly the Buyer will implement the improvement under both valuations of v. Clearly if $\tilde{v}=v$ it is in the Buyer's interest to implement the change but it is also in his interest (or at least he is indifferent about implementation) to do so even if $\tilde{v}=0$. This is because the Buyer does not pay c and when $\tilde{v}=0$ he sets his investment level at zero so implementing the design change even in these circumstances does not make him worse off. In short the Buyer gets zero if he implements the quality change and zero if he does not. The Seller, on the other hand, is made worse off if $\tilde{v}=0$ since he would incur cost c, without compensation, and thus he would wish to renegotiate ex post (at time B) his original promise to spend c at time B.

Should $\tilde{v}=v$, it is obvious that total surplus is maximised with the design change being implemented, which is the status quo. Thus, there will be no renegotiation and the Buyer will gain the full amount v because he can impose the improvement on the Seller; that is, he can get the Seller to pay the improvement costs, c, without having to compensate him.

If $v=0$, then the status quo is not efficient since it would be better if the quality improvement did not take place. This means that renegotiation will take place. The Seller wants to avoid paying c. Here it is assumed that the Nash bargaining solution determines the division of c. The Seller pays the Buyer one half of c, which clearly is better than paying all of c.

Therefore, the Buyer can determine his level of specific investment by maximising his expected surplus with respect to π:

$$\max_{\pi} \Delta S_B = \pi v + (1-\pi)\frac{c}{2} - \frac{\pi^2}{2}.$$

The first-order condition reduces to

$$v - \frac{c}{2} = \pi^{***} \quad > \pi^{\star}.$$

This gives the optimal investment of the Buyer as

$$\begin{aligned} I^{***} &= \frac{(\pi^{***})^2}{2} \\ &= \frac{(v-\frac{c}{2})^2}{2} \quad > I^{\star}. \end{aligned}$$

This shows that the Buyer now 'overinvests'. The reason being that when the value of the improvement is v the buyer does not have to pay the cost c, the Seller bares this cost without compensation, and given that the Buyer does not internalise this production cost he overinvests in the activity that makes production more likely.

The expected joint surplus is

$$\begin{aligned} \Delta S^{***} &= \left[\Delta S_B^{***}\right] + \Delta S_S^{***} \\ &= \left[\pi^{***} v + (1-\pi^{***})\frac{c}{2} - \frac{(\pi^{***})^2}{2}\right] \\ &\quad - \pi^{***} c - (1-\pi^{***})\frac{c}{2} \\ &\quad \text{(note that } \Delta S_S^{***} \text{ is a negative number)} \\ &= \pi^{***}(v-c) - \frac{(\pi^{***})^2}{2}. \end{aligned}$$

Substituting in the value for π^{***} gives

$$\Delta S^{***} = \frac{1}{2}v^2 - vc + \frac{3}{8}c^2 \quad < \Delta S^{\star}.$$

Math aside: This follows from the fact that

$$\begin{aligned}\Delta S^{***} &= \pi^{***}(v-c) - \frac{(\pi^{***})^2}{2}\\ &= \pi^{***}\left(v - c - \frac{1}{2}\pi^{***}\right)\\ &= \pi^{***}\left(v - c - \frac{1}{2}v + \frac{1}{4}c\right)\\ &= \pi^{***}\left(\frac{1}{2}v - \frac{3}{4}c\right)\\ &= \left(v - \frac{1}{2}c\right)\left(\frac{1}{2}v - \frac{3}{4}c\right)\\ &= \frac{1}{2}v^2 - \frac{3}{4}vc - \frac{1}{4}vc + \frac{3}{8}c^2\\ &= \frac{1}{2}v^2 - vc + \frac{3}{8}c^2.\end{aligned}$$

and $\Delta S^{\star}$ can be written as

$$\begin{aligned}\Delta S^{\star} &= \frac{1}{2}(v-c)^2\\ &= \frac{1}{2}(v^2 - 2vc + c^2)\\ &= \frac{1}{2}v^2 - vc + \frac{1}{2}c^2 \quad > \Delta S^{***}.\end{aligned}$$

Note that

$$\begin{aligned}&\text{if} \quad v \geq 2c\\ &\text{then} \quad \Delta S^{***} \geq \Delta S^{**}.\end{aligned}$$

Math aside: To see this note that

$$\begin{aligned}\Delta S^{***} \geq \Delta S^{**} &\Rightarrow \frac{1}{2}v^2 - vc + \frac{3}{8}c^2 \geq \frac{3}{8}(v-c)^2\\ &\Rightarrow \frac{1}{2}v^2 - vc + \frac{3}{8}c^2 \geq \frac{3}{8}(v^2 - 2vc + c^2)\\ &\Rightarrow \frac{1}{2}v^2 - vc + \frac{3}{8}c^2 \geq \frac{3}{8}v^2 - \frac{6}{8}vc + \frac{3}{8}c^2\\ &\Rightarrow \frac{1}{2}v^2 - vc \geq \frac{3}{8}v^2 - \frac{6}{8}vc\\ &\Rightarrow \frac{1}{2}(v^2 - 2vc) \geq \frac{3}{8}(v^2 - 2vc)\end{aligned}$$

which is true when $v^2 \geq 2vc$ or $v \geq 2c$.

This means that if the gains that result from the improvement in quality are large enough, then Buyer control is preferred to both Seller control or having separate firms. The advantage of Buyer control is that it encourages investment by the Buyer. But because he does not take into account the costs, c, the Buyer overinvests relative to the first best outcome.

In the special case of $v \geq 2c$ the Buyer will be willing, and able, to pay the Seller a fixed amount at time A to obtain the right to make the decision about the improvement.

> *Math aside:* To see this note that
>
> $$\Delta S^{***} \geq \Delta S^{**} \quad \text{by assumption}$$
> $$\Rightarrow \Delta S_B^{***} + \Delta S_S^{***} \geq \Delta S_B^{**} + \Delta S_S^{**}$$
> $$\Rightarrow \Delta S_B^{***} - \Delta S_B^{**} \geq \Delta S_S^{**} - \Delta S_S^{***}$$
>
> which means the increase in Buyer surplus is enough to buy the Seller out. See below.

This amounts to the Buyer buying the Seller's firm. The Seller will be able to demand an amount equal to the difference in his expected profits, $\Delta S_S^{**} - \Delta S_S^{***}$, in return for letting the Buyer make the improvement decision. (The deviation of Equation (105.1) starts at the bottom of the page.)

$$\Delta S_S^{**} - \Delta S_S^{***} = \frac{1}{4}(v^2 + 2c). \tag{105.1}$$

In summary, if $v \geq 2c$ then the Buyer is willing to purchase the Seller's firm in Period A for a price of $\frac{1}{4}(v^2 + 2c)$ so that he can make the decision about the quality improvement.

Ownership in the sense of GHM means the Buyer gains residual control rights over the Seller's firm, or more precisely the residual control rights over the non-human assets of the Seller's firm. The residual control rights are, however, limited in this case to deciding whether or not to make the quality improvement in period B. The fact that the Buyer can make this decision by fiat means that the Seller's improvement costs, c, are not being internalised in *Case III* as they were in Equation (100.1) of *Case I*. This explains why despite the fact that the two firms are integrated joint profits are less than those in the first-best (*Case I*) outcome.

> *Math aside:* Equation (105.1) follows from
>
> $$\Delta S_S^{**} = \frac{1}{4}(v - c)^2$$
> $$= \frac{1}{4}(v^2 - 2vc + c^2)$$
> $$= \frac{1}{4}v^2 - \frac{1}{2}vc + \frac{1}{4}c^2$$

$$
\begin{aligned}
\Delta S_S^{***} &= -\pi^{***}c - (1-\pi^{***})\frac{1}{2}c \\
&= -\pi^{***}c - \frac{1}{2}(c - \pi^{***}c) \\
&= -\pi^{***}c - \frac{1}{2}\left(c - \left(v - \frac{1}{2}c\right)c\right) \\
&= -\pi^{***}c - \frac{1}{2}\left(c - vc + \frac{1}{2}c^2\right) \\
&= -c\left(v - \frac{1}{2}c\right) - \frac{1}{2}\left(c - vc + \frac{1}{2}c^2\right) \\
&= -vc + \frac{1}{2}c^2 - \frac{1}{2}c + \frac{1}{2}vc - \frac{1}{4}c^2 \\
&= -\frac{1}{2}vc + \frac{1}{4}c^2 - \frac{1}{2}c \\
\Delta S_S^{**} - \Delta S_S^{***} &= \frac{1}{4}v^2 - \frac{1}{2}vc + \frac{1}{4}c^2 + \frac{1}{2}vc - \frac{1}{4}c^2 + \frac{1}{2}c \\
&= \frac{1}{4}v^2 + \frac{1}{2}c \\
&= \frac{1}{4}(v^2 + 2c).
\end{aligned}
$$

A crucial assumption for the models just presented is the non-contractibility of both the cost c and the value of the improvement $\tilde{v}$. If we were to make the assumption that either c and/or $\tilde{v}$ were contractible then, despite the non-verifiability of the Buyer's specific investments, we could still write a complete contract on c and $\tilde{v}$, which would result in the first-best optimum given by (100.2) being achieved. The contract would allow the Buyer the right to enforce a design change whenever he pays for the production costs c.

One of the fundamental ideas underlying the whole Grossman-Hart-Moore approach is that because contracts are incomplete the ownership of unique (alienable) assets, which are central to the production process, provides power to the owner since ownership allows control over those assets. But where does power come from if there are no critical alienable assets? For example, what if all of the critical assets are human-capital? Rajan and Zingales (1998, 2001a) attempt to answer this question by suggesting that power flows from control of critical resources; that is, resources that are in short supply. These resources need not be just property, they can also be strategies, ideas or skills. When a person intrinsically possesses such a resource, then they can have power directly; but power can also come from specialisation. A person can specialise their human capital to the firm and thus become valuable. They may also attract other skilled people since these people are more productive when working with that person. In these ways controlling one critical resource can become a way of controlling other resources. Given that the share of the surplus that a person gets from their power often depends more on their specific investment than on any ownerships returns, developing mechanisms for encouraging complementarities between resources can give better incentives than ownership. Examples of such mechanisms are internal organisation, work rules and incentive schemes. While ownership can legally associate inanimate assets with a firm, complementarities link inalienable assets, such as human capital, to the critical resources at the centre of a firm. Here an organisation – the domain of transactions controlled by authority rather than by prices – consists of the critical resource as well as the agents and other resources tied to it by complementarities. Rajan and Zingales use the term 'organisation' rather than 'firm' because an economic organisation may have different boundaries from the legally defined 'firm'.

This raises the following question: Why is the allocation of power so important?

> First, the allocation of power affects incentives. Whenever contracts are incomplete or can be easily renegotiated, power serves as a credible currency with which an internal party who has to take a self-denying action is assured future compensation. Second, the allocation of power can determine the range of feasible actions a party has. The powerful head of the bond-trading group in an investment bank can allocate roles so that members of the group will work together smoothly, and without overlap. Finally, the allocation of power today can affect the constellation of power in the future, and thus the future efficiency of the organization.
>
> (Rajan and Zingales 2001b: 207)

The basic assumption defining this grouping is that in many cases it is difficult, if not impossible, to write complete state-contingent contracts. In such circumstances, people will often rely on informal agreements sustained by the value of future relationships; that is, relational contracts. These theories form the fourth subgroup of the incomplete contracts category.

4.1.1.2.4 THE RELATIONAL (OR IMPLICIT) CONTRACTS APPROACH

The underlying idea in the relational contract theory of the firm is that there are differences in the way that relational contracts function between firms (outscoring) and within firms (an employment agreement).

Baker, Gibbons and Murphy (2002) (BGM) make the point that relational contracts occur both within and between firms, and they argue that the difference between them lies in what happens if the relational contract breaks down. An independent contractor can leave the relationship and take the assets belonging to it with him, which an employee cannot do.

In BGM, an independent contractor can, if he wants, sell the finished product elsewhere while an employee does not own the finished product and thus cannot leave the relationship with the asset or the product. The strength of the threat to discontinue the relationship determines the implementability of relational contracts.

As an example consider a situation where the market for the good is highly volatile. In this case, a relational contract may be unworkable since the supplier has an incentive to violate the relational contract when the market price is high. If the supplier is part of the firm, then such an option does not exist and the relational contract that holds the internal transfer 'price' constant may be self-enforcing.[25] The relational contracting theory can be seen as being related to Williamson's idea that the resolution of disputes is more easily achieved within firms them between firms in the sense that mechanisms for dispute resolution can be seen as a feature of a system of self-enforcing relational contracting within the firm.

4.1.1.2.5 THE FIRM AS A COMMUNICATION-HIERARCHY

The last of the subgroups identified by Foss, Lando and Thomsen is 'the firm as a communication-hierarchy' subgroup. Work within this category exploits the idea that one function of the firm is to adapt to and process new information. Marschak and Radner (1972) made a seminal contribution on team theory that offered a new approach to economic organisation. For Marschak and Radner, incentive conflicts were of little concern and they instead emphasised coordination and communication in their theory. Radner (1992) is a classic summary of work on coordination in a team environment. Here, the firm is viewed as a communications network designed to minimise both the cost of processing new information and the costs associated with the dispersing information among the members of the firm. Clearly, communication is costly in that it takes time for people to absorb new information that they have been sent. But this time can be reduced by having particular agents specialising in the processing of particular types of information. In the model developed by Bolton and Dewatripont (1994), for example, each agent handles a particular type of information with the different types being aggregated via the communications network. Teams, firm-like structures, arise when the benefits to specialisation are greater than the costs of communication. Garicano (2000) argues that a knowledge-based hierarchy is one way to organise the acquisition of knowledge when matching problems with those who know how to solve them is costly. In such an organisation, production workers acquire knowledge about the most common problems that are confronted and specialised problem solvers deal with the more exceptional cases.

The major problem with this approach to the firm is that it cannot explain the boundaries of the firm. The theory does not explain why communication hierarchies can exist within firms but not between firms.

4.1.1.3 General criticisms

In addition to the criticisms that have been levelled against each of the theories discussed in this section separately, there have been a number of more fundamental arguments made against the general approach underlying these theories.

One of the most common of these is that the incentive-based transaction costs theory has been made to carry too much of the weight of explanation in the theory of the firm. Most of the attention in the previous approaches has been on the hold-up problem and its ex ante consequences but coordination problems not involving incentive conflicts are surely of equal importance for the design of organisations. Team theory attempts to develop a formal treatment of some topics not well-treated within the contemporary economics of organisations. Considerations of issues such as the costs of communicating, communication channels, delays in information transmission and the such like help explain things like the economic function of corporate culture. Relational contract theory also, to a degree, takes up the challenge of dealing with these 'softer' type issues.

Bounded rationality is an important unresolved issue in much of the material discussed previously. One obvious question given bounded rationality is: How are efficient types of organisation selected? One common approach is to assume that agents can rationally calculate pay-offs associated with alternative types of economic organisations and choose the efficient one. An obvious problem with this is that such an assumption is hard to square with the idea of incomplete contracts. As incompleteness of contract often relies on some form of unforeseen contingencies, implying that people are boundedly rational, it is not clear how the necessary pay-offs can be calculated.

Another issue raised by critics involves the fact that the differences in productive capabilities of firms have been suppressed in the modern theory. While the neoclassical approach of seeing the firm as a production function is inadequate, so is the idea that technology can be ignored altogether. The critics emphasise that firms have differential productive capabilities and that this may influence economic organisation. In short, the contemporary theory of the firm ignores technology.

Finally, there are the implications of the Maskin and Tirole (1999) critique of the incomplete contracts for the theory of economic organisation. These are discussed next.

4.1.2 Recent developments within the mainstream

Here we look at three recent contributions to the theory of the firm that can be seen as attempts to extend the range of topics that the mainstream literature can address.

We first consider an addition to the 'incomplete contracting' classification, the 'reference point' approach to the firm. Importantly, the reference point approach dispenses with the assumption that renegotiation always leads to ex post efficiency. Within this new framework, even ex post trade is only partially contractible. We then examine two contributions that do not fit neatly into the Foss, Lando and Thomsen classification: the Spulber (2009) theory and the Foss and Klein (2012) approach. Significantly these last two approaches attempt to integrate the theory of the entrepreneur with the theory of the firm.

4.1.2.1 The reference point approach

We now add another group of papers to the Foss, Lando and Thomsen incomplete contracting classification: the reference point theory.[26] This approach arose, in part, as a response to the Maskin and Tirole (1999) critique of theory of incomplete contracts.[27] Maskin and Tirole argue that information which is observable to the contracting parties but not to a third party; for example, the courts – such, so-called, non-verifiable information is normally assumed to be the reason for contractual incompleteness in the 'firm as an ownership unit' approach – can be made verifiable to the third party by the use of ingenious revelation mechanisms. The contracting parties write into their contract a game which when played gives the appropriate incentives for them to truthfully reveal their private information in equilibrium.

Here we give greater detail about the use of mechanisms to overcome problems of incomplete contracts due to the indescribability or unforeseeable nature of the state of the world. The model that will be discussed next comes from Maskin (2002: 727–30). Consider a situation where two agents wish to trade a single indivisible good for which agent 1 is the producer and agent 2 is the consumer. The time line for the relationship between the agents consists of three periods. At date 0 the agents meet and formulate a contract which delineates the terms on which the good will be produced and traded. Then at date 1, agent 1 undertakes R&D, denoted e_1, which determines the properties of the good and thus determines the value of the good to agent 2. Denote this value as $v(e_1)$. Also at this time agent 2 undertakes the development of an intermediate input, e_2, that will assist in the production of the good in such a way as to decrease the costs of production, $c(e_2)$, for agent 1. Assume that $\frac{dv(e_1)}{de_1} > 0$ and $\frac{dc(e_2)}{de_2} < 0$; that is, an increase in R&D by one agent helps the other agent. At the final date, date 2, the properties of the good and the characteristics of the intermediate input are realised with agent 1 producing the good using the input and agent 2 taking delivery of it and paying agent 1 in accordance with the contract. The pay-offs for the two agents are given by their von Neumann-Morgenstern utility functions: pay-offs for agent 1 are given by $u_1(p - c(e_2) - e_1)$ and for agent 2 they are denoted $u_2(v(e_1) - p - e_2)$ where p is the price of the good. Maskin makes the standard assumption that the R&D investments, e_1 and e_2, the private benefits, v and the costs, c are not verifiable to an outside party but are symmetric information to the contracting agents at date 2. A state of the world is the combination of the properties of the good and the characteristics of the intermediate input. As is usual in the literature, the state of the world is assumed to be verifiable to a contract enforcer ex post; that is, it is verifiable at date 2.

Maskin denotes the efficient levels of investment by agents 1 and 2, assuming that trade takes place, as $e_1^\star$ and $e_2^\star$, respectively. $e_1^\star$ and $e_2^\star$ are defined as

$$e_1^\star = \arg\max_{e1} v(e_1) - e_1 \quad \text{and} \quad e_2^\star = \arg\min_{e2} c(e_2) + e_2.$$

Assume $v(e_1) - e_1 > c(e_2) + e_2$, which implies that production and trade are optimal. In a world of complete contracts agents 1 and 2 could foresee the state of nature corresponding to $e_1^\star, e_2^\star$ and write it into the contract along with penalties large enough to ensure both agents complied with the contract; that is, in a complete contract, the agents could describe the characteristics of the intermediate input corresponding to e_2 and the good with the properties corresponding to e_1. Penalties sufficient to induce compliance with these conditions would also be part of the complete contract.

The motivation for the incomplete contracts approach is the inability to describe the appropriate properties and characteristics in advance and thus the inability to write a compete contract. The major point of the Maskin and Tirole critique is that despite contractual incompleteness the optimal outcome can be reached via the design of a suitable 'mechanism'. The idea is to induce the two agents to reveal the values of v and c, and to use this information as a substitute for information about the physical characteristics. Maskin gives the following mechanism as an example of a contract that the agents could negotiate and sign at date 0 and implement at date 2.

> *Stage (i)*: Agent 1 announces $\hat{c}$ and agent 2 announces $\hat{v}$ (where the hats denote the possibility that the agents may not announce truthfully, i.e., we may have $\hat{c} \neq c(e_2)$ or $\hat{v} \neq v(e_1)$).
>
> *Stage (ii)*: Agent 1 can "challenge" agent 2's announcement. If the challenge is made,
>
> (a) agent 2 must pay a fine f to agent 1, and then
>
> (b) agent 1 offers agent 2 the choice between
>
> $$(q^\star, p^\star) \text{ and } (q^{\star\star}, p^{\star\star});$$
>
> where
>
> $$q^\star, q^{\star\star} \in \{0, 1\}$$
>
> and
>
> $$(\star) \quad q^\star \hat{v} - p^\star > q^{\star\star}\hat{v} - p^{\star\star}.$$
>
> Note that $(\star)$ implies that agent 2 will choose $(q^\star, p^\star)$ if he has been truthful (i.e., $\hat{v} = v(e_1)$).
>
> The challenge "succeeds" if agent 2 chooses $(q^{\star\star}, p^{\star\star})$ (since agent 2 is then shown to have lied), in which case $(q^{\star\star}, p^{\star\star})$ is implemented. That is, agent 1 produces and delivers $q^{\star\star}$ units of the good (with characteristics corresponding to the realized state of the world, assumed to be verifiable) for price $p^{\star\star}$. In this case, the mechanism concludes at this point.
>
> The challenge "fails" if agent 2 chooses $(q^\star, p^\star)$ (since agent 2 is then shown to have told the truth), in which case $(q^\star, p^\star)$ is implemented, i.e., agent 1 delivers $q^\star$ units of the good with characteristics corresponding to the realized state and receives price $p^\star$. Furthermore, agent 1 must pay a fine of $2f$

for having challenged unsuccessfully. In this case, the mechanism concludes at this point.

If agent 1 does not make a challenge, then the mechanism moves to Stage (iii).

Stage (iii): Agent 2 can challenge agent 1's announcement. Such a challenge is handled completely symmetrically to that of Stage (ii). And if it occurs, the mechanism then concludes.

If neither agent makes a challenge, then the mechanism moves to Stage (iv).

Stage (iv): Agent 2 delivers the input with properties corresponding to the realized state. Agent 1 produces and delivers a unit of the good with characteristics corresponding to the realized state and receives price $p(\hat{v}, \hat{c})$, where

$$p(\hat{v}, \hat{c}) = \hat{v} + \hat{c} + k$$

and k is a constant. The mechanism then concludes.

(Maskin 2002: 728–9)

To see how this mechanism works note that if $\hat{v} \neq v(e_1)$ – that is, $\hat{v}$ is not truthful – then there exists $(q^\star, p^\star)$ and $(q^{\star\star}, p^{\star\star})$ satisfying $(\star)$ such that

$$(\star\star) \quad q^\star v(e_1) - p^\star < q^{\star\star} v(e_1) - p^{\star\star}$$

which means agent 1 can successfully challenge a claim by agent 2 if and only if 2 has in fact been untruthful. From $(\star\star)$ it is clear that agent 2 will pick $(q^{\star\star})$. In addition if the fine f is large enough agent 1 does have an incentive to challenge successfully. Remember agent 1 is paid f by agent 2. On the other hand if agent 2 is truthful 1 will not challenge given that if he does he would expect the challenge to fail. In this case he would receive f from agent 2 but would now have to pay $2f$.

This means that should agent 2 be untruthful he would expect to be challenged and thus he has the incentive to announce $\hat{v} = v(e_1)$. Similarly agent 1 has the incentive to be truthfully and set $\hat{c} = c(e_2)$.

What remains is to show that the agents will be willing to agree to the contract and that it induces an optimal allocation. To demonstrate this we just need to show that each agent wishes to set $e_i = e_i^\star$ and that they receive a non-negative pay-off from doing so.

We know that each agent will be truthful at date 2 and thus agent 1 will maximise

$$p(v(e_1), c(e_2)) - c(e_2) - e_1$$

at date 1. Given the definition of $p(v, c)$ this equals

$$(\star\star\star) \quad v(e_1) + k - e_1,$$

for which the maximum is $e_1^\star$ regardless of e_2 and k. Furthermore as we have $v(e_1^\star) - e_1^\star - c(e_2^\star) - e_2^\star > 0$ we can set k to be such that both agents get positive pay-offs in equilibrium. This completes the argument.

Such results undermine the non-verifiability approach to incomplete contracts. To deal with this Hart and Moore (2008) developed the 'reference point' approach to contracts. A simple application of the reference point theory to the theory of the firm can be found in Hart and Moore (2007) (HM). We deal with this paper in some detail because the reference point literature is still relatively new and, thus, is not as well known as the theories considered up to this point.[28]

The basic ideas underlying the reference point theory can be outlined as follows. Consider a situation where a buyer B wants a good from a seller S at some future date 1. Assume the good is a homogeneous widget. Also assume that there is a 'fundamental transformation' between dates 0 and 1; that is, what starts as a situation of perfect competition at date 0 evolves into one of bilateral monopoly by date 1. The parties meet and contract at date 0 but there is uncertainty about the state of the world at this time. This uncertainty is resolved shortly before date 1. There is symmetric information throughout but the state of the world is not verifiable. A date 0 contract can be thought of as specifying a set of possible price-quantity pairs which form the set of possible outcomes of B and S's date 1 transaction. Note that the outcomes cannot be state contingent since the state itself is not verifiable. A mechanism for choosing from among the set of possible outcomes may also be included as part of the date 0 contract.

Importantly for the HM story, the date 0 contract acts as a 'reference point' for the contracting parties feelings of entitlement at date 1. Neither party feels entitled to an outcome not included in the contract. The contract is seen as 'fair' since it was negotiated under the competitive conditions prevailing at date 0.[29] Problems can arise, however, when choosing among the different outcomes allowed under the contract. HM suppose that each party feels entitled to their best possible outcome allowed under the contract.[30] This means that it is likely that at least one of the parties, if not both, will feel disappointed or aggrieved by the actual outcome.

A second important assumption built into the HM theory is that outcomes are not perfectly contractible, even at date 1. Each party has the freedom to choose between perfunctory performance (a low level of performance) and consummate performance (a higher level of performance) but only perfunctory can be contracted on. Consummate performance will be provided if the party feels well treated but each party will 'shade' if they feel aggrieved. Note that 'shading' is where a party chooses to perform at the (contractible) perfunctory level rather than the (uncontractible) consummate level.

To make matters a little more precise, suppose that if the outcome that is chosen from those available under the contract causes S to feel aggrieved by \$$k$ – that is, S's actual payment is \$$k$ less than S's best possible outcome – then S will shade on her performance to such a degree that B's pay-off falls by θk. θ being an exogenously given parameter where $0 < \theta \leq 1$. A similar situation with regard to shading pertains to B. There is a symmetry here, both B and S can shade and θ is the same for both. Shading cannot occur if there is no trade.

Assume further that B's value of the widget at date 1 is v and that S's cost of production is zero but there is an opportunity cost of r. That is, trade with B means S foregoes an alternative income of r. B cannot trade the widget for r. Thus, trade is efficient if and only if $v \geq r$. At date 0, v and r are random variables with a probability distribution which is common knowledge. Also, no third party is able to tell who is at fault if trade does not take place at date 1. This means that trade is voluntary. Given these assumptions Hart and Moore (2008) are able to show that it is only the difference between the trade price and the no-trade price that matters and that it is possible to normalise the no-trade price to zero. HM also assume that lump-sum transfers can be used to carry out any redistribution of surplus at date 0.

The simplest case to consider is that where there is no uncertainty as to the value of v and r; that is, they are constants, and $v > r$. In this situation, the first-best can be achieved. All that has to happen is that the parties agree, at date 0, that S will supply the widget to B at date 1 for a given price, p, where $r < p < v$. This contract would ensure trade and would result in no aggrievement because both parties receive the best outcome permitted under the contract. Note that the contract only specifies one outcome, trade at price p.

While this form of contract achieves the first-best, not all contracts, even in this no uncertainty world, do so. For example, consider a contract that specifies that the trade price can be anything in the range $[r, v]$ and that B will choose the price. Here B will choose the lowest price possible, $p = r$, at date 1. Note, however, that this will cause S to be aggrieved since the best possible price for her, $p = v$, was not chosen and thus she will shade resulting in a deadweight loss of $\theta(v - r)$. This follows from the fact that S's best outcome is $p = v$ while the actual outcome is $p = r$ and thus S is aggrieved by the amount $v - r$ which means she shades, thereby lowering B's pay-off, by an amount $\theta(v - r)$. This is the deadweight loss. B does not shade because she receives her best outcome.

Things are more interesting, however, if v and r are uncertain. In this case any contract which specifies a single trading price, p, will ensure trade if and only if $v \geq p \geq r$; that is, if and only if both parties gain from trade. The problem is that as v and r are now stochastic, it cannot be guaranteed that it is possible to find a single p that lies between v and r whenever $v > r$. HM point out that under such conditions a contract that specifies a range of trading prices $[\underline{p}, \overline{p}]$ can be superior to a single price contract.

Hart and Moore (2008) show that it is not necessary to go beyond a contract which specifies a no-trade price of zero, as before, a trading price range of $[\underline{p}, \overline{p}]$ and lets B choose the price. The advantage of the large price range is that it makes it more likely that B can find a price between v and r whenever $v \geq r$. The cost is that there are typically many feasible prices between v and r when $v \geq r$ and B will pick the lowest price. This means that S will feel aggrieved that B did not pick the highest price and will therefore shade, resulting in a deadweight loss. The optimal contract will trade off these two effects.

Thus far one important issue has been ignored. If $v > r$ but there is no price in the range $[\underline{p}, \overline{p}]$ such that $v \geq p \geq r$, then it would be expected that the parties would renegotiate their contract. But renegotiation does not change the analysis in any fundamental way, as is shown in Hart and Moore (2008).

Next HM turn to the issue of ownership. Up to this point HM have implicitly assumed that B and S are separate entitles; that is, they are 'non-integrated'. Now suppose that B acquires S's firm (S's non-human assets) at date zero. This is interpreted as 'integration'. It amounts to saying that B now owns and possesses the widget. HM take this to mean that B can get someone other than S to produce the widget, at zero cost, at date 1. It is assumed that S's human capital, along with the widget, is still needed to realise the opportunity cost, r. Keep in mind that S gets zero if she has only their own human capital to work with and that to get r, S requires both her human and non-human assets (or equivalently the widget). Effectively, for S to earn r, B must sell the widget back to S. If no trade occurs, then B earns v since she already owns the widget, while if trade does occur, then S earns r but pays p. Trade is now efficient if and only if $r \geq v$; trade is still voluntary. In this situation a contact consists of a zero no-trade price and a range of trading prices $[\underline{p}, \overline{p}]$, with S choosing the price. S will choose the smallest price such that $r \geq \underline{p} \geq v$, whenever $r > v$.

In place of a complete analysis of non-integration versus integration, HM makes a number of observations on the difference between them. Assume that $v > r$ with probability 1. Then, as was previously noted, it may be impossible to achieve the first-best. The reason being that in order to ensure trade with probability 1 it may be necessary to have a range of trading prices, but this results in aggrievement and shading whenever there is more than one price satisfying $v \geq p \geq r$. On the other hand, integration can achieve first-best because the status-quo has been transformed into one where B owns the widget, which is the efficient outcome. S is irrelevant and does not or cannot shade.

The situation is reversed if $v < r$ with probability 1: now integration is inefficient because a range of prices is required to ensure that B trades the widget to S. This results in aggrievement and thus shading whenever there are a number of feasible prices in the range while for non-integration the status-quo point has S possessing the widget which is efficient and does not give rise to shading.

The HM model can be thought of as capturing the idea that integration is useful for ensuring input supply in an uncertain world. When $v > r$ but v and r vary, non-integration is usually inefficient; that is, either trade will not take place when it should or there will be shading, while integration results in the first-best outcome.

The papers making up the reference point approach to the firm have demonstrated that the trade-off between contractual rigidity and flexibility has important implications for the organisation of firms. The unifying feature shared by the reference point papers is the application of the idea that contracts act as a reference point for feelings of aggrievement and thus acts of shading. The Hart and Moore (2008) theory and its extensions provide an explanation for the existence of long-term contracts in the absence of relationship-specific investments, which are assumed in most of the incomplete contracts approaches to the firm. In addition, the reference point theory can shed new light on the roles of the employment relationship and authority. In work extending the theory, Hart (2009) reintroduces assets into the model and shows that previously hard to explain observations in the empirical literature on contracting and integration can be explained by the reference point approach. Hart and Holmström (2010) offers a theory of firm scope. They provide an analysis that moves the focus of the theory away from the role of non-human assets in determining a firm's boundaries towards a theory where the activities undertaken by the firm determine the firm's scope.

The papers utilising the reference point approach rest on strong (ad hoc) behavioural assumptions which have only limited experimental support and, thus far, no direct empirical backing. There are concepts in the behavioural literature, such as reference dependent preferences, the self-serving bias or reciprocity, which are broadly consistent with the reference point model but, as already noted, the experimental/empirical support for the model is, at best, limited. An important topic for future work in the reference point literature on contract theory is to show that the ad hoc nature of the behavioural assumptions used within it are consistent with utility-maximising behaviour.

One empirical issue with the reference point literature is that aggrievement and shading are hard to measure empirically. This makes empirical evaluation difficult, to say the least.

In addition, on the theory side, an assumption made with regard to shading is that the reason for aggrievement does not affect the amount of shading that takes place, clearly it could. If one party thinks that another agent's behaviour is opportunistic, then they may react differently than if they feel the other agent's action is the result of external factors. The first case could result in more shading than the second.

Also the theory has an inherent human capital bias. The reliance on aggrievement and shading could be seen as limiting the applicability of the theory to areas relatively dependent on human capital. In firms in which production is mainly dependent on non-human capital, which cannot be aggrieved and cannot shade, the theory may be of less value. In addition, for areas where it is possible to write contracts that cover most of, if not all of, the relevant actions – thereby reducing the likelihood of aggrievement and the ability to shade if aggrievement does occur – the theory would be of more limited usefulness. In other words the theory is less applicable to situations where the set of actions which defines consummate, as opposed to perfunctory, performance is small. Thus the theory seems to have greater potential when applied to firms who have a greater dependence on human capital and where monitoring is ineffective.

This human capital bias is important when, to take one example, Hart and Holmström (2010: 511) state that "[. . .] giving private benefits a pivotal role in the analysis moves the focus of attention away from assets toward activities in the determination of firm boundaries".

More correctly, they have moved the focus of attention away from asset ownership to human capital utilisation. They tie the 'unit' to the manager in such a way that an expansion of activities requires the addition of extra managers (human capital). What happens if, for example, the activities the firm undertakes can be expanded by simply expanding the range of physical capital the firm employs? There is no basis for an increase in the level of aggrievement and shading and, therefore, Hart and Holmström's reference point model would say that the boundaries of the firm would not have changed but the firms activities have increased.

Within the reference point approach, firms or divisions within firms, are fundamentally individuals and, thus, it can be asked if it can it be applied to more sophisticated organisational firms? Questions also have to be asked about where a reference point comes from? And, how can we pin it down? Do reference points have to be the same at the contractual performance stage as they were at the contractual negotiation stage? If they can change, then when, how and why do they?

4.1.2.2 Spulber 2009

Another recent contribution to the theory of the firm, but one which can be seen as being outside – even if related to – the post-1970 mainstream, and thus a contribution that does not fit neatly into the Foss, Lando and Thomsen classification, is Spulber (2009). If we think of the mainstream theory of the firm as being concerned with three basic topics to do with the existence, boundaries and internal organisation of the firm, then Spulber's book is somewhat outside of the mainstream but the issues that it deals with are related closely enough to those of the mainstream to justify a brief overview. Spulber's framework offers insights into a number of important issues missing from the mainstream and thus lays the groundwork for future research in both the theory of the firm and industrial organisation more generally. The three mainstream topics are mentioned in Spulber's book but they are not the main focus of his analysis. For Spulber "*The Theory of the Firm* seeks to explain (1) why firms exist, (2) how firms are established, and (3) what firms contribute to the economy" (Spulber 2009: ix). Particular issues which are a focus of Spulber's framework but with which the mainstream does not deal, or at least does not deal with fully, include a theory of the entrepreneur and a theory of market creation. Spulber's book is an attempt to create a general approach to microeconomics in which entrepreneurs, firms, markets, and organisations are all endogenous. This makes his intended contribution wider than that of the mainstream theory of the firm.

Spulber's basic framework is illustrated in Figure 118.1.

For Spulber a firm is defined "[. . .] to be a transaction institution whose objectives differ from those of its owners. This separation is the key difference between the firm and direct exchange between consumers" (Spulber 2009: 63).[31] Note that under this definition organisations such as clubs, basic partnerships, many family firms, worker cooperatives, not-for-profit organisations and public enterprises are not firms. The fundamental reason being that the objectives of these types of organisations cannot be separated from those of their owners. This separation of the objectives of owners and the firm also justifies the profit maximisation objective. Consumers who are the owners of the firm, obtain income via the firm's profits and thus want profit maximisation so that they can maximise their consumption (utility).

Along with firms come three other players in Spulber's story: consumers, organisations and markets. Consumers are individuals who consume the goods and services generated within the economy. Organisations are transaction institutions whose objectives cannot be separated from those of their owners. Markets are transaction mechanisms that bring buyers and sellers together.

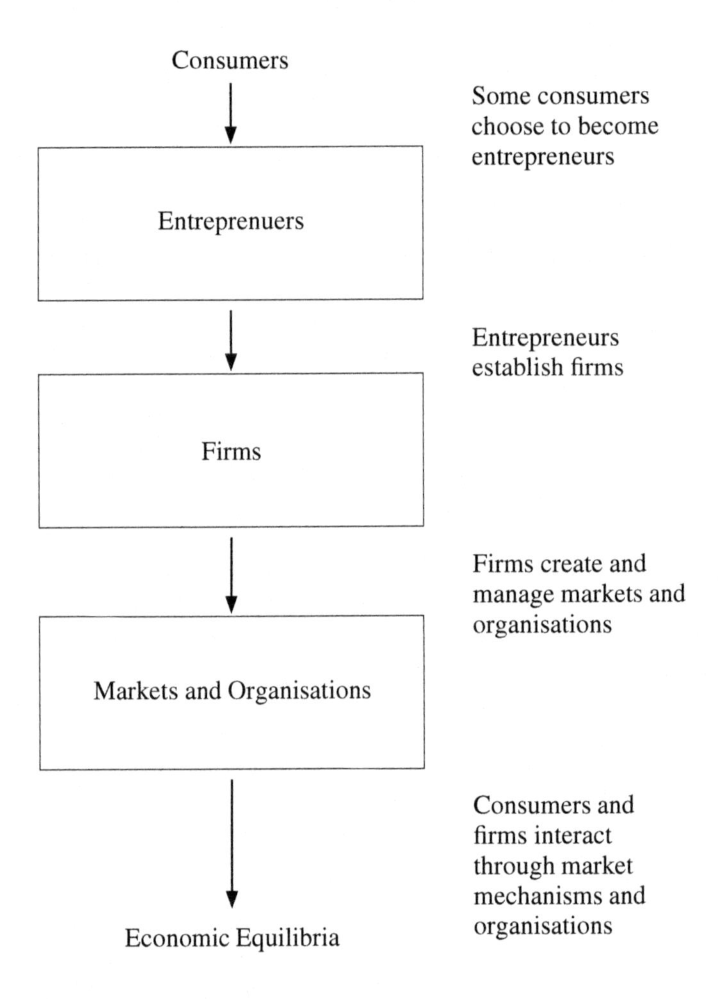

Figure 118.1.

Source: Spulber 2009: Figure 1.1. Microeconomics with endogenous entrepreneurs, firms, markets and organizations, p. 2.

For Spulber the entrepreneur is important because it is their efforts that leads to the creation of firms. The interaction of available market opportunities and the individual's preferences, endowments and other such characteristics leads the consumer to take on the role of entrepreneur. The individual is an entrepreneur for the time it takes to establish the firm. Assuming that the firm is successfully established, the entrepreneur's role changes to that of an owner of the firm. Ownership is valuable in so far as it provides returns to the (former) entrepreneur. This change from entrepreneur to owner is in Spulber's terms, 'the fundamental shift' (Spulber 2009: 152). The important point is that before the change from entrepreneur to owner, the objectives of the organisation cannot be separated from those of the (then) entrepreneur. The start-up enterprise is not a fully formed firm because of this. After the fundamental shift has occurred, the entrepreneur is now the owner and the firm's objectives are separate from those of the owner, which means a firm has now been fully established.

In addition to firms other organisations can be formed that allow consumers to enjoy the advantages of joint production. Such advantages include economies of scale, public goods, common property resources and externalities. Unlike the firm, the objectives of the consumer organisation reflect the consumption objectives of the members of the organisation. A problem with a consumer organisation is that it can experience inefficiencies due to free riding. Firms overcome such problems by separating the objectives of the organisation from the consumption objectives of its owners and thereby inducing profit maximisation. Profit maximisation may not, however, achieve full efficiency due to problems such as allocative inefficiencies that result from market power. Thus the comparison between a firm and a consumer organisation depends on the trade-off between profit maximisation and free riding. When the number of consumers is small, free riding problems tend to be small and thus a consumer organisation may be more efficient than a firm.

Given that we have firms, firms can create markets. Firms can act as intermediaries and in doing so they increase the gains from trade and reduce transactions costs when consumers are separated by time, distance and uncertainty. Firms create markets by providing centralised mechanisms for matching consumers – in their roles as buyers and sellers – in a more efficient manner than decentralised exchange can achieve. Market making firms are required to buy and sell at any moment meaning that buyers and sellers avoid the costs involved with trading delays and the risk of being unable to find a trading partner. In the world of financial markets, market-making firms provide liquidity by being ready to buy and sell financial assets. Additional transaction efficiencies are bought about by market-making firms being able to consolidate trades which allows traders to reduce the costs involved with having to find multiple trading partners or with having mismatched trades. Firms can also avoid the problems inherent with complex bartering arrangements by simplifying the trading process via the use of posted prices. Supply and demand can be equated in a market by firms adjust their buying and selling behaviour; thereby, reducing potential losses due to market imbalances. Thus market creation is endogenous.

Spulber offers insights into a number of issues that the mainstream theory of the firm does not deal with well, if at all. The discussion of issues such as the role of the entrepreneur and the creation of markets are important issues that lie outside of the mainstream of the theory of the firm, at least as far as the mainstream is conceived of here. Such issues do, however, raise questions for the future of the theory of the firm and the theory of industrial organisation.

There are a number of issues that have been raised about the Spulber approach to the firm. Hart (2011), for example, notes that there are a number important institutions that would be considered firms by most people but may not pass Spulber's requirement that, to be a firm, the firm's objectives should differ from those of its owners.

Bill Gates is still a significant owner of and is quite involved in Microsoft, so is Microsoft a firm? In addition, there is the question of how do we determine that the objectives of the firm do differ from those of the owners? How can we learn what the objective function of a firm is? Who do we ask?

Hart also asks is the Spulber requirement empirically relevant?

> Suppose that I want to know whether a public company A is likely to engage in value-reducing acquisitions. We know from much research in corporate finance that it may be significant whether company A has a large shareholder or whether company A's CEO has substantial stock options, but whereas the first may disqualify the company as a firm according to Spulber's test, the second does not.
>
> (Hart 2011: 109)

In addition Hart asks if Spulber's approach yields any useful theoretical insights. For example, Spulber sees a standard worker cooperative as not being a firm since its objectives cannot be separated from those of its owners, but a cooperative with a membership fee is a firm because the two objective functions can be separated. Hart argues that both forms of worker cooperative are firms, but one turns out to be more efficient than the other. What are the advantages of Spulber's argument?

There is also the issue of the difference in primitives between the standard literature and Spulber. Spulber supposes that different organisations have different objective functions whereas the standard approach is to derive an organisation's behaviour from primitives such as governance structure, managerial incentives, culture and so on.

4.1.2.3 Foss and Klein 2012

A second recent approach to the firm that does not fit well into the Foss, Lando and Thomsen classification but which also emphasises the entrepreneur is that of Foss and Klein (2012) (FK).[32] FK see their work as offering a theory of the entrepreneur[33] centred around a combination of Knightian uncertainty and Austrian capital theory. While such a basis places their work outside the conventional theory of the firm, FK see themselves "not as radical, hostile critics, but as friendly insiders" (Foss and Klein 2012: 248).

To understand the FK theory, first consider the one-person firm. For FK it is the incompleteness of markets for 'judgement' that explains why an entrepreneur has to form their own firm. Here 'judgement' refers to business decision making in situations involving Knightian uncertainty; that is, circumstances in which the range of possible future outcomes, let alone the likelihood of any individual outcome, is unknown. Thus decision-making about the future must rely on a kind of understanding that is subjective and tacit, one that cannot be parameterised in a set of formal, explicit decision-making rules. But if this is so, how can we tell great/poor judgement from good/bad luck?

A would-be entrepreneur may not be able to communicate to others just what his 'vision' of a new way to satisfy future consumer desires is in such a manner that other people would be able to assess its economic validity. If the nascent entrepreneur cannot verify the nature of his idea, then they are unlikely to be able to sell their 'expertise' across the market – as a consultant or advisor – or become an employee of a firm utilising his 'expertise' due to adverse selection/moral hazard problems and thus he will have to form his own firm to commercialise this 'vision'. This reasoning for the formation of a firm is not entirely without precedence. Working within a standard property rights framework Rabin (1993) and Brynjolfsson (1994) show that an informed agent may have to set up a firm to benefit from their information for adverse selection and moral hazard reasons, respectively.

In addition, the inability to convey his 'vision' to capital markets will limit an entrepreneur's ability borrow to finance the purchase of any non-human assets the entrepreneur requires. This means the the entrepreneur cannot be of the Kirznerian penniless type. Non-human assets are important because judgemental decision making is ultimately about the arrangement of the non-human capital that the entrepreneur owns or controls. Capital ownership also strengthens the bargaining position of the entrepreneur relative to other stakeholders and helps to ensure that the entrepreneur is able to appropriate the rents from his 'vision'.

Turning to the multi-person firm, FK argue that the need for experimentation with regard to production methods is the underlying reason for the existence of the firm. Given that assets have many dimensions or attributes that only become apparent via use, discovering the best uses for assets or the best combination of assets requires experimenting with the uses of the assets involved. Thus entrepreneurs seek out the least-cost institutional arrangement for experimentation. Using a market contract to coordinate collaborators leaves the entrepreneur open to hold-up, collaborators can threaten to veto any changes in the experimental set-up unless they are granted a greater proportion of the quasi-rents generated by the project. By forming a firm and making the collaborators employees, the entrepreneur gains the right to redefine and reallocate decision rights among the collaborators and to sanction those who do not utilise their rights effectively. This means that the entrepreneur can avoid the haggling and redrafting costs involved in the renegotiation of market contracts. This can make a firm the least-cost institutional arrangement for experimentation.

With regard to the boundaries of the firm, FK argue that when firms are large enough to conduct activities exclusively within its borders – so that no reference to an outside market is possible – the organisation will become less efficient since the entrepreneur will not be able to make rational judgements about resource allocation. When there are no markets for the means of production, there are no monetary prices and thus the entrepreneur will lack the information they need about the relative scarcity of resources to enable them to make rational decisions about resource allocation and whether entrepreneurial profits exists. This implies that as they grow in size, and thus do more internally, firms become less efficient due to the increasing misallocation of resources driven by the lack of market prices. But the boundaries of firms seem to be such that firms stop growing before outside markets for the factors of production are eliminated and market prices become unavailable. So while this idea can explain why one big firm cannot produce everything it seems less able to tell us why the boundaries of actual firms are where they are. Real firms seem to be too small for the lack of outside markets and prices to be driving large inefficiencies.

For FK the internal organisation of a firm depends on the dispersion of knowledge within the firm. The entrepreneur will typically lack the information or knowledge to make optimal decisions. So the entrepreneur has to delegate decision-making authority to those who have, at least more of, the necessary information or knowledge. In doing this the firm is able to exploit the locally held knowledge without having to codify it for internal communication or motivating managers to explicitly share their knowledge. But the benefits of delegation in terms of better utilisation of dispersed knowledge need to be balanced against the costs of delegation such as duplication of effort – due to a lack of coordination of activities, moral hazard, creation of new hold-up problems and incentive alignment.

The things that set FK apart from the mainstream are the importance given in their theory to the entrepreneur and that they develop their theory utilising a combination of Knightian uncertainty and Austrian capital theory. But, unlike Spulber (2009), the questions they set out to answer are standard in that they want to explain the existence, boundaries and organisation of the firm.

4.1.3 Summary

The classification utilised so far in this chapter is based upon that of Foss, Lando and Thomsen (2000) and partitions the post-1970 mainstream theory of the firm into two general groups: (1) principal–agent type models; and (2) incomplete contracts models. Each of these general groups can be subdivided to give an elementary organisational structure for the contemporary theory of the firm. The principal agent groups contains three sub-groups: (1) the nexus of contracts view; (2) the firm as a solution to moral hazard in teams approach; and (3) the firms as an incentive system view. Meanwhile, the incomplete contracts group contains five subgroups: (1) the authority view; (2) the firm as a governance mechanism; (3) the firm as an ownership unit; (4) implicit contracts; and (5) the firm as a communication-hierarchy.

We expanded the incomplete contracting group by adding a new sixth subgroup: 'the reference point approach'. Two other new approaches to the theory of the firm, which do not fit easily into the Foss, Lando and Thomsen classification but can be seen as being closely related to the contemporary theories, were then discussed: Spulber (2009) and Foss and Klein (2012). The Foss and Klein approach to the firm, like that of Spulber but unlike the more standard approaches, emphasises the role of the entrepreneur.[34] Foss and Klein wish to explain the formation of, determination of the boundaries of and the internal organisation of the firm. Spulber seeks to explain why firms exist, how firms are established, and what firms contribute to the economy. He sets out to create an approach to microeconomics in which entrepreneurs, firms, markets, and organisations are all endogenous. The Spulber and Foss and Klein contributions open important new lines of inquiry for the theory of the firm since *Hamlet* really does need the Prince of Denmark.[35]

4.2 Reference points, property rights and transaction costs

Among the contemporary mainstream economic approaches to the theory of the firm, the transaction costs and property rights theories are the dominant frameworks, with the reference point approach representing the most likely challenger to their status. In this section we consider the relationships between the two dominant theories and the newer reference point approach. We also succinctly examine the relationship between the 'old' property rights theories and the contemporary theories.

To begin, one problem with the formalisation of transaction cost models is how to characterise the somewhat nebulous concept of 'transaction costs'. One method suggested in the reference point literature is to approximate transactions costs by 'shading costs'. In Hart (2008: 406), for example, it is argued that shading costs are akin to 'haggling costs' – a kind of transaction cost – while in Hart and Moore (2008: 4–5) it is stated that shading costs can be seen as a shorthand for other kinds of transaction costs, such as rent-seeking and influence costs, as well as haggling costs. But just how fully shading costs capture transaction costs and thus how well the reference point approach formalises the transaction cost theory is open to debate. Just how well, for example, shading costs capture the costs of ex post maladaptation and haggling, both these costs being emphasised in the transaction cost literature, is an open question.

Williamson (2000: 605–6) argues that one of the most important differences between the property rights approach to the theory of the firm and the transaction cost theory is that the property rights theory introduces inefficiencies at the ex ante investment stage while the transaction-cost approach emphasises inefficiencies due to ex post haggling and maladaptation.[36] In the property rights approach there are no ex post inefficiencies due to the assumption of common knowledge and costless ex post bargaining. The difference is summarised by Gibbons (2010: 283) as:

> The model in question is Grossman and Hart's (1986) [the property rights model], which explores an alternative to Williamson's (2000: 605) emphasis

> that "maladaptation in the contract execution interval is the principal source of inefficiency". Instead, in the Grossman-Hart model, there is zero maladaptation in the contract execution interval, and the sole inefficiency is in endogenous specific investments.
>
> It is striking how different the logic of inefficient investment can be from the logic of inefficient haggling. In their pure forms envisioned here, the two can be seen as complements. For example, the lock-in necessary for Williamson's focus on inefficient haggling could result from contractible specific investments chosen at efficient levels. But by assuming efficient bargaining and hence zero maladaptation in the contract execution interval, Grossman and Hart focused attention on non-contractible specific investments and hence discovered an important new determinant of the make-or-buy decision: in the Grossman-Hart model, an important benefit of non-integration is that both parties have incentives to invest; in Williamson's argument, an important cost of non-integration is inefficient haggling. In short, the two theories are simply different.

This emphasis on ex post haggling and maladaptation can be interpreted as reflecting a view that internal organisation is better at reconciling the conflicting interest of the parties to a transaction and facilitating adaptation to changing supply and demand conditions when such cost are high.

In so much as contracting in the reference point approach is imperfect, even ex post, the reference point theory can be seen as a movement away from the ex ante inefficiencies of the property rights theory and back towards the ex post efficiencies of the transaction cost theory. The imperfect nature of ex post contracting in the reference point approach is, as Hart (2008: 294) points out, "[...] a significant departure from the standard contracting literature. The literature usually assumes that trade is perfectly enforceable ex post (e.g. by a court of law). Here we are assuming that only perfunctory performance can be enforced: consummate performance is always discretionary", and thus inefficiencies can arise ex post. The development of a tractable model of contracts and organisational form that exhibits ex post inefficiency is one of motivations for advancing the reference point approach in the first place (Hart and Moore 2008: 4). Hart's interpretation of the reference point theory is that this theory can, in a sense, "[...] be viewed as a "merger" of the transaction cost and property rights literatures" (Hart 2011: 106).

The fact that the reference point approach does not assume that relationship specific investments are made by the contracting parties is another difference between the property rights theory and the reference point approach. Invoking relationship specific investments is standard in the property rights theory. This is not to say that relationship specific investments cannot be introduced into the reference point theory, they can, Hart (2013) is an example where this is done, but, in general, the reference point theory does not rely on such investment.

Williamson's concept of the 'fundamental transformation' is of prime importance for the reference point approach.[37] The change from an ex ante competitive market to an ex post bilateral setting is what Williamson (1985: 61–3) terms the 'fundamental transformation'. Hart and Moore argue that such a transformation provides a rationale for the idea that contracts are reference points. "A competitive ex ante market adds objectivity to the terms of the contract because the market defines what each party brings to the relationship. HM assume that the parties perceive a competitive outcome as justified and accept it as a salient reference point" (Fehr, Hart and Zehnder 2009: 562). This is an idea which finds experimental support: see papers such as Fehr, Hart and Zehnder (2009), Fehr, Hart and Zehnder (2011) and Hoppe and Schmitz (2011).

But we must also be aware that important features of the transaction-cost theory may still have been left out. When discussing some opportunities for the future of transaction-cost economics, Robert Gibbons (2010: 283) notes that "[. . .] it may be that Hart and Moore's (2008) "reference points" approach is a productive path. Time will tell [. . .]". Hart (2011: 106) concludes "[w]hether this merger [resulting in the reference point theory] will be successful remains to be seen".

There is, in addition to the matters just discussed, an issue to do with the relationship between the contemporary property rights approach and the 'old property rights approach' (e.g. Alchian 1965b, Demsetz 1967, Barzel 1997) and its outgrowth the nexus of contracts view of the firm (see pages 63–64 for a brief outline). Foss and Foss (2001) characterise the differences between the two approaches in terms of the basic questions that they attempt to answer. For the old property rights approach the question is: From the economic viewpoint, what does it mean to own an asset? While for the contemporary theory the question is: Does it matter *who* owns an asset? It is this latter question that is most relevant to issues to do with the theory of the firm.

One important difference between the frameworks utilised by the two groups is the reliance on complete contracts by the old property rights theorists as opposed to the modern theories which assume incomplete contracts. Contemporary authors argue that under complete contracts ownership has no meaning, there are no residual control rights, and thus from the modern viewpoint the application of the old property rights theory to theory of the firm is problematic.

But, as Foss and Foss (2001) note, there are several shortcomings with the contemporary theories that are highlighted by approaching these theories from the viewpoint of the old property rights framework. This process stresses some of the differences between the two approaches. First, the meaning of asset ownership is not clearly delineated within the current property rights scheme. In addition, they argue that the contemporary theories are built on extreme assumptions such as the idea that ownership is perfectly and costlessly enforceable, which implies that the issue of the meaning of asset ownership under less than costless enforcement is avoided. But we should keep in mind that the reference point approach assumes that contracts are only partially enforceable.

Foss and Foss (2001) also contend that there are problems with the contemporary approach regarding such ideas as the ownership of assets that have multi-attributes – it may be more useful to think in terms of ownership of attributes rather than of assets; the composite nature of ownership with respect to rights – there are use rights, income rights, rights to exclude and rights to alienate assets and so on, combinations of which can make up ownership; and the distinction between formal (the right to decide) and real (the effective control over decisions) authority.[38]

4.3 The theory of privatisation

An often neglected topic in the theory of the firm is that of state-owned firms[39] and asset sales.[40] But as Hart (2003: C69) makes clear, there are close parallels between the theories of the firm and of privatisation.

> Let me begin by discussing the very close parallel between the theory of the firm and the theory of privatisation. In the vertical integration literature one considers two firms, A and B. A might be a car manufacturer and B might supply car-body parts. Suppose that there is some reason for A and B to have a long-term relationship (e.g., A or B must make a relationship-specific investment). Then there are two principal ways in which this relationship can be conducted. A and B can have an arms-length contract, but remain as independent firms; or A and B can merge and carry out the transaction within a single firm. The analogous question in the privatisation literature is the following. Suppose A represents the government and B represents a firm supplying the government or society with some service. B could be an electricity company (supplying consumers) or a prison (incarcerating criminals). Then again, there are two principal ways in which this relationship can be conducted. A and B can have a contract, with B remaining as a private firm, or the government can buy (nationalise) B.

Also, "[. . .] the issues of vertical integration and privatisation have much more in common than not. Both are concerned with whether it is better to regulate a relationship via an arms-length contract or via a transfer of ownership" (Hart 2003: C70). Thus, we can think about the nationalisation/privatisation decision of the government in a similar way to the integration/spin-off decision of the private firm, conceptually both decisions are about determining the boundaries of an organisation.

4.3.1 Background

Privatisation as an important economic and political issue is a relatively recent phenomenon. Even the word is of recent origin, dating back to only around 1959.[41] Before the Thatcher government came to power in the United Kingdom in 1979 and started implementing the first, widely known, privatisation programme during the 1980s, very few people anywhere around the world had heard of privatisation or knew what it meant.

While there were attempts at economic reform involving denationalisation[42] during the period 1900 to the mid-to-late 1970s such asset sales were sporadic and limited, and there were no systematic, on going, asset sales programmes until 1974 when the first wave of genuine privatisation[43] started in Chile,[44] a few years before the United Kingdom's privatisation programme got under way.

A number of commentators have argued that the early privatisation programmes were not so much the result of the deliberate implementation of a preplanned strategy founded on a well developed theoretical base but rather were ad hoc policies developed in practice, evolving over time, with the theory catching up later.

This argument is commonly made with respect to the Thatcher government's privatisation programme in the United Kingdom. Bortolotti and Siniscalco (2004: 5) state that, "[c]uriously, the United Kingdom embarked on the first large-scale privatization programme in the late 1970s largely on faith, as the main privatization theories were not yet developed". Pirie (1988: 9–10) notes,

> It is highly significant that the election manifesto which the Conservatives put forward under Mrs Thatcher in 1979 referred to the sale of only the shipbuilding and aerospace industries and the National Freight Corporation. The fact that dozens of pieces of privatization have been successfully implemented indicates that the British government developed the techniques in practice. Privatization in Britain was not the end-result of an ideological victory in the world of ideas; it was something which was so successful in practice that the government did more of it.

Arguing in a similar vein Veljanovski (1989: vii) writes,

> The remarkable thing about the whole [privatisation] process is that it was unpredictable, and it followed no coherent over-arching strategy. Privatisation evolved, each sale was self-contained and each pattern of disposing of assets, from the legal requirements to the terms of sale, was *ad hoc*.

In a review of the Thatcher government's economic policies Samuel Brittan (Brittan 1989: 6) goes so far as to argue that privatisation became an important policy plank for the Conservative government simply because it was easier to carry out than other policies: "[. . .] privatization was hardly mentioned in the 1979 Conservative manifesto, except for shipbuilding, aerospace and National Freight. But it became a major thread when it was found easier to carry out than many other Conservative aspirations."[45]

In addition, Kay and Thompson (1986) lay the charge that privatisation in the United Kingdom lacked any clear rationale. They summed up their view in the title of their paper 'Privatisation: A Policy in Search of a Rationale'. They argue that

> [. . .] the reality behind the apparent multiplicity of objectives [of privatisation in the United Kingdom] is not that the policy has a rather sophisticated rationale, but rather that it is lacking any clear analysis of purpose or effects; and hence any objective which seems achievable is seized as justification.
>
> (Kay and Thompson 1986: 19)

Following the increased importance of privatisation in practice came a, belated, increase in interest from economists. By the early 1980s the role of the state in the economy was being increasingly questioned and it was at this time that the first formal theoretical and empirical investigations of privatisation began to appear. There were, of course, discussions of the proper role of the state before this time[46] with consideration of the economic consequences of privatisation going back at least as far as Adam Smith. On the sale of crown lands Smith (1776: 824, Book V Chapter II Part II) famously wrote:

> In every great monarchy of Europe the sale of the crown lands would produce a very large sum of money, which, if applied to the payment of the public debts, would deliver from mortgage a much greater revenue than any which those lands have ever afforded to the crown. [...] The crown might immediately enjoy the revenue which this great price would redeem from mortgage. In the course of a few years it would probably enjoy another revenue. When the crown lands had become private property, they would, in the course of a few years, become well improved and well cultivated. The increase of their produce would increase the population of the country by augmenting the revenue and consumption of the people. But the revenue which the crown derives from the duties of customs and excise would necessarily increase with the revenue and consumption of the people.

In the period, roughly, between the Second World War and the 1980s there was some, if not vigorous, debate as to the correct economic role of government, including state ownership of firms, but there was little or no formal modelling of either privatisation[47] or nationalisation[48] despite the prevalence of state ownership at this time. As late as 1989 George Yarrow (Yarrow 1989: 52) could write:

> Unfortunately, at the theoretical level, economic analysis has not accorded a high priority to the question of the likely effects of ownership on industrial performance. Despite a number of distinguished contributions from [the old] property rights theorists, the literature is much less well developed than in other areas of the subject. Thus, as an examination of economics textbooks will show, it is hard to find convincing *positive* theories of public enterprise behaviour. This may be because of factors such as the complexities arising from international differences in the frameworks of accountability and control for state industries but, whatever the cause, the point is simply that, on this issue, the cupboard is remarkably bare.

During this period many governments and economists favoured,[49] for various reasons, at least some degree of state ownership of firms. Megginson and Netter (2001: 323) note that:

> The Depression, World War II, and the final breakup of colonial empires pushed government into a more active role, including ownership of production and provision of all types of goods and services, in much of the world. In Western Europe, governments debated how deeply involved the national

> government should be in regulating the national economy and which industrial sectors should be reserved exclusively for state ownership. Until Margaret Thatcher's conservative government came to power in Great Britain 1979, the answer to this debate in the United Kingdom and elsewhere was that the government should at least own the telecommunications and postal services, electric and gas utilities, and most forms of non-road transportation (especially airlines and railroads). Many politicians also believed the state should control certain "strategic" manufacturing industries, such as steel and defense production.

Scitovsky (1952: 374) argues that concerns over the power of private monopolies explains the creation of state-owned monopolies in telephone, telegraph and public utilities in most European countries during this period. But monopoly was not the only reason for public ownership. As Vickers and Yarrow (1988: 125) point out, when dealing with the case of the United Kingdom, there were a number of other motivations for state control:

> British Petroleum (BP), in which a controlling interest was acquired by the Government before the First World War with the object of securing fuel oil products for the Navy; the British Sugar Corporation, created by the Government in 1936 to promote domestic production of beet sugar for reasons of national security; Cable and Wireless, acquired in two stages (1938 and 1946) with a view to extending state ownership in telecommunications activities; Short Brothers and Harland (aircraft and aircraft components), acquired during the Second World War because the company was not being operated efficiently and the Government was not prepared to see it collapse; Rolls-Royce and British Leyland (now the Rover Group), both taken into public ownership in the 1970s to mitigate the consequences of impending bankruptcy.

As far as the UK nationalisations of the 1940s are concerned, Jewkes (1948: 145) is sceptical of there being any economic basis for them, "[b]ut the experience of the British Labour Government in the first years of office suggests that, in fact, no objective economic principles were being applied in choosing industries for nationalisation". Millward (1997: 215), on the other hand, put forward the hypothesis that these nationalisations can be explained by

> a The infrastructure industries of electricity, gas, water, transport, and communications display the classic problems of natural monopoly and externalities on a substantial scale and this explains why in many western countries, and in Britain specifically from the middle of the nineteenth century, they were subject to increasing government control.
>
> b The failure of arm's length regulation of the infrastructure industries in the interwar period explains why in the 1940s public control took the form of public ownership and why this had support over a wide political spectrum.

c Manufacturing, commerce, and agriculture did not have problems of natural monopoly and externalities on anything like the same scale and were left largely in private ownership.

d The fundamental class division between wage earners and owners of capital to be found in the neo-Marxist characterizations of capitalist society played a limited role in the 1940s drive to public ownership and had a clear manifestation only in that large industry whose working conditions and economic fortunes in the nineteenth and twentieth centuries appeared to suffer most from the cold winds of market forces-the coal industry.

e The election of a Labour government in 1945, and its commitment to economic planning together with the specific historical context of reconstruction following the Second World War go a long way to explaining the particular institutional arrangements which emerged in the public sector, specifically the nationwide dimension of public ownership, the legal form of the public corporation, the means of achieving coordination within the fuel and transport sectors, and the nationalization of the Bank of England.

Writing in 1953 Jewkes notes that, "[i]t is only recently that the claim has been made that nationalization is a more efficient way of organizing an industry than is possible whilst it remains in private hands" (Jewkes 1953: 616).[50]

Carlson (1994: 77) makes the case for defence policy as the motivation behind the first (partial) nationalisation of an incorporated company in Sweden:

> The state's first major involvement in the incorporated company form was initiated in 1907, under Lindman's Conservative government, when the state become half-owner of the mining company LKAB. This action of the Conservatives was dictated largely by considerations of defence policy.

In the US context, Troesken and Geddes (2003) argue that for the case of the municipal acquisition of waterworks in the period 1897–1915, the data supports the explanation that municipalities were unable to credibly precommit to not expropriating value from the private water companies once investments were made, resulting in a rational reduction in investment in water provision by private companies. This rational underinvestment was then used by local governments as a pretext for municipalising the private water companies. Similar results were found for the municipalising of gas companies in the United States. Troesken (1997) argues that the data are consistent with commitment and small market theories of public ownership. The commitment hypothesis, again, refers to the inability of municipalities to be able to credibly precommit to not expropriating value from the private companies once investments were made, while the small market hypothesis argues that in small towns the inadequate consumer demand prevents suppliers from exploiting scale economies and from recouping their large capital investments.

Towards the more radical end of the spectrum of views of economists, Joseph A. Schumpeter argued in his book *Capitalism, Socialism and Democracy* that, in

England at least, an extensive programme of nationalisation could accomplish a big step forward towards socialism. His list of industries ready for nationalisation included the Bank of England; insurance; inland transport, in particular railroads and trucking; mining, in particular coal mining; the production, transmission and distribution of electricity; iron and steel; and, the building and building material industries. He added to this list a number of other industries – the armaments or key industries, movies, shipbuilding, trade in foodstuffs – that could also, for 'special, mostly non-economic reasons', be nationalised. In addition he noted that 'as an economist' he had no objection to make to land nationalisation (Schumpeter 1950: 228–31).

It is interesting to note that much of what Schumpeter recommended came to pass within a short period after the publication of the first edition of his book. The first edition appeared in 1942 and the Bank of England was nationalised in 1946, road and rail transport in 1948, the coal industry in 1947, electricity in 1948 and the iron and steel industry in 1951 (and again in 1967).

Shleifer (1998: 133) sums up the prevailing thinking among the majority of more mainstream economists as "[...] economists were quick to favor government ownership of firms as soon as any market inequities or imperfections, such as monopoly power or externalities, were even suspected". The instigator of the standard tax/subsidy approach to correcting negative/positive externalities, Arthur Cecil Pigou, favoured the nationalisation of some industries including "[...] certainly the manufacture of armaments, probably the coal industry, and possibly the railways" in addition to the Bank of England (Pigou 1937: 138). On the basis of fears about monopoly power Sir W. Arthur Lewis (Lewis 1949: 101) argued for the nationalisation of land, mineral deposits, the generation of electricity, telephone service, insurance and the motor car industry. Similar concerns led James Meade (Meade 1948: 68) to suggest that the iron and steel, and chemical industries, to take just two examples, should not 'long escape socialization'. On the other side of the English Channel, Maurice Allais (Allais 1947: 66) went as far as to recommend the trial nationalisation of a small number of the most important firms in each industry to make possible a comparison of public and private ownership. But Allais was not alone in making this suggestion, back on the English side of the channel, Arthur Lewis (Lewis 1949: 102) argued in a similar vein:

> There is a case for having some private firms in industries mainly nationalised, to act as a check on the efficiency of the public firms, and to provide an outlet for ideas which the public firms might suppress (this is particularly important in a country dependent on foreign trade). And equally there is a good case for public firms in many industries that are largely in private hands, to serve similarly as a yardstick and as an opportunity for experiments.

There was, however, also a minority view which was sceptical about state ownership. Jewkes (1965: 13–14) agues that state-owned industries could nothelp but be politicised:[51]

> Thus it is claimed that a government may take responsibility for some new public service but take the whole operation 'out of politics' and thereby escape any increase in its own administrative burdens. [...] Experience in the past twenty years suggests that view is naïve. Nationalization has not taken industries out of the political area. It has pushed them more firmly into it.

By the late-1970s to early-1980s the sceptical minority was becoming larger, with the mood turning against government ownership among both politicians and economists. One reason for the move by politicians, albeit at different times in different countries, towards a more pro-privatisation position was simply the bad experiences that many governments, world-wide, had injured with state-owned firms. See Appendix 4, page 175 for a brief discussion of some of the more egregious examples of poor performance of state-owned enterprises (SOEs) around the world at different times. As far as economists were concerned,

> In the eighties the opinions of many public economists began intensively to deviate from the Musgravian view which has long been prevalent. The allocation of resources became the field of central interest. [...] Theories of public enterprises similarly began to concentrate on the question of how a regulating government could give the best incentives for efficient production in the firm. Internal subsidization was increasingly considered undesirable, as was any form of pricing with redistributive features. Furthermore, stabilization by public enterprises fell into disapproval. [...] This view on allocation, distribution, and stabilization dismissed many of those arguments in favor of public enterprises [...] in particular the desirability of distributional and stabilization politics of public firms.
>
> (Bös 1994: 21)

One factor driving the change in thinking of economists was the slow accumulation of empirical evidence[52] that suggested that private firms were, by and large, more efficient than public firms. The theoretical question this raised was: Why is the performance of state-owned and private firms different?

4.3.2 Definitions of privatisation

Privatisation can be, and has been, defined in many ways. Jackson and Price (1994: 5) list the following activities as those which could make up a definition of privatisation:

1 The sale of public assets,
2 Contracting out,
3 Deregulation,
4 Opening up state monopolies to greater competition,

5 The private provision of public services,
6 Joint capital projects using public and private finance, and
7 Reducing subsidies and increasing or introducing user charges.

Parker (2004: 2) cautions against such a wide ranging definition of privatisation,

> The term 'privatisation' has been used variously to describe state asset sales, the contracting out of government services, public-private partnerships, and certain other reforms involving the reduction in direct state provision of goods and services. However, arguably it is very misleading to refer to changes, such as contracting out and public-private partnerships, as privatisation because the state remains primarily responsible for deciding the outputs and sometimes the inputs, instead of the market.

Former British Chancellor of the Exchequer Nigel Lawson (Lawson 1993: 198) defines privatisation as "[. . .] almost the same thing as denationalization. 'Almost' because industries such as the telephone service, which had always been in the State sector, and thus never been through a process of nationalisation in the first place, were transferred to the private sector".

Newbery (2006: 4) gives a 'British definition' of privatisation:

> The British definition of privatisation is the transfer of ownership and control by the state (central or local government) to private owners. In practical terms that means selling at least 50% of the voting shares, in most cases with the objective of selling 100%, bearing in mind the financial advantages of selling in stages at successively higher prices.

López-de-Silanes, Shleifer and Vishny (1997: 447) give an 'American definition':

> In the United States, "privatization" mainly refers to the contracting out by the government of local public services to private provides. A city or county government may contract with a private company to pick up garbage, to keep city parks clean, to manage its hospitals, to provide ambulance services, to run schools and airports, or to even provide police and fire protection.

The theoretical literature has tended to concentrate on items 1. (the 'British definition') and 2. (the 'American definition') in the list of seven possible definitions given previously, and one of these two definitions is used in each of the papers discussed later on.

4.3.3 The post-1980 theory of privatisation

During the first ten years, 1980–1990, efforts to explain the empirical results consisted of either informal, somewhat ad hoc, models[53] of the advantages of bringing market pressure and institutions to bear on state-owned firms, or formal models which, in the main, utilised a principal–agent framework to analyse the differences between public and private firms.[54] The major problem with these formal frameworks is that they assume that contracts are either complete or comprehensive and so cannot credibly address the issue of ownership and thus cannot satisfactorily explain why privatisation/nationalisation should make any difference to the operations of a firm.

It turns out that incomplete contracts are in fact a necessary condition to explain the differences between the two forms of ownership. In a world of complete or comprehensive contracts there is no difference between private and state-owned firms. In both cases the government can write a contract with the firm that will anticipate all future contingencies – it will detail the managers' compensation, the pricing policy of the firm, how changes in technology will the change the firm's products and so on – and thus the outcome under both forms of ownership will be the same. As Hart (2003: C70) explains,

> Applying this insight to the privatisation context yields the conclusion that in a complete contracting world the government does not need to own a firm to control its behaviour: any goals – economic or otherwise – can be achieved via a detailed initial contract. However, if contracts are incomplete, as they are in practice, there is a case for the government to own an electricity company or prison since ownership gives the government special powers in the form of residual control rights.

This intuition about the importance of complete contracts to the equivalence of firm performance has been formalised into a series of Neutrality Theorems. These theorems establish the conditions under which private or public ownership of productive assets is irrelevant for the final allocation of resources. Consider first the 'fundamental privatisation theorem' due to Sappington and Stiglitz (1987).[55] Assume that the government's aim is to simultaneously achieve three objectives: (i) economic efficiency; (ii) equity; and (iii) rent extraction. What Sappington and Stiglitz show is that the government can design an auction scheme that will result in these three objectives being achieved, and where both public and private production give the same outcome.

The government has a 'social' valuation of the level of output. This valuation embodies the government's concerns with regard to any equity issues such as the consumption levels of the good among different classes of citizens. It is assumed that the costs of production are such that production by a single firm is optimal but there are at least two risk-neutral firms, who have symmetric beliefs about the least-cost production technology, willing to bid to be the supplier. The government auctions off the right to be the good's supplier subject to the understanding that the supplier receives a payment which equals the social evaluation.

The most efficient firm will win the contract with the highest bid, which will equal the firm's (expected) profits, and will set the production level most preferred by the government. Rent extraction is achieved since the winning bid equals the firm's profits and economic efficiency is achieved since the most efficient firm is selected as the producer and the firm produces the government's preferred (social welfare maximising) level of output.

A simple example of this mechanism is given by Bös (1991: 20). Let the payment received by the firm equal the government's social valuation, which equals the sum of consumer surplus plus revenue.[56] This induces a profit maximising firm to maximise the sum of consumer and producer surplus. This implies technological and allocative efficiency. Since the highest offer in the competitive auction is identical to the expected profit of the firm, the expected monopoly profit goes to the government. See Figure 135.1

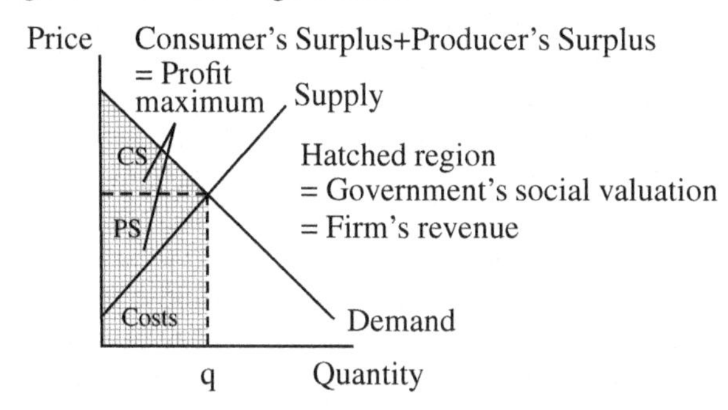

Figure 135.1.

Shapiro and Willig (1990) obtain a similar result for a setting in which a public-spirited social planner or framer decides on the nationalisation/privatisation outcome and sets up the governance structure for the enterprise.

The framer's decision is dependent upon the informational differences that exist between private and public ownership. The important pieces of information are: (i) information about external social benefits generated by the firm; (ii) information concerning the difference between the 'public interest' and the private agenda of the regulator; and (iii) information about the firm's profit level (cost and demand information).

First consider the case where the firm is state-owned. Here the firm is run by a public official that Shapiro and Willig refer to as a 'minister'. By virtue of his role in managing the enterprise, the minister receives the private information about the profitability of the enterprise. By virtue of his position in the public sector, the minister also observes information that bears on the external social benefits generated by the enterprise's operations. Given this information, the minister makes the decision about the level of investment to be made in the firm and the decision as to the level of output for the firm. The overall social welfare function that the framer seeks to maximise is the sum of external benefits plus enterprise profits where there is a magnification factor added to the profit term which equals the unit cost of raising public funds, including any distortions caused by the taxes required to finance public sector operations. The minister's objective function is that of the framer plus a term related to the private agenda of the minister where there is a weighting parameter attached to the private agenda term which measures how easily the minister can extract these benefits. This parameter can be interpreted as being a proxy for how well the political system works. The better the system, the greater the limits on what the minister can extract.

If the firm is a private company, then it is managed by a professional manager and is overseen by a regulator. The manager observes the profitability of the firm while the regulator learns the nature of the externality variable and the private agenda variable. The regulator designs a regulatory scheme that offers the expectation of a competitive rate of return on the private firm's sunk capital. The firm then maximises profit subject to the regulatory scheme while the regulator has the same objective function as the minister under state ownership. The framer's objective is to maximise the sum of the external benefits plus profits net of the cost of raising any public funds needed to make the transfers to the private company required under the regulatory scheme.

The important difference between the two ownership forms is who receives the information about cost and demand conditions. The manager is the informed party under private ownership while under public ownership the minister is informed. This means that an informational barrier is created between the firm and the government by privatisation. The advantage of this barrier is that it reduces the discretion that the minister has to interfere with the working of the firm. The disadvantage is that it makes it more difficult for the regulator to motivate the firm to pursue social welfare objectives.

When considering the neutrality results, first consider the operation of an enterprise in an environment in which there is no private information whatsoever. Suppose that all information regarding the external benefits of the enterprise and all information about the firm's profitability is contractible. Such circumstances are sufficient for the regulator to be able to put in place a set of taxes or subsidies, contingent on what will be commonly known realisations of the public costs and benefits of the enterprise's operations. These taxes and subsidies can be designed to induce the owners of the firm to operate it in such a manner as to to achieve the regulator's objectives in every contingency.

Perhaps it is not surprising that one can obtain a neutrality result in the complete absence of non-contractible private information, for in such a case there is no truly active role for the managers of the enterprise. They need only carry out the detailed instructions left by the minister or the regulator, and the manager cannot claim that there will ever be any new information or extenuating circumstances that can justify departures from that mechanical mandate.

The more interesting neutrality results arise in situations where there is private information. First assume that the private information about the firm's profitability is known only after the investment is made but the private information concerning public impacts and private agenda is known to the regulator when he must commit himself to the regulatory mechanism, before the time of the investment decision. Under these conditions, the regulator can exert sufficient indirect control over the private firm to obtain the same outcome and pay-offs as under public ownership, so the framer is indifferent between public and private enterprise. The regulator's control is secured by paying the firm according to a schedule which takes into account the sum of external benefits generated plus the private agenda of the regulator plus the smallest possible payment that will induce the firm to invest. With this schedule, the regulator induces the same actions and achieves the same pay-offs as does the minister under public enterprise. The mechanism operates by forcing the firm to internalise the objectives of the regulator.

The second distinct case occurs when the (private) information concerning both costs and public impacts is revealed only after the investment commitment must be made. Only the prior probability distributions of the private information of the regulator and the profitability of the firm are known at the time that the investment decision must be effected. After the investment has been made, but before the activity level must be chosen, the private information of the regulator will become know to him and the nature of the firm's profitability will be revealed to the manager of the enterprise. Again, the regulator's optimal payment scheme results in the same choices of activity levels and the same expected drain on the treasury that would result if the firm was run as a public enterprise.

The logic behind this result is a straightforward extension of the analysis of the first case. Here the regulator commits himself to the menu of payment schedules, with the understanding that he will choose a particular schedule from this menu after investment is made and his private information is revealed to him, but still before the activity level must be chosen by the firm. The firm is indifferent, ex ante, about which particular schedule will be chosen from the menu by the regulator because each of them offers the same zero level of expected profits, which is just enough to induce the firm to make the investment. Once the regulator learns his private information, he will be motivated to select the payment schedule corresponding to that information because that schedule is optimal given his objective function. Given this payment schedule, the firm will be motivated to choose the same activity level as it would if this were the first case considered previously, and here too this is optimal from the perspective of both the regulator and the public minister.

In the third case of neutrality the private firm knows the information about its costs before the investment decision must be made. It is assumed that there are no costs to raising public funds and thus any transfers from the treasury are not a matter of concern to the framer, the regulator or the public minister. Because the firm knows the information about its profitability and the regulator is aware of this fact, but does not know this information himself, the regulator, to assure that the investment will be made, must commit to a payment schedule or to a menu of schedules that provides non-negative profits for all demand/cost cases. Here, because of the stipulation that public funds can be raised at zero cost, this requirement poses no problem for the regulator: he is perfectly willing to add enough funds to any payment schedule to assure its profitability in the light of his indifference to transfers from the treasury.

Consequently, it is optimal for the regulator to offer the firm internalisation schedules, each with different levels of investment funds, such that these funds are sufficiently large to guarantee the firm non-negative profit, even if its profitability level is the worst possible. In the end, the regulated firm chooses the same activity levels that the public enterprise would choose, but the drain on the treasury caused by regulation is greater than that caused by public enterprise. Since in this case, however, this drain is not a matter of concern, the framer would see no difference between the performance of public and private forms of organisation.

The third neutrality result is that of Shleifer and Vishny (1994). Their starting point is the idea that politicians control SOEs in order to achieve political objectives, such as excess employment and/or high wages. In this model the politician derives benefits from this inefficient allocation of resources, as they create political support for him. If the firm is privatised, then the politician must bargain with the manager of the firm to get the outcome that he wants. Clearly the manager, who aims to maximise profits, and the politician, who wants political support, have conflicting objectives. The firm will not want to expand employment above the profit maximising level as the politician wishes to do. The politician must make a transfer, from the treasury, to the firm to induce the taking on of the extra workers. This is a problem to the politician since the transfer is costly to him because taxes need to be raised to finance the subsidy.

The Shleifer and Vishny model allows for a complete separation of income rights and control rights. There is no clear-cut dichotomy between state-owned and private firms in the model because it allows for four corporate forms:

i a SOE, the Treasury has income rights and the politician has control rights;
ii a regulated firm, the private owners have income rights, but the politician has control rights and can interfere in the operating activity of the firm;
iii a 'corporatised' firm, when the government has income rights, but the control rights are in the hand of the firm's management; and
iv a purely private firm, when the manager/owner has both income and control rights.

Given that the model has the two parties bargaining, disagreement points have to be identified. These points are focused on whether the politician or the manager controls the firm. When the politician controls the firm he has control over the manager and is able to force the profits of the firm to zero. He can use the firm's cash flow to hire extra labour, up to the point where the marginal benefits of the excess employment equals the marginal cost of raising public funds. Under control by the manager, the manager has power over the politician, and the firm produces at the efficient level (with zero excess labour) but does not receive any transfer from the Treasury.

As far as the manager and the politician are concerned, under bargaining the efficient point is reached when the level of excess employment reaches the point where the marginal political benefits equals the wage, which is the marginal cost of labour. At this point the amount of excess labour employed is lower than that under political control and the subsidy paid to the firm is higher than under private control.

The neutrality result that Shleifer and Vishny present is basically an application of the Coase Theorem to privatisation. As side payments are allowed – or more correctly in this case, when the manager and politician can freely bribe each other – then the manager and the politician will reach the jointly efficient solution no matter what the initial allocation of income and control rights.

The importance of these theorems is that they outline the conditions under which ownership of the firm does not matter. Of all the assumptions on which the irrelevance results hinge, the most important requirement is that complete contingent long-term contracts can be written and enforced. But writing complete contracts is only possible in a world of zero transaction costs. In a positive transaction costs world only incomplete contracts can be written but contractual incompleteness creates a role for ownership – making decisions under conditions not covered in the contract. It is only within such an environment that we can explain why privatisation matters; that is, why the behaviour of state-owned and private companies differ. This reliance on incomplete contracts means that the theory of privatisation can be seen as forming a part of the incomplete contracts framework explained in the previous subsection.

These results also show why the pre-1990 theoretical privatisation literature was largely unsuccessful. As noted before, this literature took a complete/comprehensive contracting perspective, in which any imperfections present in contracts arose solely because of moral hazard or asymmetric information. But as Hart (2003: C70) notes

> [...] if the only imperfections are those arising from moral hazard or asymmetric information, organisational form – including ownership and firm boundaries – does not matter: an owner has no special power or rights since everything is specified in an initial contract (at least among the things that can ever be specified). In contrast, ownership does matter when contracts are incomplete: the owner of an asset or firm can then make all decisions concerning the asset or firm that are not included in an initial contract (the owner has 'residual control rights').

Thus ownership, and therefore privatisation, only matters in an incomplete contracts world. In such an environment, the allocation of residual control rights can differ and so the behaviour of publicly owned firms will differ from that of privately owned firms.

Schmidt (1996a)[57] considers a monopolistic firm that produces a public good in a world of incomplete contracts. The Schmidt model has multiple periods with the privatisation decision being made in the initial period. That is, the government must decide whether to sell the SOE to a private owner-manager or keep it in state hands and hire a professional manager to run it. Importantly, knowledge concerning the firm's cost is private information known only by the firm's owner. Given this, privatisation amounts to a transfer of private information from the government to the private owner. In the next period the manager selects his effort level and the state of the world is then revealed. The importance of the manager's effort level is that it affects the probability of the state of the world. A high level of effort from the manager results in productive efficiency being enhanced and costs being lowered for any level of output. In the last period, the government selects the transfer scheme and pay-offs are revealed.

When the firm is a SOE the government observes the firm's realised cost function and thus can implement the first-best allocation by choosing the ex post efficient level of production. But the manager's wage will be fixed since contingent contracts cannot be written and, thus, is independent of the level of output. Given this, the manager has no incentive to exert effort and the government knowing this will, therefore, offer him only his reservation wage.

On the other hand, when the firm is in private hands the government does not know the exact cost structure of the firm. In an effort to get the private owner to produce the efficient level of output, the government must provide an incentive via the payment of an informational rent. But if transfers are costly, then it will be impossible to implement the optimal allocation and, therefore, the cost to private ownership is an inefficiently low level of production. However, given that the rent payment provides an incentive to increase effort, productive efficiency is greater.

Schmidt's main conclusion is, therefore, that when the monopolistic firm produces a good or service which provides a social benefit, there is a trade-off between allocative and productive efficiency that needs to be considered when deciding if a firm is to be privatised. Under private ownership the equilibrium production level is socially suboptimal but the incentives for better management result in cost savings. Considered overall, the welfare effect of privatisation should be positive for cases where the social benefits are small but social welfare will be greater under public ownership for those cases where production exhibits large social benefits.

An important implication of this is that a case can be made for privatisation even when the government is a fully benevolent dictator who wishes to maximise social welfare. Even if all the deficiencies of the political system could be remedied, it is still possible for privatisation to be superior to state ownership.

In the Laffont and Tirole (1991) model a firm is assumed to be producing a public good with a technology that requires investment by the firm's manager. In the case of a public firm, this investment can be diverted by the government to serve social ends. For example, the return on investment in a network could be reduced by the government if it were to allow ex post access to the general population. Such an action may be socially optimal but would expropriate part of the firm's investment. A rational expectation of such an expropriation would reduce the incentives of a public firm's manager to make the required investment. For a private firm, the manager's incentives to invest are better given that both the firm's owners and the manager are interested in profit maximisation. The cost of private ownership is that the firm must deal with two masters who have conflicting objectives: shareholders wish to maximise profits while the government purses economic efficiency. Both groups have incomplete knowledge about the firm's cost structure and have to offer incentive schemes to induce the manager to act in accordance with their interests. Obviously, the game here is a multi-principal game which results in the manager's incentives being diluted via low-powered managerial incentive schemes and low managerial rents.[58] Each principal fails to internalise the effects of their contracting on the other principal and they provide socially too few incentives to the firm's management. The added incentive for the managers of a private firm to invest is countered by the low powered managerial incentive schemes that the private firm's managers face. The net effect of these two insights is ambiguous with regard to the relative cost efficiency of public and private firms. Laffont and Tirole cannot identify conditions under which privatisation is better than state ownership.

In the Shapiro and Willig paper that was previously discussed, privatisation is considered in a context where the regulator pursues a different agenda from the framer. Assume that either information about profitability is known before the level of investment is decided upon or that there are costs to raising public funds. In these cases, the neutrality results of Shapiro and Willig do not hold. The equilibrium behaviour of the minister who is in charge of the firm is virtually unconstrained and he will set the activity levels of the firm to maximise his utility. The regulator of the private firm has a more complex problem to deal with. This involves the design of a regulatory scheme which ensures non-negative profits for the firm. Given that this is a case of optimal regulation under asymmetric information, we would expect to see the firm enjoying informational rents, which are proportional to the activity chosen. As public funds are costly to raise, these transfers are costly to the state.

The trade-off in this model is driven by how easily the public official can interfere with the operations of the firm. If the public official's objectives are the same as the (welfare maximising) framer (i.e. the public official has no private agenda), then public ownership is optimal. In this case, private ownership reduces performance since the firm extracts a positive information rent. But when there is a private agenda, then a reduction in discretion may increase welfare. Politicians find it easier to distort the operations of a firm in their favour when that firm is a SOE and under the direct control of the minister. The regulated private firm does earn a positive rent but is less subject to the control of the minister. This means that regulated private firms are likely to out-perform SOEs in poorly functioning political systems, which are open to abuse by the minister, and where the private information about the profitability of the firm is less significant.When the firm has less private information on the cost and demand conditions, it receives a lower information rent and this in turn implies that the regulator has to pay the firm less to get it to maximise social welfare.

In Boycko, Shleifer and Vishny (1996) information problems do not explain the difference between public and private firms. Here it is differences in the costs to a politician of interfering in the activities of the different types of firms that explains the effects of privatisation. The starting point of their paper is the observation that public firms are inefficient because they address political objectives rather than maximise efficiency. One common objective for a politician is employment. Maintaining employment helps the politician maintain his power base. In their model, Boycko, Shleifer and Vishny assume a spending politician, who controls a public firm, forces it to spend too much on employment. The politician does not fully internalise the cost of the profits foregone by the Treasury or by any private shareholders that the firm might have.

Boycko, Shleifer and Vishny argue that privatisation can be a strategy to reduce this inefficiency in state-owned enterprises. By privatisation they mean the reallocation of control rights over employment from politicians to a firm's managers and the reallocation of income rights to the firm's managers and private owners. The spending politician will still want to maintain employment and can use government subsidies to 'buy' excess employment at the private firm. In this model the advantage of privatisation is that it increases the political costs to maintaining excess employment. It is less costly for the politician to spend the profits of the state-owned firm on labour without remitting them to the Treasury than it is to generate new subsidies for a privatised firm. Given that voters will be unaware of the potential profits that a state firm is wasting on hiring excess labour they are less likely to object than they are to the use of taxes, which they know they are paying, to subsidise a private firm not to restructure. This difference between the political costs of foregone profits of state firms and of subsidies to private firms is the channel through which privatisation works in this paper.

Shleifer and Vishny's (1994) study is a continuation of research stated in Boycko, Shleifer and Vishny (1996). As with the 1996 paper Shleifer and Vishny assume that there is a relationship between politicians and a firm's mangers that is governed by incomplete contracts, and thus ownership becomes critical in determining resource allocation. As noted before, the Shleifer and Vishny model is a game between the public, the politicians and the firm's managers. The model derives the implications of bargaining between politicians and managers over what the firms will do. A particular focus is placed on the role of transfers between the private and state sectors, including subsidies to firms and bribes to politicians.

When considering the determinants of privatisation and nationalisation Shleifer and Vishny utilise what they term a 'decency constraint' which says that the government cannot openly subsidise a profitable firm. To do so would be seen as politicians enriching their friends. The first, obvious, point made is that politicians are always better off when they have control rights. Control brings political benefits, via excess employment, or bribes, to allow a reduction in the excess employment. Both the Treasury and the politicians prefer[59] nationalisation to subsidising a money-losing private firm. Control brings bribes and even without bribes politicians get a higher level of employment and lower subsidies when they have control. The Treasury likes the smaller subsidies that come with nationalisation. When it comes to profitable firms politicians like control or Treasury ownership because these firms have a strong incentive to restructure since the profits go to the private owners and they lose little in terms of subsides foregone due to the decency constraint. To ensure that the firms achieve political objectives, politicians need control. Given the decency constraint, politicians do not want managers who have control rights to also have large income rights since the decency constraint means that fewer subsidies are lost if employment is cut and income rights mean that the managers gain from restructuring and maximising profits. Politicians who have control prefer higher private and lower Treasury ownership since higher private ownership implies higher bribes. Without bribes, the private surplus is extracted via higher levels of employment.

Given that politicians like control, why would they ever privatise a firm? To explain privatisation the interests of taxpayers must become more prominent. Thus the decision to privatise (or not) is the result of competition between two groups of politicians: those who benefit from government spending (and bribes), and those who benefit from low taxes and support from taxpayers. We would expect privatisation to take place when the political benefits of public control are low, and the desire of the Treasury to limit subsidies is high. This is most likely to occur when the political costs of raising taxes to pay subsides is high and when the political benefits from excess employment are low.

Next we consider Hoppe and Schmitz (2010). Here the government signs a contract with a manager which stipulates that he will produce and deliver a particular good. The contract specifies the characteristics of a basic version of the good. After the contract has been signed it is possible to make an investment that increases both the quality of the good and the costs of production. It is also possible to make an investment which lowers the manager's costs and the good's quality. These, ex ante non-contractible, innovations result in modifications to the basic version of good, meaning that the actual good provided can differ from that stipulated in the contract. To be able to make these modifications, access to essential assets is required. The difference between public and private ownership is that under state ownership the government controls these assets and thus government approval is needed to be able to make any modifications. Under private ownership the decision as to what changes, if any, are made to the basic good are in the hands of the manager. In addition, two kinds of public-private partnerships are considered: (1) either both parties can veto the implementation of innovations – that is, there is joint ownership, or (2) neither party has veto power – that is, the government has the right to implement quality innovations and the manager has the right to implement cost innovations.

With regard to which investment decision should be allocated to whom, Hoppe and Schmitz show that under private ownership the manager should have control over the cost innovation decision while the relative bargaining strengths of parties should determine the quality investment decision. For public ownership the government should undertake the investment in quality decision with responsibility for cost innovation depending on the parties' bargaining powers. Under a partnership deal neither party should have veto power and cost investment should be assigned to the manager while the government should be assigned the quality investment decision. Different ownership allocations also result in different levels of investment. Under private ownership the first-best level of investment in cost reduction is achieved while there is underinvestment in quality innovations. There is a similar result for public ownership but in this case it is the investment in quality innovations that is first-best while there is underinvestment in cost reduction. In the case of a partnership with neither party having veto rights, both kinds of innovation occur.

As to which governance structure is best, this depends on the importance of the cost reductions, their effect on quality reductions, the importance of quality reductions, their effect on cost increases and the bargaining strength of the parties. Hoppe and Schmitz (2010: 260) explain,

> Roughly speaking, if one party has a sufficiently large bargaining power, then the extent of the underinvestment in one task (which is the only disadvantage

> of ownership by a single party) becomes arbitrarily small, so that a partnership cannot be optimal. In contrast, if the parties' bargaining powers are almost equal, then the underinvestment problem under single ownership will turn out to be most severe, which makes ownership by a single party less attractive. Whether private or public ownership will be preferred depends on the relative strengths of the side effects caused by the innovations. If the side effect of the cost (quality) innovation becomes very large, so that inducing cost (quality) investment is relatively unimportant, then public (private) ownership is optimal (because then the first-best investment in the important innovation is induced). In contrast, if the side effects of both innovations almost disappear, then a partnership with no veto power must be optimal, because overinvestment (which is the partnership's drawback compared to single ownership) is no longer a problem.

There are two points worth noting about the Hoppe and Schmitz framework. The first is that, unlike a number of the other papers considered here, their model does not rely on informational asymmetries. The second is that their paper is rare in that it allows for the ex ante allocation of investment tasks in addition to ownership rights.

The final paper to be considered is Hart, Shleifer and Vishny (1997). Once again, in this paper information problems are not the driving force of the analysis of contracting out. The provider of a service, either public or private, can invest his time in improving the quality of the service or reducing the cost of the service. The important assumption is that investments in cost reduction have negative effects on quality. Investments are non-contractible ex ante. For the case where the provider is a government employee, he must obtain approval from the government to implement any innovation that he has created. Given that the government has residual rights, the employee will gain only a fraction of the return on his investment. This gives him weak incentives to innovate.

If the service provider is an independent contractor – that is, the service has been contracted out – then he will have stronger incentives to both cut costs and improve quality because he keeps the returns to his investment. The downside to private provision is that the incentives to cut costs are strong and the provider does not fully internalise the negative effects on quality of the reductions in cost.

With public provision the incentive for excessive cost cutting are reduced, as are the incentives for innovation and quality improvements. Costs are always lower under private ownership but quality may be higher or lower under a private owner. Hart, Shleifer and Vishny argue that the case for public provision is generally stronger when:

i non-contractible cost reductions have large deleterious effects on quality;
ii quality innovations are unimportant; and
iii corruption in government procurement is a severe problem.

On the other hand, their argument suggests that the case for privatisation is stronger when:

- i quality-reducing cost reductions can be controlled through contract or competition;
- ii quality innovations are important; and,
- iii patronage and powerful unions are a severe problem inside the government.

4.3.4 Summary

The theoretical literature on privatisation has only been able to explain why ownership matters for firms since around 1990. Before then the privatisation literature, such as it was, followed the then contemporary theory of the firm literature and relied on a complete or comprehensive contracts framework which is, as the Neutrality Theorems make clear, unable to differentiate between public and private ownership.

It was only in the post-1990 period that the property rights (or incomplete contracting) approach to the theory of the firm was applied to privatisation and a literature began to emerge that could explain performance differences between SOEs and private firms.

As these post-1990 privatisation theories utilise a framework based upon the incomplete contracts approach to the theory of the firm, many of the criticisms of the latter group of theories carry over to the former group. To note just three examples: the Maskin and Tirole (1999) critique of incomplete contracts applies just as well to the theory of privatisation as to the theory of the firm. In addition, questions can be raised as to whether the firm in the theory of privatisation is an organisation or an individual. Also, the contradiction between bounded rationality and incomplete contracts is as problematic for the theory of privatisation as it is for the theory of the firm more generally.

4.4 Conclusion

A useful classification of the post-1970 mainstream literature on the theory of the firm can be constructed by seeing the theories forming this literature as being derived from the breaking of either of two of the assumptions embedded in the standard neoclassical general equilibrium model. One group of theories corresponds to the breaking of the assumption that there are no asymmetries in the information available to contracting parties and thus no principal–agent type problems. The second group of theories violates the assumption that agents can costlessly write contracts.

Both these groupings take a Coaseian approach to explaining aspects of the firm in so far as they both set out to answer questions about the existence, boundaries and/or internal organisation of the firm. These were the questions asked, for the first time, in Coase (1937). Famously, part of Coase's answer to these questions was to point out that firms can only exist in a world of positive transaction costs.[60] This assumption of positive transaction costs separates the current incomplete contracting theories of the firm, including the theory of privatisation, from the neoclassical model of the 'firm' which was developed, implicitly, within a zero transaction cost framework. The principal–agent theories can be differentiated from the neoclassical theory by their emphasis on monitoring and incentives issues, which do not arise in the symmetric information neoclassical framework.

Notes

1 Coase has argued that the rekindling of interest in 'The Nature of the Firm' from the 1970s on owed much to the popularity of 'The Problem of Social Cost'.

> Why has there been this renewed interest in the 1970s and 1980s in questions which I raised some fifty years ago? Barzel and Kochin have argued in an unpublished paper that the interest now being shown in "The Nature of the Firm" reflects the influence of my article "The Problem of Social Cost", published in the October 1960 issue of the *Journal of Law and Economics*, and that the recent literature on the organization of industry which is seemingly derived from "The Nature of the Firm" is in fact much more an outgrowth of the argument in "The Problem of Social Cost". [...] However, unlike "The Nature of the Firm", "The Problem of Social Cost" was an immediate success. It was soon cited and extensively discussed, and this continues to be the case. I do not wish to discuss why these two articles, using so similar an approach, should have been received so differently, but I agree with Barzel and Kochin that the popularity of "The Problem of Social Cost" must have played a very important part in rekindling interest in "The Nature of the Firm".
>
> (Coase 1988b: 34–5)

2 For other surveys of the contemporary, Coaseian, approaches to the firm see Ricketts (2015) for a brief, chapter length, introduction or for an advanced, graduate level, discussion see Gibbons and Roberts (2013). For something between these extremes see Foss (2000), Foss, Lando and Thomsen (2000) and Ricketts (2002).

3 The standard practice of including agency theory as part of the theory of the firm is followed here, although strictly speaking such theories are not about the existence and boundaries of firms (Hart 1989).

4 More precisely, contracts can be incomplete for two reasons: the first is that the contract is 'insufficiently state contingent' in that its terms are not optimal in all possible states of the world, while the second is where the contract is 'obligationally incomplete' in that it has a gap or missing provision. For example, a contract may state that a supplier must provide one widget in all states of the world rather than the optimal number of widgets, which varies with the state of the world; or it may not specify what is to happen if a supplier's factory is destroyed in an earthquake. Something not discussed here is the question as to why parties would write an incomplete contract. See Halonen-Akatwijuka and Hart (2013) for consideration of this point.

5 The Arrow-Debreu framework was not originally conceived as a theory of contracting per se, but rather it was seen as an analytical apparatus for modelling competitive equilibria. However, the efficiency properties associated with trade involving complete contingent claims contracts – that is, contracts specifying the price, date, location and physical characteristics of a commodity for every future state of nature – made such contracts the standard against which other, more realistic, contracts are compared.

6 In a later work, Alchian has stated that this assertion is incorrect (Alchian 1984: 38) while Demsetz (1995: 37) claims the idea "is a mere aside" in their paper.

7 A problem with the Alchian and Demsetz story is that the monitor need not be the owner of the firm; that is, he need not have control rights and be the residual income claimant.

It is possible for the monitor to be hired by the team members, rather than the other way round. A specific reward could be paid to the monitor after he has provided the contracted for monitoring services. McManus (1975) provides an anecdote that illustrates this idea:

> Anecdote told by Steve Cheung: On the Yangtze River in China, there is a section of fast water over which boats are pulled upstream by a team of coolies prodded by an overseer using a whip. On one such passage an American lady, horrified at the sight of the overseer whipping the men as they strained at their harness, demanded that something be done about the brutality. She was quickly informed by the Captain that nothing could be done: 'Those men own the right to draw boats over this stretch of water and they have hired the overseer and given him his duties'.
>
> (McManus 1975: 341, footnote 3)

There is also the possibility that the monitor could be an employee of another firm which specialises in providing monitoring services.

8 Importantly Holmström ignores team synergies by assuming an additive production function.
9 Budget balancing means that the incentive scheme has to fully distribute the revenues among the team members.
10 McAfee and McMillan (1991: 562) describe the problem and one solution mechanism as

> The principal offers to pay each of the n agents 100 percent of any marginal increase in team output. Clearly this gives each agent the appropriate incentive to exert effort. It does, however, result in the principal's total variable payment being n times the value of output. To balance this, the fixed part of the payment function must be negative: in fact, in this case each agent's fixed payment is set equal to the expected value of output minus the agent's production cost, so that the agents earn zero rents on average. Thus the optimal contract has the principal initially (before production takes place) collecting money from the agents, and then (after the production process) paying each agent the full value of the team's output. In other words, in the presence of moral hazard, the principal achieves his ideal outcome by, at the margin, breaking the budget: by eliminating the requirement that the marginal payments sum to one, and by manipulating the lump-sum payments instead of the marginal payments [...].

11 If we restrict ourselves to differentiable rules there is a simpler proof, see Border (2004: 3).
12 See, for example, Bolton and Dewatripont (2005: 37) and Buhai (2003: 3). Gibbons and Roberts (2013: 2) write, "Herbert Simon (1951) offered perhaps the first formal model in organizational economics, [...]".
13 For a discussion of an "updated theory of the employment relation" see Bolton and Dewatripont (2005: 490–8).
14 For *W* this will affect, say, the pleasantness of the work while for *B* this will determine the product to be produced involving *W*'s labour.
15 The model in Bolton and Dewatripont (2005: 490–8) introduces both these ideas.
16 Wernerfelt (1997: 490) introduces the game forms with three simple examples:

> 1 As a typical day unfolds, you learn that you will need several services from your secretary. In principle, the two of you could contract over the provision of each service as its nature becomes clear. However, under such an arrangement

you would spend a lot of time negotiating. We therefore have the institution normally called the employment relationship under which the secretary has agreed to supply ex ante unspecified services for a certain number of hours.

2 Consider what happens if a general contractor remodels your house. You may change your mind during construction, but because these adaptations are infrequent they are typically handled through negotiation on an as-needed basis.

3 Suppose next that you are at H & R Block getting help with your tax return. While at the store, you may realize that you need additional services: there may be more schedules to file or you may want to prepay part of next year's taxes. In this case you know the price of each adaptation ex ante and no new negotiation is needed. Since the number of possible adjustments is small, the price list governs adaptation cheaply.

17 Williamson (1975), for example, makes use of Simon (1951) in Chapters 4 and 5.

18

> The Fundamental Transformation is perhaps the most distinctive intertemporal regularity within the TCE setup. It refers to the transformation of a large numbers bidding competition at the outset into a small numbers supply relation during contract implementation and at contract renewal intervals for transactions that are supported by significant investments in transaction specific assets. Such bilateral dependencies present the parties with contractual hazards for which, as discussed above, governance supports are introduced to effect hazard mitigation in cost effective degree.
>
> (Williamson 2007: 11)

19 In more general terms Oliver Williamson characterises selective intervention as

> This would obtain if bureaucratic intervention between the semiautonomous parts of a hierarchical enterprise occurred only but always when there is a prospect of expected net gain. Because promises to intervene selectively lack credibility, selective intervention is impossible. If it were otherwise, everything would be organized in one large firm. Because, however, selective intervention is impossible, hierarchies are unable to replicate market incentives.
>
> (Williamson 1996a: 379)

20 See Aghion and Holden (2011), Bolton and Dewatripont (2005: Chapter 11), Hart (1989) and Moore (1992) for more detailed introductions. See Aghion, Dewatripont, Legros and Zingales (2014a) for five survey papers presented at a conference in the honour of the 25th anniversary of the publication in 1986 of the paper 'A Theory of Vertical and Lateral Integration' by Grossman and Hart.

21 Having control rights over an asset means that you can decide all uses of the asset that are not inconsistent with prior contracts, custom or law.

22 Residual control rights are those rights associated with being able to use the asset under conditions not specified in the contract.

23 For additional discussion of this model see Furubotn and Richter (2005: 251–8).

24 Assume that time A lump-sum payments are used to allocate the surplus.

25 Self-enforcing here means that each party lives up to the other party's expectation in fear of retaliation and the breaking down of cooperation.

26 Hart (2008) offers an intuitive introduction to the reference point approach to the theory of contracts.

27 See Maskin (2002) and Aghion and Holden (2011: 190–3) for non-technical discussions.

28 For a more detailed discussion of the reference point literature see Walker (2013).

29 This is an important point for all the papers in the reference point approach. See Fehr, Hart and Zehnder (2011) for experimental evidence related to this issue.

30 Such an extreme assumption is not necessary for the analysis but does simplify the workings.

31 This suggests that some form of trade is a necessary, but not sufficient, condition for a firm to exist since without trade consumption and production must coincide, that is, the objectives of the producer and consumer will be the same. The coincidence of consumption and production in a world without trade, or at least a world with little trade, was noted as a potential problem by McDonald and Snooks (1986) in their analysis of manorial production in Domesday England:

> In the absence of trade, all the goods produced on the manor will he consumed on the manor. Such a situation makes it difficult to interpret the results of our production function estimates, because it becomes difficult to draw a distinction between the manor as a unit of production and as a unit of consumption: manorial production behaviour will be inextricably combined with the lord's consumption preferences (or utility function). The underlying reason is that the implicit prices of output reflect both the production and the consumption behaviour of the manor, rather than just the costs of manorial production.
>
> (McDonald and Snooks 1986: 99)

In such a situation the manor could not be considered a firm under Spulber's definition.

32 For a more complete survey see Foss, Klein and Linder (2015). For an expanded discussion of the judgement-based approach to entrepreneurship see Forum (2015).

33 Here an entrepreneur is seen as a businessman who invests financial and non-human resources in the hope of gaining profits.

34 For more on the relationship between the theory of the firm and entrepreneurship see Foss, Klein and Bylund (2012).

35 For any clarification that is needed see the conclusion (page 156) for William Baumol's famous comment.

36 Holmström and Roberts (1998: 75–9) and Tadelis and Williamson (2013: 183–4) also discuss the differences between transaction cost economics and the property rights theory. Whinston (2003) looks at the empirical differences between the two theories.

37 Given the importance of fundamental transformation to the analysis of economic organisation Williamson (1985: 63) asks why this notion was ignored for so long. In footnote 23 he gives three reasons:

> One explanation is that such transformations do not occur in the context of comprehensive, once-for-all contract – which is a convenient and sometimes productive contracting fiction but imposes inordinate demands on limited rationality. A second reason is that the transformation will not arise in the absence of opportunism – which is a condition that economists have been loath to concede. Third, even if bounded rationality and opportunism are conceded, the fundamental transformation appears only in conjunction with an asset specificity condition, which is a contracting feature that has only recently been explicated.

38 See Foss and Foss (2015) for extension of the 2001 paper that argues that the move from the old to the modern property rights theory has some of the features of a Kuhnian 'loss of content' of paradigmatic change.

39 On the economics of public enterprise see Aharoni (1986), Vogelsang (1990), Lawson (1994) and Horn (1995: Chapter 6). For a short overview from a law and economics perspective see Ogus (1994: Chapter 13). For the development of a modern Marxist economic theory of public ownership see Roemer (1989, 1994: Essay 13).

40 Hart (1995: 11–12), for example, has a short section entitled 'An omitted topic: public ownership'. Hart writes

> A very important topic not considered concerns the optimal balance between public and private ownership. [...] This issue has always been a central one in the economic and political debate, but it has attracted new attention in the last few years as major industries have been privatized in the West and the socialist regimes in Eastern Europe and the former Soviet Union have dissolved.

41 The second edition of the Oxford English Dictionary gives an etymology of the word dating back to 1959:

> **1959** *News Chron.* 28 July 2/6 Erhard selected the rich Preussag mining concern for his first experiment in privatization. **1960** *Ibid.* 22 Apr. 11/5 Complete privatization was opposed by the Socialists . . because they feared . . the little man selling out his shares to the big capitalists. **1970** *Observer* 25 Jan. 1/6 He foresaw 'privatization' of many sectors of industry now in public ownership. **1970** J. COTLER in I. L. Horowitz *Masses in Lat. Amer.* xii. 440 If rural marginality allows for the . . privatization of State power, the political sphere demands . . a new line of social integration. **1976** *National Observer* (US) 1 May B6/3 The contrast between then and now measures the tendency towards privatization and withdrawal of our commitments from the open, public arena that has occurred during the twentieth century. **1976** *Globe & Mail* (Toronto) 12 Dec. 5/7 Privatization in the handing over of elements of the public service to the private sector is threatening the livelihoods of thousands of public servants. **1977** *Ibid.* 20 Jan. 6/1 The Government published a working paper . . which set out some possibilities ... including this: "The possibility of the private sector providing goods or services that are now provided through government enterprise and programs." The government, it seemed was toying with the idea of 'privatization'. **1979** *New Statesman* 6 July 14/3 This political formula of controlled privatization depends on not too many people finding the stringent limits on expression spiritually intolerable.

According to Yergin and Stanislaw (1998: 114) the word 'privatisation' is due to Peter Drucker, and the expression 'reprivatisation' does appear in Drucker (1969: 218). But the concept of reprivatisation has a wider meaning than that commonly associated with the term privatisation, reprivatisation "need not mean 'return to private ownership'" (Drucker 1969: 220). For Drucker what is important is that institutions should not be *run* by government but should be autonomous. However, these institutions could still be owned by governments.

An early use of the term 'privatisation' in the United Kingdom can be found in Howell (1970: 8, footnote 1). This is a pamphlet written by the then Conservative MP, David Howell about the problems of reform which would face an incoming Conservative government, published more than ten years before Margaret Thatcher made privatisation a household word. Howell thought the word "unusually ugly" and "hideously clumsy" and added, "[s]omething better must be invented". Clearly nothing was.

42 See Megginson (2005: 14–15).

43 More correctly this is the first post-1900 privatisation programme. There were privatisation programmes before 1900. For example, over the period from 1874–1896 the Japanese government privatised 26 large SOEs (Morck and Nakamura 2007).

44 On the Chilean privatisation programme see Bitran and Sáez (1994), Hachette and Luders (1993) and Luders (1991).

45 The view that privatisation was not part of the Thatcher government's original objectives but was more a piece of political opportunism has been challenged by former British Chancellor of Exchequer Nigel Lawson. Lawson (1993: 199) has written,

> The limited and low-key reference to denationalization in the 1979 manifesto has led many commentators [...] to suppose that privatization was not part of our original programme and emerged as an unexpected development into which we stumbled by happy accident. They could not be more mistaken. The exiguous references in the 1979 Conservative manifesto reflected partly the fact that little detailed work had been done on the subject in Opposition; partly that the enthusiasts for privatization were Keith Joseph, Geoffrey Howe, John Nott, David Howell and me, rather than Margaret [Thatcher] herself; and, perhaps chiefly Margaret's understandable fear of not frightening the floating voter. But privatization was a central plank of our policy right from the start.

46 For discussions of the role of the state including state ownership of firms see, for example, Mill ([1848] 1909: Book 5), Boon (1873), Harper (1886), Adams (1887), Bemis and Outerbridge (1891), Ely (1894), Marshall (1907), Keynes (1926), Pigou (1937), Hayek (1944), Jewkes (1948, 1953, 1965), Meade (1948), Lewis (1949), Davies (1952), Friedman (1962), Olson (1974: 327–31) and White (2012).

47 Heldman (1951) does consider the economic problems of denationalisation, concluding that "[...] denationalisation would not be an easy policy to carry out, because of the variety and complexity of the issues that would require attention".

48 Lewis (1949: Chapter 8), for example, discusses nationalisation but stops short of formally modelling it.

49 Shleifer (1998: 135n1 and 138) argues that economists pre-war and pre-depression were more sceptical about state ownership; Alfred Marshall is one example:

> The same may be said of the undertakings of Governments imperial and local: they also may have a great future before them, but up to the present time the taxpayer who undertakes the ultimate risks has not generally succeeded in exercising an efficient control over the businesses, and in securing officers who will do their work with as much energy and enterprise as is shown in private establishments.
>
> (Marshall 1920b: 253–4)

> Starting from the fact that the growth of the national dividend depends on the continued progress of invention and the accumulation of expensive appliances for production; we are bound to reflect that up to the present time nearly all of the innumerable inventions that have given us our command over nature have been made by independent workers; and that the contribution from Government officials all the world over have been relatively small.
>
> (Marshall 1920b: 593)

> A Government could print a good edition of Shakespeare's works, but it could not get them written. When municipalities boast of their electric lighting and power, they remind me of the man who boasted of "the genius of my Hamlet" when he has but printed a new edition of it. The carcase of municipal electric works belongs to the officials; the genius belongs to free enterprise.
>
> (Marshall 1907: 22)

Carlson (1994: 83) portrays Eli Heckscher's view of state ownership, in 1918, as

> Heckscher also considered the time ripe for new reflections on state enterprises. If his reasoning prior to the war had laid stress on proposals for improvements to enable state enterprises to live up to the more stringent requirements now being imposed on them, he was now (S*v*T 1918: 520) clear "that it is a contraction and not an expansion of state business activity, even such as existed before the war, that we need". The criterion which Heckscher (1918, pp. 6–7, 21–23) propounded for

> the choice between state and private enterprise was now: who will best serve the interests of the consumer? And the answer (just as with Cassel) was that private firms in a competitive environment always have a sword of Damocles hanging over them which keeps efficiency alive and weeds out incompetent companies by natural selection – "survival of the fittest". In the case of publicly-owned corporations, however, "their survival or death really has no connection at all with their capacity for managing their affairs" but is decided on "political grounds or [by] prejudices concerning the expediency or otherwise of state production". Because state-owned corporations do not live under the sword, what they supply is not automatically adapted to market demand, and they are not compelled to develop new techniques and products. "For state monopolies the watchword, more or less inevitably, is the well-known phrase *Quieta non movere* – don't ruffle the prevailing calm". And on the occasions when they do experiment, it is often popular fancies and not the prospect of profit that are the guiding star.

White (2012: 22–5) argues differently. In his view many economists of the time, including Alfred Marshall, desired an increase in the scope of government intervention in the economy.

> Marshall's own view was that various influences, among which he listed the increasing professionalism of government bureaus and the socialist ideas of the "noble if weird" Robert Owen, "have co-operated with technical progress to enlarge the scope for the beneficial intervention of Government since Mill's death even more than during his long life".
>
> (White 2012: 23)

For Marshall such interventions included municipal ownership of public utilities (Marshall 1907: 22). In the United States, Richard T. Ely supported the nationalisation of telegraph, telephones, railways, forests, arable lands and large manufacturing plants (Ely 1899: 10).

50 Jewkes adds that

> The claim that nationalization represents a more efficient manner of running industry and of translating decisions regarding prices and investment into actions can best be examined in terms of the fundamental changes introduced in any industry subjected to nationalization. They are:
>
> 1 The nationalized industry is a larger operating unit than those it replaced. From this arises the claim for the economies of scale.
> 2 The nationalized industry is monopolistic. Out of this arises the claim that it can adopt more complete integration and coordination of related functions.
> 3 The nationalized industry is not operated for private profit. From this it is asserted that price and investment policy can be made more rational and that the collaboration between different classes of workers in the industry can be made more willing, smoother and, thereby, fruitful.
>
> (Jewkes 1953: 617)

51 The problem of politicisation of public firms had been noted before. Baker (1899), for example, pointed out, with respect to waterworks in cities around the United States, that "[t]he absence of political considerations, generally speaking, from the management of private works, is undoubtedly a great advantage" (Baker 1899: 41) and "[p]rivate companies . . . certainly will not be accursed of lowering rates unduly for political effect, as cities sometimes do" (Baker 1899: 42).

52 For surveys of the results of empirical studies of privatisation see Bortolotti and Siniscalco (2004), Kikeri and Nellis (2004), Megginson (2005), Megginson and Netter (2001), Sheshinski and López-Calva (2003), Shirley and Walsh (2000) and Yarrow (1986). See also the 'Forum on privatisation' in CESifo (2005). Gupta, Shiller, Ma and Tiongson (2001) is a survey of the literature on the effects of privatisation on job loses and wages. A survey on privatisation in transition countries is Havrylyshyn and MacGettigan (1999). Claessens and Djankov (2002) look at privatisation in Eastern Europe. The Latin American experience is covered in Chong and López-de-Silanes (2003, 2005) and Nellis (2003b). Privatisation in Sub-Saharan Africa is discussed in Nellis (2003a). A survey on privatisation in the developing world, in general, is Parker and Kirkpatrick (2003). For studies of the European experience with privatisation see Parker (1999) and Köthenbürger, Sin and Whalley (2006), which contains chapters on Austria, Denmark, Finland, France, Germany, Italy, Ireland, The Netherlands, Spain and the United Kingdom. For other views on the British privatisation experience see Pollitt (1999), Part 2 of Vickers and Yarrow (1988) and Yarrow (1993). On the French experience see Dumez and Jeunemaitre (1994) and Schmidt (1999). On the politics of privatisation in Britain and France see Suleiman (1990). Gökgür (2006) looks at the case of Turkey. La Porta and López-de-Silanes (1999) analyse the Mexican privatisation program. For a discussion of privatisation in Malaysia see Sun and Tong (2002). For differing viewpoints on the privatisation experience in Russia see Boycko, Shleifer and Vishny (1995), Kokh (1998), Nellis (1999), Radygin (2003) and Brown, Earle and Gelbach (2013). The performance of newly privatised firms in China is studied in Wei, Varela, D'Souza and Hassan (2003). See Hodge (2003), King and Pitchford (1998) and Mead and Withers (2002) for discussions of privatisation in Australia and Duncan and Bollard (1992), Duncan (1996) and Barry (2002) for discussions of the New Zealand case. In addition see Table 1.3, pages 22–4, in Megginson (2005) for a more comprehensive listing of country studies describing national privatisation programs.

53 For overviews of this literature see Bös (1989a), Domberger and Piggott (1986), Rees (1994), Yarrow (1986) and Yeaple and Moskowitz (1995).

54 For examples see Bös and Peters (1991a,b). For summaries of this literature see Bös (1991) and Vickers and Yarrow (1988). See Bös (1986, 1987) and Bös and Peters (1988) for examples of papers which develop models of privatisation within the 'Boiteux tradition' of public enterprises. Haskel and Szymanski (1992) develop a firms/workers bargaining theory of privatisation. Bös (1989b, 2000) model privatisation as a cooperative game between the government, a trade union and the private shareholders.

55 Martimort (2006) discusses this theorem in detail and gives conditions for it to hold under complete contracts.

56 This is the total area under the demand curve for a given quantity.

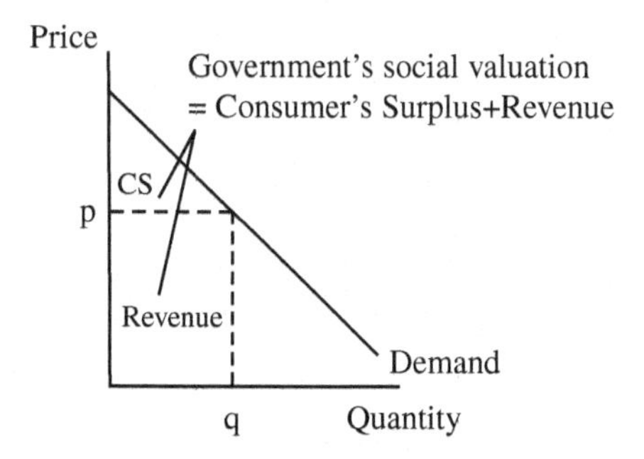

This area is called 'gross consumer surplus' by Varian (2014: 256).

57 Schmidt (1996a) is variant of Schmidt (1996b). Schmidt (1996b) considers the case of privatisation to an employee manager while Schmidt (1996a) applies to the case of privatisation to an owner-manager. While this second case is less realistic, it is simpler and does not require the assumption that the manager is an empire builder that is utilised in Schmidt (1996b).

58 Technically, the multi-principal distortion is similar to the double marginalisation on two complementary goods sold by noncooperative monopolists.

59 As a SOE the Treasury has income rights and the politician has control rights.

60 The importance of positive transactions costs is the theme that links Coase's two most famous papers. As Demsetz (1996: 565) notes,

> 'The Problem of Social Cost' (Coase, 1960) is R. H. Coase's most cited and most influential work. It is noted for, among other things, demonstrating the importance of incorporating transaction cost into the analysis of externalities and into the analysis of markets more generally. This theme, that markets are not free, is also found in the classic 'The Nature of the Firm' (Coase, 1937), so that, taking the perspective offered by both works, transaction cost turns out to be important whether one is analysing allocation through the price system or through the firm.

In fact the notion of positive transaction costs has importance beyond linking Coase's two most important papers, and providing the foundation for the contemporary theory of the firm. As Martin Ricketts has written,

> The founding insight – that transacting was not a costless activity – led, with considerable lags, to detailed analysis of the economics of contract, the economics of property rights (the entities being traded), the economics of information, legal economics (the processes and rules under which exchange takes place) and the economics of collective decision making (public choice).
>
> (Ricketts 2015: 46)

The foundation of the New Institutional Economics and the economic analysis of law is Coase's investigation of the implications of the positive transaction cost framework. As Veljanovski (2015a: 23) notes,

> Coase's work did not lead to a revolution in economics or public policy in the same sense that Keynes' General Theory did. Yet it did progressively stimulate two distinct intellectual developments: New Institutional Economics on the one hand and the economic analysis of law on the other.

For an evaluation of Coase's contribution to economics more generally see Veljanovski (2015b).

5 Partial versus general equilibrium

A final point about the models of the firm discussed in this book is that they illustrate a general issue to do with post-1970 microeconomics; namely, the retreat from the use of general equilibrium (GE) models.[1]

As early as 1955 Milton Friedman was suggesting that to deal with "substantive hypotheses about economic phenomena" a move away from Walrasian towards Marshallian analysis was required. When reviewing Walras's contribution to GE, as developed in his *Elements of Pure Economics*, Friedman argued,

> Economics not only requires a framework for organizing our ideas [which Walras provides], it requires also ideas to be organized. We need the right kind of language; we also need something to say. Substantive hypotheses about economic phenomena of the kind that were the goal of Cournot are an essential ingredient of a fruitful and meaningful economic theory. Walras has little to contribute in this direction; for this we must turn to other economists, notably, of course, to Alfred Marshall.
>
> (Friedman 1955: 908)

By the mid-1970s microeconomic theorists had largely turned away from Walras and back to Marshall, at least in so far as they returned to using partial equilibrium analysis to investigate economic phenomena such as strategic interaction, asymmetric information and economic institutions.

All of the models considered in this book are partial equilibrium models,[2] but in this regard the theory of the firm is no different from most of the microeconomic theory developed since the 1970s. Microeconomics such as incentive theory, incomplete contract theory, game theory, industrial organisation, organisational economics etc, has largely turned its back, presumably temporarily, on GE theory and has worked almost exclusively within a partial equilibrium framework.[3] This illustrates the point made in Chapter 1 that there is a close relationship between the economic mainstream and the theory of the firm; when the mainstream forgoes general equilibrium, so does the theory of the firm.[4]

One major path of influence from the mainstream of modern economics to the development of the theory of the firm has been via contract theory. But contract theory is an example of the mainstream's increasing reliance on partial equilibrium modelling. Contract theory grew out of the failures of GE. As Salanié (2005: 2) has argued,

> The theory of contracts has evolved from the failures of general equilibrium theory. In the 1970s several economists settled on a new way to study economic relationships. The idea was to turn away temporarily from general equilibrium models, whose description of the economy is consistent but not realistic enough, and to focus on necessarily partial models that take into account the full complexity of strategic interactions between privately informed agents in well-defined institutional settings.

The Foss, Lando and Thomsen classification scheme utilised in Chapter 4 clearly illustrates the movement of the current theory of the firm literature away from GE towards partial equilibrium analysis. The scheme divides the contemporary theory into two groups based on which of the standard assumptions of GE theory is violated when modelling issues to do with the firm. The theories are divided into either a principal–agent group, based on violating the 'symmetric information' assumption, or an incomplete contracts group, based on the violation of the 'complete contracts' assumption. The reference point approach extends the incomplete contracts grouping to situations where ex post trade is only partially contractible.

The introduction of the entrepreneur, as in the models proposed by Spulber and by Foss and Klein, also challenges, albeit in a different way, the standard GE model since, as William Baumol noted more than 40 years ago, the entrepreneur has no place in formal neoclassical theory.

> Contrast all this with the entrepreneur's place in the formal theory. Look for him in the index of some of the most noted of recent writings on value theory, in neoclassical or activity analysis models of the firm. The references are scanty and more often they are totally absent. The theoretical firm is entrepreneurless – the Prince of Denmark has been expunged from the discussion of *Hamlet*.
>
> (Baumol 1968: 66)

The reasons for this are not hard to find. Within the formal model the 'firm' is a production function or production possibilities set, it is simply a means of creating outputs from inputs. Given input prices, technology and demand, the firm maximises profits subject to its production plan being technologically feasible. The firm is modelled as a single agent who faces a set of relatively uncomplicated decisions, such as what level of output to produce, how much of each input to utilise and so on. Such 'decisions' are not decisions at all, they are simple mathematical calculations, implicit in the given conditions. The 'firm' can be seen as a set of cost curves and the 'theory of the firm' as little more than a calculus problem. In such a world there is a role for a 'decision maker' (manager) but no role for an entrepreneur.

The necessity of having to violate basic assumptions of GE theory so that we can model the firm, suggests that as it stands GE cannot deal easily with firms, or other important economic institutions. Bernard Salanié has noted that,

> [. . .] the organization of the many institutions that govern economic relationships is entirely absent from these [GE] models. This is particularly striking in the case of firms, which are modeled as a production set. This makes the very existence of firms difficult to justify in the context of general equilibrium models, since all interactions are expected to take place through the price system in these models.
>
> (Salanié 2005: 1)

This would suggest that to make GE models a ubiquitous tool of microeconomic analysis – including the analysis of issues to do with non-market organisations such as the firm – developing models which can account for information asymmetries, contractual incompleteness, strategic interaction, the existence of institutions and the like is not so much desirable as essential. One catalyst for the development of such a new approach to GE is that partial equilibrium models can obscure the importance of the theory of the firm for overall resource allocation, a point which is more easily appreciated in a GE framework.

Notes

1 When discussing the influence of Gerard Debreu on economics Düppe (2010: 2–3) nicely sums up the fate of GE as well,

> From the point of view of today Debreu's influence on the body of economics could be called zero, in that general equilibrium theory (GET) is the economics of yesterday. While GET had mirrored most analytic advances in economic theory before Debreu, after Debreu most theoretical innovations came as alternatives to GET (from game theory to complexity theory).

Historian of economic thought Roger Backhouse writes that "[i]n the 1940s and 1950s general-equilibrium theory [. . .] became seen as the central theoretical framework around which economics was based" (Backhouse 2002: 254) and that by the "[. . .] early 1960s, confidence in general-equilibrium theory, and with it economics as a whole, as at its height, with Debreu's *Theory of Value* being widely seen as providing a rigorous, axiomatic framework at the centre of the discipline" (Backhouse 2002: 261), but

> [. . .] there were problems that could not be tackled within the Arrow-Debreu framework. These include money (attempts were made to develop a general-equilibrium theory of money, but they failed), information, and imperfect competition. In order to tackle such problems, economists were forced to use less general models, often dealing only with a specific part of the economy or with a particular problem. The search for ever more general models of general competitive equilibrium, that culminated in *Theory of Value*, was over.
>
> (Backhouse 2002: 262)

One set of particularly problematic results for general equilibrium are the Sonnenschein-Mantel-Debreu (SMD) theorems,

> In part because of a conviction that progress could not be made in general equilibrium theory, there was a substantial redirection in economic theory. As the results in SMD theory became well known, for example through Wayne Shafer and Hugo Sonnenschein's survey (1982), economists began to question the centrality of general equilibrium theory and put forward alternatives to it. Thus in the ten years following the Shafer-Sonnenschein survey, we find a number of new directions in economic theory.
>
> (Rizvi 2006: 230)

2 When characterising the difference between partial and general equilibrium models Gale (2000: 38–9) describes partial equilibrium in the following terms,

> [...] partial equilibrium analysis, that amalgam of handy short cuts that allows economists to isolate particular phenomena and study them on the back of a virtual envelope, ignoring the fact that an economy is a complex system in which "everything affects and is affected by everything else". It may not he pure, but it is very practical.

He describes the 'elegant theory' of GE as a theory in which "[...] the interaction of individual agents and individual markets throughout the economy are aggregated to provide a precise account of the equilibrium of the entire economy. It may not be practical, but it is very pure"(Gale 2000: 39).

3 This is not to say there has been no work at all on GE within these areas. For examples of work on the GE approach to firms see Kihlstrom and Laffont (1979), Dreze (1985) and Zame (2007). For a survey of imperfect competition in GE see Hart (1985). On the GE approaches to the multinational firm see Markusen and Maskus (2001). For a discussion of the Arrow-Debreu model when faced with moral hazard and adverse selection see Guesnerie (1992). For a look at effects to provide strategic foundations for GE see Gale (2000). On the GE approach to tax and to international trade see, for example, Shoven and Whalley (1984), Creedy (1997), Jones (2011) and Woodland (2011). There has also been much work on computable general equilibrium analysis, see Böhringer, Rutherford and Wiegard (2003) and Sue Wing (2004) for overviews.

4 Arrow (1971) discusses the pre-1970 GE approach to the firm.

6 Conclusion

Even though firms may be, in practice, as old as farming – and even if not that old, 'firms', of some description, are at least two to three thousand years old – attempts at the formulation of a theoretical explanation for the existence, boundaries and organisation of firms only go back, at the most, to the 1920s or 1930s, while the current mainstream approach to the theory of the firm is even more recent having been developed only since the 1970s. During the period, roughly, from 1930–1970 the mainstream theory of the firm was the neoclassical model in which the firm is seen as a production function or production possibilities set, simply a means of transforming inputs into outputs. Given the available technology, a vector of input prices, and a demand schedule, the firm maximises money profits subject to the constraint that its production plans must be technologically feasible. For the pre-1930 neoclassical period there was no generally accepted theory of the firm. None of the then contemporary schools of thought offered an exhaustive analysis of the firm. Before that the classical economists only had a theory of aggregate production. The emphasis in classical economics was on macroeconomic questions centred around economic growth.[1] This resulted in less interest being shown in purely microeconomic issues, including firm level production.

When discussing the post-1930 neoclassical model of the firm Jensen and Meckling write,

> While the literature of economics is replete with references to the "theory of the firm", the material generally assumed under that heading is not actually a theory of the firm but rather a theory of markets in which firms are important actors.
>
> (Jensen and Meckling 1976: 306)

The move from a 'theory of markets with firms' to a 'theory of the firm' is the major change that has taken place within the mainstream approach to the theory of the firm over the theory's history.[2] What we have seen since the 1970s is a movement away from the theory of the firm being seen as developing a component of price theory, namely the component which asks – How does a producer act in its factor and product markets? – to the theory being concerned with the firm as an important institution in its own right.

Mark Roe (1994: vii) sums up much of this change when he writes,

> Economic theory once treated the firm as a collection of machinery, technology, inventory, workers, and capital. Dump these inputs into a black box, stir them up, and one got outputs of products and profits. Today, theory sees the firm as more, as a management structure. The firm succeeds if managers can successfully coordinate the firm's activities; it fails if managers cannot effectively coordinate and match people and inputs to current technologies and markets. At the very top of the firm are the relationships among the firm's shareholders, its directors, and its senior managers. If those relationships are dysfunctional, the firm is more likely to stumble.

The post-1970 changes to the theory of the firm have also made possible the development of a theory of privatisation. Before around 1990, despite a number of contributions from the 'old property rights' theorists, economic analysis did not accord a high priority to the question of the likely effects of ownership on industrial performance.

It was only after 1990 that the contemporary theory of the firm was applied to the theory of privatisation and we started to develop a greater appreciation for when and why ownership matters for the performance of a firm. These new privatisation theories highlight the importance of incomplete contracts for understanding the boundary between state-owned and privately owned firms, in addition to their importance for explaining the boundaries between firms and between firms and markets.

While the post-1970 theory of the firm literature has began the task of developing a genuine understanding of the firm, and closely related issues, it has yet to coalesce around one model or even one group of models. Even within the contemporary mainstream there are a number of competing models, to say nothing of those we could add into the mix if we were to consider the heterodox literature. As Bylund (2016: 1–2) explains,

> [...] there are several notable theories that each provide a different explanation and rationale for the business firm. [...] [T]here are several different definitions of what the firm supposedly is. [...] But each one must necessarily be incomplete, since it doesn't capture all of what the other definitions capture.

One can be forgiven for thinking that the current situation with regard to the modelling of the firm is much like a group of blind men trying to describe an elephant, each man can tell you about the part he can feel while remaining unaware of the rest of the animal. Each of the current theories tells us something about the firm, but none can tell us everything.

When thinking about the development of the theory of the firm from the 'past' to the 'present' a rudimentary history would read: the classical economists had a theory of aggregate production but no theory of firm level production, the neoclassical economists had a theory of firm level production but no theory of the firm and it has only been since the advent of the contemporary, post-1970, literature that a start has been made on developing a genuine theory of the firm's existence, boundaries and internal structure.

Today we also see attempts at integrating the theory of the entrepreneur and the development of markets with the theory of the firm. Questions to do with the importance of 'judgement' to the role of the entrepreneur with regard to the existence and organisation of firms, as well as the importance of the entrepreneur to the formation of firms and through them the creation of markets are now being considered.

The introduction of such elements may seem, on the surface, to be anti-mainstream but these new theories still utilise many mainstream ideas and thus are not so much attempts to subvert the contemporary theory as attempts to broaden the range of topics that the theory can handle. It can be argued that the discussion of the entrepreneur, the formation of firms, and via them the creation of markets, has now, finally, become a respectable mainstream activity. Alfred Marshall's comments, made at the end of the nineteenth century, about the development of economics in general apply with full force to the specific case of the development of the theory of the firm at the beginning of the twenty-first century:

> Some of the best work of the present generation has indeed appeared at first sight to be antagonistic to that of earlier writers; but when it has had time to settle down into its proper place, and its rough edges have been worn away, it has been found to involve no real breach of continuity in the development of the science. The new doctrines have supplemented the older, have extended, developed, and sometimes corrected them, and often have given them a different tone by a new distribution of emphasis; but very seldom have subverted them.
>
> (Marshall, 1920: v)

Notes

1 When discussing classical macroeconomics Thomas Sowell writes,

> Classical economics was much more than a miscellaneous collection of theories and doctrines. Its particular theories and policy prescriptions revolved around a single central concern: economic growth. Unlike modern growth theory, classical economists were not primarily concerned with the adjustments of the economy to the growth process, but with how such a process could be generated and sustained. The full title of Adam Smith's classic included the nature and *causes* of the wealth of nations.
>
> (Sowell 2006: 22)

When writing about classical microeconomics Sowell says, "Classical microeconomics revolved as much around economic growth as did classical macroeconomics" (Sowell 2006: 22). and "Classical allocation and distribution theory, like classical macroeconomics, reflected a preoccupation with secular growth" (Sowell 2006: 48).

2 It could be argued that the mainstream theory of the firm has changed while the orthodox (neolcassical) theory has not.

Appendix 1: the particular expenses curve

It was noted in Chapter note 33, page 46, that the notion of a 'particular expenses curve' (PEC) can be utilized in an explanation of the representative firm. Blaug (1997: 367–72) discusses Marshall's concept of the particular expenses curve and he notes that the curve is a cumulative array of the average costs of different firms.[1] Note that this means that the PEC is not a supply curve; that is, it is not a cumulative array of the marginal costs of the firms in the industry.

As an example consider a short-run equilibrium where the price is equal to the marginal costs of an intra-marginal producer and the average cost of a marginal firm. See Figure 162.1.

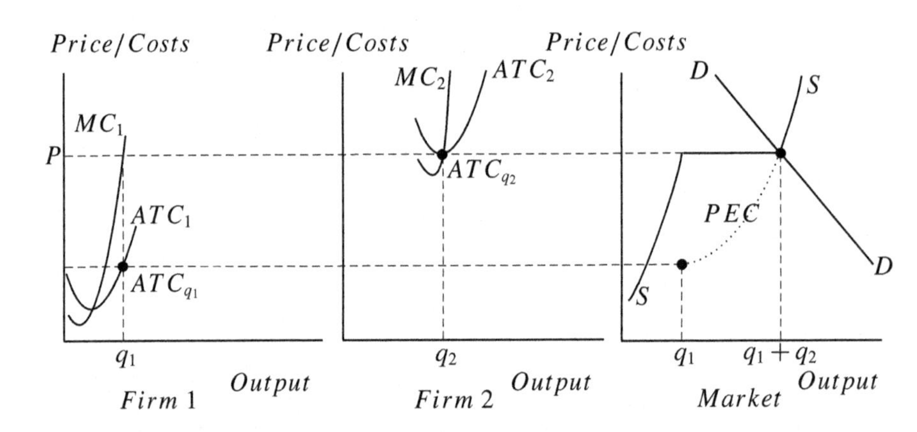

Figure 162.1.

Here there are two firms; one, a low cost intra-marginal firm – firm 1 – and one the marginal firm – firm 2. The price, P, is given by the intersection of the market supply and demand curves which occurs at the equilibrium quantity of $q_1 + q_2$. At P firm 2's $MC_2 = ATC_2$ $(= P)$ and the firm produces an output of q_2. Firm 1 is more efficient than firm 2 and thus $P = MC_1 > ATC_1$. Output is q_1. The PEC includes the points (ATC_{q_1}, q_1) and $(ATC_{q_2}, q_1 + q_2)$. The change from using dots to represent the PEC to using a curve to do so implies the addition of many (an infinite number of) extra firms with efficiencies between firm 1 and firm 2.

In general, the PEC shows the average total costs of the firms involved in the production of the output for a given market price-output combination with the firms arranged in order of efficiency from left to right, with the most efficient firm on the left and the marginal (least efficient) firm at the right. Since this must be true for any market price-output combination, with each firm producing a different output and incurring different average total costs for each market price-output combination, it follows that there is a PEC for each point on the short-period supply for the industry. The end point of the PEC shows the marginal (and average) cost of producing for the marginal firm. It follows that the industry supply curve is the locus of the end points of the PECs. See Figure 163.1

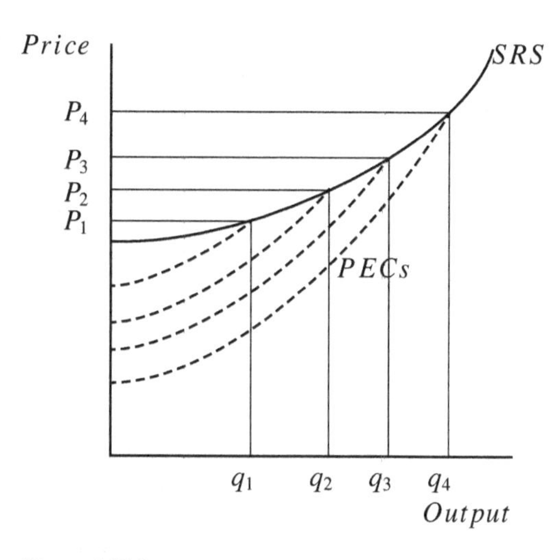

Figure 163.1.

Source: Blaug (1997): Figure 10.7, p. 368.

While this discussion has been in conducted terms of the short-run, the notion of a PEC can be equally well applied to the long-run. In fact, it was this latter application which interested Marshall (Blaug 1997: 368–72).

Marshall (1920b: 811) argues that the difference between the PEC and a normal supply curve is that in the former we do, and in the latter we do not, take the general economies of production as fixed and uniform throughout. The PEC is based on the assumption that all firms have access to the internal and external economies which belong to the market level of production while for the supply curve a firm's internal and external economies are determined by its level of production. For example, for the PEC in Figure 162.1 firm 1 can take advantage of the internal and external economies associated with the market level of output $q_1 + q_2$. For the supply curve the internal and external economies for firm 1 are those associated with the output level q_1.

Note

1 See Viner (1932: 43–6) for another discussion. Viner defines the curve as follows:

> To a curve representing the array of actual average costs of the different producers in an industry when the total output of the industry was a given amount, these individual costs being arranged in increasing order of size from left to right, Marshall gave the name of "particular expenses curve", and American economists have called such curves "bulk-line cost curves", "accountants' cost curves", and "statistical cost curves".
>
> (Viner 1932: 44; footnotes removed)

Appendix 2: Simon (1951)

Proof of Theorem 80.1

Let T_m be this greatest value. The proof has two parts. In the first it is shown that if $T(x) = T_m$ for (x, w), then there is no point preferred to (x, w). The second part deals with the situation where $T(x') < T_m$ and shows that there is a point (x, w), with $T(x) = T_m$, that is preferred to (x', w'). These two parts complete the proof.

(1) Suppose that $T(x, w) = T_m$. Consider any other point (x', w') with $T(x', w') \leq T_m$. Given that $T_m \geq T(x', w')$ we know from the definition of T that $a_2 S_1 + a_1 S_2 \geq a_2 S_1' + a_1 S_2'$ or, rearranging things,

$$a_2(S_1 - S_1') - a_2(S_2' - S_2) \geq 0. \tag{165.1}$$

For (x', w') to be preferred to (x, w) we must have

$$(S_1 - S_1') \leq 0 \quad \text{and} \quad (S_2' - S_2) \geq 0. \tag{165.2}$$

But given that $a_1 > 0$ and $a_2 > 0$ both (165.1) and (165.2) can only hold if $S_1 = S_1'$ and $S_2 = S_2'$. Therefore, (x', w') cannot be preferred to (x, w).

(2) Assume that $T(x', w') < T_m$. Let x be such that $T(x) = T_m$.

Also let $w = \left(\frac{1}{T(x')}\right)\{F_1(x)S_2(x', w') - F_2(x)S_1(x', w')\}$.

(Remember that we just need one w such that there is a point (x, w), with $T(x) = T_m$, which is preferred to (x', w').)

Then

$$\begin{aligned}
S_1(x, w) &= F_1(x) - a_1 w \text{ (from Equation (78.1))} \\
&= F_1(x) - a_1\left(\frac{1}{T(x')}\right)\left\{F_1(x)S_2(x', w') - F_2(x)S_1(x', w')\right\} \\
&= \left(\frac{1}{T(x')}\right)\left\{F_1(x)T(x') - a_1 F_1(x)S_2(x', w') + a_1 F_2(x)S_1(x', w')\right\} \\
&\qquad (T(x') = a_2 S_1(x', w') + a_1 S_2(x', w')) \\
&= \left(\frac{1}{T(x')}\right)\left\{F_1(x)a_2 S_1(x', w') + F_1(x)a_1 S_2(x', w')\right.
\end{aligned}$$

$$- a_1 F_1(x) S_2(x', w') + a_1 F_2(x) S_1(x', w')\}$$

$$(F_1(x)a_1 S_2(x', w') \text{ and } -a_1 F_1(x) S_2(x', w') \text{ cancel})$$

$$= \left(\frac{1}{T(x')}\right) \{F_1(x) a_2 S_1(x', w') + a_1 F_2(x) S_1(x', w')\}$$

$$= \left(\frac{1}{T(x')}\right) \{a_2 F_1(x) + a_1 F_2(x)\} S_1(x', w')$$

$$(T(x) = a_2 F_1(x) + a_1 F_2(x))$$

$$= \left(\frac{1}{T(x')}\right) T(x) S_1(x', w')$$

$$(T(x) = T_m \text{ by assumption})$$

$$= \left(\frac{1}{T(x')}\right) T_m S_1(x', w') > S_1(x', w') \qquad \left(\text{given that } \frac{T(m)}{T(x')} > 1\right)$$

Similarly it can be shown that $S_2(x, w) > S_2(x', w')$. Hence (x, w) is preferred to (x', w'). ■

Derivation of $T_X - \mathcal{E}[T(x_a)]$ (Equation (82.4))

Utilising the definitions given previously (see pages 77–82), in particular Equation (82.3) and Equation (82.1), $T_X - \mathcal{E}[T(x_a)]$ can be written as

$$\begin{aligned}
&\int_{F_1(x_a)=-\infty}^{\infty} \int_{F_1(x_b)=F_1(x_a)}^{\infty} (a_2 F_1(x_b) + a_1 \beta) p(F_1(x_a), F_1(x_b)) dF_1(x_b) dF_1(x_a) \\
&+ \int_{F_1(x_b)=-\infty}^{\infty} \int_{F_1(x_a)=F_1(x_b)}^{\infty} (a_2 F_1(x_a) + a_1 \alpha) p(F_1(x_a), F_1(x_b)) dF_1(x_a) dF_1(x_b) \\
&- a_2 \int_{-\infty}^{\infty} \int_{-\infty}^{\infty} F_1(x_a) p(F_1(x_a), F_1(x_b)) dF_1(x_a) dF_1(x_b) - a_1 \alpha. \qquad (166.1)
\end{aligned}$$

First note that $-a_2 \int_{-\infty}^{\infty} \int_{-\infty}^{\infty} F_1(x_a) p(F_1(x_a), F_1(x_b)) dF_1(x_a) dF_1(x_b) - a_1 \alpha$ can be rewritten as

$$\begin{aligned}
&- \int_{F_1(x_b)=-\infty}^{\infty} \int_{F_1(x_a)=-\infty}^{F_1(x_a)=F_1(x_b)} a_2 F_1(x_a) p(F_1(x_a), F_1(x_b)) dF_1(x_a) dF_1(x_b) \\
&- \int_{F_1(x_b)=-\infty}^{\infty} \int_{F_1(x_a)=F_1(x_b)}^{\infty} a_2 F_1(x_a) p(F_1(x_a), F_1(x_b)) dF_1(x_a) dF_1(x_b) \\
&- \int_{F_1(x_b)=-\infty}^{\infty} \int_{F_1(x_a)=-\infty}^{F_1(x_a)=F_1(x_b)} a_1 \alpha p(F_1(x_a), F_1(x_b)) dF_1(x_a) dF_1(x_b) \\
&- \int_{F_1(x_b)=-\infty}^{\infty} \int_{F_1(x_a)=F_1(x_b)}^{\infty} a_1 \alpha p(F_1(x_a), F_1(x_b)) dF_1(x_a) dF_1(x_b). \qquad (166.2)
\end{aligned}$$

Also note that

$$\int_{F_1(x_b)=-\infty}^{\infty}\int_{F_1(x_a)=F_1(x_b)}^{\infty}(a_2F_1(x_a)+a_1\alpha)p(F_1(x_a),F_1(x_b))dF_1(x_a)dF_1(x_b)$$

can be rewritten as

$$\int_{F_1(x_b)=-\infty}^{\infty}\int_{F_1(x_a)=F_1(x_b)}^{\infty}a_2F_1(x_a)p(F_1(x_a),F_1(x_b))dF_1(x_a)dF_1(x_b)$$
$$+\int_{F_1(x_b)=-\infty}^{\infty}\int_{F_1(x_a)=F_1(x_b)}^{\infty}a_1\alpha p(F_1(x_a),F_1(x_b))dF_1(x_a)dF_1(x_b). \qquad (167.1)$$

Adding (166.2) to (167.1) and using (166.1) we see that $T_X-\mathcal{E}[T(x_a)]$ can be expressed as

$$\int_{F_1(x_a)=-\infty}^{\infty}\int_{F_1(x_b)=F_1(x_a)}^{\infty}(a_2F_1(x_b)+a_1\beta)p(F_1(x_a),F_1(x_b))dF_1(x_b)dF_1(x_a)$$
$$-\int_{F_1(x_b)=-\infty}^{\infty}\int_{F_1(x_a)=-\infty}^{F_1(x_a)=F_1(x_b)}a_2F_1(x_a)p(F_1(x_a),F_1(x_b))dF_1(x_a)dF_1(x_b)$$
$$-\int_{F_1(x_b)=-\infty}^{\infty}\int_{F_1(x_a)=-\infty}^{F_1(x_a)=F_1(x_b)}a_1\alpha p(F_1(x_a),F_1(x_b))dF_1(x_a)dF_1(x_b) \qquad (167.2)$$

which can, in turn, be written as

$$\int_{F_1(x_a)=-\infty}^{\infty}\int_{F_1(x_b)=F_1(x_a)}^{\infty}a_2F_1(x_b)p(F_1(x_a),F_1(x_b))dF_1(x_b)dF_1(x_a)$$
$$+\int_{F_1(x_a)=-\infty}^{\infty}\int_{F_1(x_b)=F_1(x_a)}^{\infty}a_1\beta p(F_1(x_a),F_1(x_b))dF_1(x_b)dF_1(x_a)$$
$$-\int_{F_1(x_b)=-\infty}^{\infty}\int_{F_1(x_a)=-\infty}^{F_1(x_a)=F_1(x_b)}a_2F_1(x_a)p(F_1(x_a),F_1(x_b))dF_1(x_a)dF_1(x_b)$$
$$-\int_{F_1(x_b)=-\infty}^{\infty}\int_{F_1(x_a)=-\infty}^{F_1(x_a)=F_1(x_b)}a_1\alpha p(F_1(x_a),F_1(x_b))dF_1(x_a)dF_1(x_b). \qquad (167.3)$$

The second and fourth lines of Equation (167.3) are

$$\int_{F_1(x_a)=-\infty}^{\infty}\int_{F_1(x_b)=F_1(x_a)}^{\infty}a_1\beta p(F_1(x_a),F_1(x_b))dF_1(x_b)dF_1(x_a)$$

$$- \int_{F_1(x_b)=-\infty}^{\infty} \int_{F_1(x_a)=-\infty}^{F_1(x_a)=F_1(x_b)} a_1 \alpha p(F_1(x_a), F_1(x_b)) dF_1(x_a) dF_1(x_b)$$

$$= a_1 \beta \int_{F_1(x_a)=-\infty}^{\infty} \int_{F_1(x_b)=F_1(x_a)}^{\infty} p(F_1(x_a), F_1(x_b)) dF_1(x_b) dF_1(x_a)$$

$$- a_1 \alpha \int_{F_1(x_b)=-\infty}^{\infty} \int_{F_1(x_a)=-\infty}^{F_1(x_a)=F_1(x_b)} p(F_1(x_a), F_1(x_b)) dF_1(x_a) dF_1(x_b).$$

Given that the integrals

$$\int_{F_1(x_a)=-\infty}^{\infty} \int_{F_1(x_b)=F_1(x_a)}^{\infty} p(\cdot) dF_1(x_b) dF_1(x_a)$$

and (168.1)

$$\int_{F_1(x_b)=-\infty}^{\infty} \int_{F_1(x_a)=-\infty}^{F_1(x_a)=F_1(x_b)} p(\cdot) dF_1(x_a) dF_1(x_b)$$

integrate to give the same region (it is explained in the following that they both give the probability of being above the 45° line in the following figure) it is possible to rewrite this equation as

$$a_1 \beta \int_{F_1(x_a)=-\infty}^{\infty} \int_{F_1(x_b)=F_1(x_a)}^{\infty} p(F_1(x_a), F_1(x_b)) dF_1(x_b) dF_1(x_a)$$

$$- a_1 \alpha \int_{F_1(x_a)=-\infty}^{\infty} \int_{F_1(x_b)=F_1(x_a)}^{\infty} p(F_1(x_a), F_1(x_b)) dF_1(x_b) dF_1(x_a)$$

$$= a_1(\beta - \alpha) \int_{F_1(x_a)=-\infty}^{\infty} \int_{F_1(x_b)=F_1(x_a)}^{\infty} p(F_1(x_a), F_1(x_b)) dF_1(x_b) dF_1(x_a)$$

$$= \int_{F_1(x_a)=-\infty}^{\infty} \int_{F_1(x_b)=F_1(x_a)}^{\infty} a_1(\beta - \alpha) p(F_1(x_a), F_1(x_b)) dF_1(x_b) dF_1(x_a). \quad (168.2)$$

The third line of (167.3) is

$$- \int_{F_1(x_b)=-\infty}^{\infty} \int_{F_1(x_a)=-\infty}^{F_1(x_a)=F_1(x_b)} a_2 F_1(x_a) p(F_1(x_a), F_1(x_b)) dF_1(x_a) dF_1(x_b).$$

We know that (how we know this is explained below)

$$\int_{F_1(x_a)=-\infty}^{\infty} \int_{F_1(x_b)=F_1(x_a)}^{\infty} a_2 F_1(x_a) p(\cdot) dF_1(x_b) dF_1(x_a)$$

$$= \int_{F_1(x_b)=-\infty}^{\infty} \int_{F_1(x_a)=-\infty}^{F_1(x_a)=F_1(x_b)} a_2 F_1(x_a) p(\cdot) dF_1(x_a) dF_1(x_b) \quad (168.3)$$

which means that the third line can be rewritten as

$$-\int_{F_1(x_a)=-\infty}^{\infty}\int_{F_1(x_b)=F_1(x_a)}^{\infty} a_2F_1(x_a)p(F_1(x_a), F_1(x_b))dF_1(x_b)dF_1(x_a). \tag{169.1}$$

By using Equations (168.2) and (169.1), we can rewrite (167.3) to get

$$\begin{aligned}
&\int_{F_1(x_a)=-\infty}^{\infty}\int_{F_1(x_b)=F_1(x_a)}^{\infty}(a_2F_1(x_b)-a_2F_1(x_a))p(F_1(x_a), F_1(x_b))dF_1(x_b)dF_1(x_a)\\
&\quad+\int_{F_1(x_a)=-\infty}^{\infty}\int_{F_1(x_b)=F_1(x_a)}^{\infty} a_1(\beta-\alpha)p(F_1(x_a), F_1(x_b))dF_1(x_b)dF_1(x_a)\\
&=\int_{F_1(x_a)=-\infty}^{\infty}\int_{F_1(x_b)=F_1(x_a)}^{\infty}((a_2F_1(x_b)-a_2F_1(x_a))+a_1(\beta-\alpha))\cdot\\
&\qquad\qquad p(F_1(x_a), F_1(x_b))dF_1(x_b)dF_1(x_a)\\
&=\int_{F_1(x_a)=-\infty}^{\infty}\int_{F_1(x_b)=F_1(x_a)}^{\infty}(a_2(F_1(x_b)-F_1(x_a))+a_1(\beta-\alpha))\cdot\\
&\qquad\qquad p(F_1(x_a), F_1(x_b))dF_1(x_b)dF_1(x_a) \qquad (169.2)
\end{aligned}$$

(which is Equation (82.4)).

The following figure helps explain why

$$\int_{F_1(x_a)=-\infty}^{\infty}\int_{F_1(x_b)=F_1(x_a)}^{\infty} p(\cdot)dF_1(x_b)dF_1(x_a)$$

equals (Equation (168.1))

$$\int_{F_1(x_b)=-\infty}^{\infty}\int_{F_1(x_a)=-\infty}^{F_1(x_a)=F_1(x_b)} p(\cdot)dF_1(x_a)dF_1(x_b).$$

The dashed 45 degree line is the $F_1(x_a) = F_1(x_b)$ line. The hatched region is where $F_1(x_b) > F_1(x_a)$. Moreover,

$$\int_{F_1(x_b)=F_1(x_a)}^{F_1(x_b)=\infty} p(\cdot)dF_1(x_b)$$

represents the probability of the dark gray column and thus

$$\int_{F_1(x_a)=-\infty}^{\infty}\int_{F_1(x_b)=F_1(x_a)}^{\infty} p(\cdot)dF_1(x_b)dF_1(x_a)$$

represents the probability of being in the hatched region.

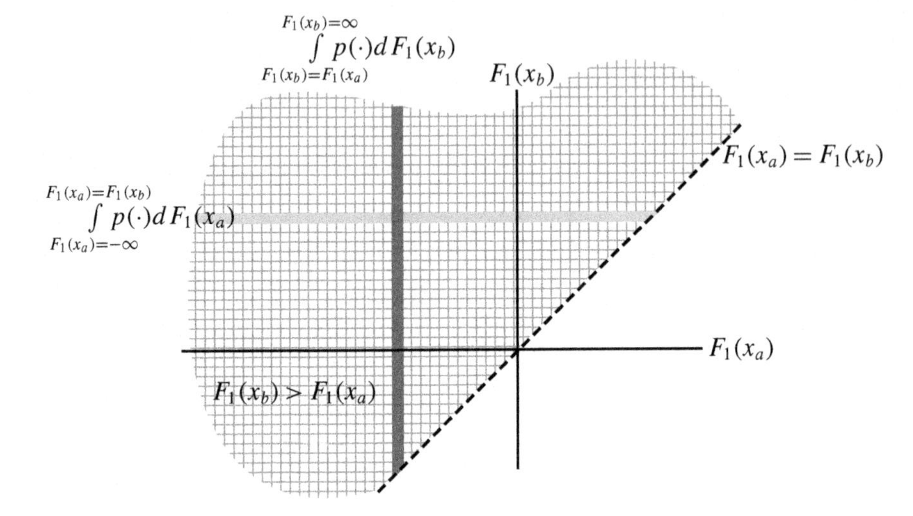

On the other hand

$$\int_{F_1(x_a)=-\infty}^{F_1(x_a)=F_1(x_b)} p(\cdot)dF_1(x_a)$$

is represented by the light gray area and

$$\int_{F_1(x_b)=-\infty}^{\infty} \int_{F_1(x_a)=-\infty}^{F_1(x_a)=F_1(x_b)} p(\cdot)dF_1(x_a)dF_1(x_b)$$

is also the probability of being in the hatched area.

Mathematically, it is easy to see that

$$\int_{F_1(x_a)=-\infty}^{\infty} \int_{F_1(x_b)=F_1(x_a)}^{\infty} p(\cdot)dF_1(x_b)dF_1(x_a)$$

equals (Equation (168.1))

$$\int_{F_1(x_b)=-\infty}^{\infty} \int_{F_1(x_a)=-\infty}^{F_1(x_a)=F_1(x_b)} p(\cdot)dF_1(x_a)dF_1(x_b)$$

since the difference between the top and bottom lines of Equation (168.1) is that the order of integration has been reversed, and the limits of integration have been changed in the bottom line to ensure that both the top and bottom lines integrate over the hatched region in the previous diagram.

Why does Equation (168.3) hold? That is, why does

$$\int_{F_1(x_a)=-\infty}^{\infty} \int_{F_1(x_b)=F_1(x_a)}^{\infty} a_2 F_1(x_a) p(\cdot) dF_1(x_b) dF_1(x_a)$$

equal (Equation (168.3))

$$\int_{F_1(x_b)=-\infty}^{\infty} \int_{F_1(x_a)=-\infty}^{F_1(x_a)=F_1(x_b)} a_2 F_1(x_a) p(\cdot) dF_1(x_a) dF_1(x_b)?$$

With reference to the previous diagram, note that the top line of Equation (168.3) can be interpreted as giving the (scaled, by a_2) expected value of $F_1(x_a)$ over the hatched region above the 45° line.

When changing the order of integration, as is done when moving from the top line of Equation (168.3) to the bottom line, we have to change the limits of integration to ensure that the bottom line also integrates over the hatched region. This explains the change in the limits of integration between the top and bottom lines of Equation (168.3). The new limits of integration in the bottom line makes certain that the bottom line also gives the scaled expected value of $F_1(x_a)$ for the region above the 45° line.

Appendix 3: monotone comparative statics

The following results are drawn from the lectures notes of Van Zandt (2002), which are based on the original work by Milgrom and Shannon (1994), Topkis (1998) and Vives (1999).

We start with the definition of increasing differences.

Let $X \subset \mathbb{R}$ and $Y \subset \mathbb{R}$. Let $u : X \times Y \to \mathbb{R}$.

DEFINITION 1. The function u has *increasing differences* in (x, y) if, for $x^L, x^H \in X$ such that $x^H > x^L$ and for $y^L, y^H \in Y$ such that $y^H > y^L$, we have

$$u(x^H, y^H) - u(x^L, y^H) \geq u(x^H, y^L) - u(x^L, y^L). \tag{172.1}$$

If this inequality is always strict, then u has strictly increasing differences in (x, y).

Van Zandt makes three relevant remarks following on from the definition.

REMARK 1. The interpretation of inequality (172.1) is that "the extra value of increasing x is higher when y is higher". However, this property is symmetric with respect to x and y. The inequality

$$u(x^H, y^H) - u(x^H, y^L) \geq u(x^L, y^H) - u(x^L, y^L) \tag{172.2}$$

is just a rearrangement of inequality (172.1), but its interpretation is that "the extra value of increasing y is higher when x is higher". One can check whichever inequality falls out more naturally in an application.

REMARK 4. Suppose that X is convex (i.e., is an interval) and that u is continuously differentiable in x. Then u has increasing differences in (x, y) if and only if $\frac{\partial u(x,y)}{\partial x}$ is non-decreasing in y. If also this partial derivative is strictly increasing in y (except perhaps at isolated values of x), then u has strictly increasing differences. (We can reverse the roles of x and y. For example, if Y is convex and u is differentiable in y, then u has increasing differences in (x, y) if and only if $\frac{\partial u(x,y)}{\partial y}$ is non-decreasing in x.)

and

REMARK 5. Suppose that X and Y are both convex and that u is twice continuously differentiable in (x, y). Then u has increasing differences in (x, y) if and only if

$$\frac{\partial^2 u(x, y)}{\partial x \partial y} \geq 0 \tag{173.1}$$

for all $x \in X$ and $y \in Y$. If inequality (173.1) is strict (except perhaps at isolated values of x or y), then u has strictly increasing differences.

These results have one decision variable and one parameter. What happens with multiple decision variables and parameters?

Start with an expanded set-up. Let $X = X_1 \times \cdots \times X_m$ be a set of m choice variables, where $X_i \subset \mathbb{R}$ for $i = 1, \ldots, m$. Let $Y = Y_1 \times \cdots \times Y_n$ be a set of n parameters, where $Y_j \subset \mathbb{R}$ for $j = 1, \ldots, n$. Let $u : X \times Y \to R$ be a utility function. Let $\varphi : Y \to X$ be the solution correspondence for the utility maximisation problem. That is, for $y \in Y$,

$$\varphi(y) = \arg\max_{x \in X} u(x, y).$$

The takeaway result here is given by Van Zandt's Theorem 3.

THEOREM 3. Suppose that

1. u has strictly increasing differences in (x_i, y_j) for $i \in \{1, \ldots, m\}$ and $j \in \{1, \ldots, n\}$;

   and

2. u has increasing differences in (x_i, x_k) for $i, k \in \{1, \ldots, m\}$ such that $i \neq k$.

Then, for $y^L, y^H \in Y$ such that $y^H > y^L$ and for $x^L \in \varphi(y^L)$ and $x^H \in \varphi(y^H)$, we have $x^H \geq x^L$.

But what about cases, like the proof of Proposition 96.1, where an increase in a parameter causes the choice variable to go down?

First note that the definition of strictly decreasing differences is the same as Definition 1 of strictly increasing differences except that the inequality is reversed. A function $f(x, y)$ has strictly decreasing differences in (x, y) if and only if $-f(x, y)$ has strictly increasing differences in (x, y).

Thinking in terms of Remark 5, the condition for the cross-partial derivative becomes $\frac{\partial^2 u(x,y)}{\partial x \partial y} \leq 0$.

For concreteness, suppose that there are two decision variables and one parameter, with the objective function $u(x_1, x_2, y)$.

The important result here is Van Zandt's Theorem 4.

THEOREM 4. Suppose that

1. u has strictly decreasing differences in (x_i, y) for $i \in \{1, \ldots, m\}$;

   and

2. u has increasing differences in (x_i, x_k) for $i, k \in \{1, ..., m\}$ such that $i \neq k$.

Then, for $y^L, y^H \in Y$ such that $y^H > y^L$ and for $x^L \in \varphi(y^L)$ and $x^H \in \varphi(y^H)$, we have $x^H \leq x^L$.

Now thinking about the proof of Proposition 96.1 in terms of Theorem 4, first note that in the proposition there are two choice variables, $\{z, G\}$, and two parameters, $\{\sigma, \rho\}$. Second, realise:

(i) that the conditions $\frac{\partial^2 S}{\partial z \partial \rho} < 0$ and $\frac{\partial^2 S}{\partial z \partial \sigma} < 0$ and the need for $\frac{\partial S}{\partial \rho}$ and $\frac{\partial S}{\partial \sigma}$ to be decreasing in G are requirement 1;

and

(ii) the condition that $\frac{\partial S}{\partial z}$ is increasing in G is requirement 2.

Appendix 4: examples of poor SOE performance

One of the motivating forces for reform of state-owned enterprises was a history of under performance by these firms worldwide. Some of the more notorious cases of poor SOE performance that have been publicised include:

McDonald (1991) outlines the case of the Hindustan Fertiliser Corporation in Haldia, West Bengal, India. By 1991 the firm had been operating for twelve years and employed twelve hundred workers. Yet up to that time the enterprise had not produced a single kilogram of fertiliser for sale!

The Economist (*Economist* 1994) details similar experiences in Italy:

> One example was a rolling mill at Bagnoli near Naples built by Italy's state-owned steel company ILVA. Designed to create jobs in a depressed area where the Christian Democrats were strong, the plant, which took nearly a decade to complete, was never used. In Sardinia, another area of high unemployment, politicians made ENI, a state chemicals and energy conglomerate, refit a coal mine, only to leave the miners idle but on the payroll.

In France, the near-bankruptcy of then state-owned bank Crédit Lyonnais is another example. In 1997 the French finance minister Dominique Strauss-Kahn admitted that the bank had probably lost around Ffr100 billion (around US$17 billion). The bank had to be bailed out three times in the 1990s. The total cost to the French taxpayer of the whole debacle has been estimated at between US$20 and US$30 billion. See the Economist (1997) for more on the affair.

With regard to the experience of the steel industry in the United Kingdom, Aylen (1988: 2) writes that in

> 1980/1 the [British Steel] Corporation made a total loss of £1 billion on a turnover of just under £3 billion, earning a place for a while in the *Guinness Book of Records*. [. . .] By 1980 British Steel was fundamentally uncompetitive, with cost per tonne almost a third above those of West German producers, and by rights should not have survived.

About coal, Vickers and Yarrow (1988: 331) could write,

> In recent years, mostly as a consequence of the combination of overinvestment in new capacity and the relatively slow rate of closure of inefficient collieries, the NCB [National Coal Board]'s continued viability has depended upon large injections of Government finance. In 1983–1984, for example, operating losses were covered by subsidies, known as deficit grants, amounting to £875 million.

During a House of Commons debate on nationalisation, denationalisation and renationalisation in 1991 the then Financial Secretary to the Treasury, Francis Maude, said of the British experience with nationalised industries:

> I do not wish to dwell on the record of nationalised industries in Britain. It is a sad and depressing saga in our nation's life. We all remember the British Steel Corporation, with its losses of 1 million every day of the year. We all remember British Telecom being in the Guinness Book of Records for the largest loss ever. We all remember the sloppy standards, the waiting lists for telephones, the ever-rising prices, the dingy tale of failure, the contempt for the customer, the craven management and the political interference.
>
> (Maude 1991)

The World Bank (World Bank 1995: 33–5) notes that in

> Turkey, Turkiye Taskorumu Kurmu, a state-owned coal mining company, lost the equivalent of about $6.4 billion between 1986 and 1990. Losses in 1992 worked out to about $12,000 per worker, six times the average national income. Yet health and safety condition in the mine were so poor that a miners' life expectancy was forty-six years, eleven years below the national average. [. . .] In the Philippines, the performance of the National Power Corporation steadily deteriorated from 1985 until the early 1990s. In 1990 the capital region alone lost an estimated $2.4 billion in economic output due to power outages. By 1992–1993, electricity was shut off about seven hours a day in many parts of the country. In Bangladesh, in 1992 the state sugar milling monopoly had twice as many office workers as it needed, or about 8,000 extra employees. [. . .] Meanwhile, sugar cost twice as much on the open market in Bangladesh as it did internationally. In Tanzania, the state-owned Morogoro shoe factory, built in the 1970s with a World Bank loan, never manufactured more than about 4 percent of its supposed annual capacity.

Kikeri, Nellis and Shirley (1992: 2) state that

> Of particular concern to governments is the burden that loss-making SOEs place on hard-pressed public budgets. SOE losses as a percentage of gross domestic product (GDP) reached 9 percent in Argentina and Poland in 1989;

through the 1980s about half of Tanzania's 350 SOEs persistently ran losses that had to be covered from public funds; in Ghana from 1985–1989 the annual outflow from government to fourteen core SOEs averaged 2 percent of GDP; and in China about 30 percent of SOEs were loss-making in 1991. The losses have important consequences: Mexico's minister of finance has noted that a fraction of the $10 billion in losses incurred by the state-owned steel complex would have been enough to bring potable water, sewerage, hospitals, and educational facilities to an entire region of the country (Aspe 1991).

References

Adams, Henry C. (1887). 'Relation of the State to Industrial Action', *Publications of the American Economics Association*, 1(6) January: 7–85.

Aghion, Philippe and Richard Holden (2011). 'Incomplete Contracts and the Theory of the Firm: What Have We Learned Over the Past 25 Years?', *Journal of Economic Perspectives*, 25(2) Spring: 181–97.

Aghion, Philippe, Mathias Dewatripont, Patrick Legros, and Luigi Zingales (eds.) (2014a). 'Grossman & Hart at 25', *Journal of Law, Economics, and Organization*, 30(suppl. 1) May: i1–i175.

Aghion, Philippe, Mathias Dewatripont, Patrick Legros, and Luigi Zingales (2014b). 'Introduction', *Journal of Law, Economics, and Organization*, 30(suppl. 1) May: i1–i12.

Aharoni, Yair (1986). *The Evolution and Management of State Owned Enterprises*, Cambridge, MA: Ballinger Publishing Co.

Alchian, Armen (1965a). 'The Basis of Some Recent Advances in the Theory of Management of the Firm', *Journal of Industrial Economics*, 14(1) November: 30–41.

Alchian, Armen (1965b). 'Some Economics of Property Rights', *Il Politico*, 30(4): 816–29.

Alchian, Armen (1984). 'Specificity, Specialization, and Coalitions', *Journal of Institutional and Theoretical Economics*, 140(1) March: 34–49.

Alchian, Armen and Harold Demsetz (1972). 'Production, Information Costs and Economic Organization', *American Economic Review*, 62(5) December: 777–95.

Allais, Maurice (1947). 'Le Problème de la Planification dans une Économie Collectiviste', *Kyklos*, II: 48–71.

Allen, Douglas and Dean Lueck (2002). *The Nature of the Farm: Contracts, Risk, and Organization in Agriculture*, Cambridge, MA: MIT Press.

Allen, G. C. (1929). *The Industrial Development of Birmingham and the Black Country, 1860–1927*, London: George Allen & Unwin Ltd.

Antràs, Pol (2014). 'Grossman-Hart (1986) Goes Global: Incomplete Contracts, Property Rights, and the International Organization of Production', *Journal of Law, Economics, and Organization*, 30(suppl. 1) May: i118–i175.

Antràs, Pol (2016). *Global Production: Firms, Contracts, and Trade Structure*, Princeton, NJ: Princeton University Press.

Antràs, Pol and Stephen R. Yeaple (2013). 'Multinational Firms and the Structure of International Trade', *National Bureau of Economic Research*, NBER Working Papers No. 18775, February. Available from NBER: www.nber.org/papers/w18775 [accessed 27 April 2016].

Appleby, Joyce (2010). *The Relentless Revolution: A History of Capitalism*, New York: W.W. Norton & Company.

Arena, Lise (2011). 'From Economics of the Firm to Business Studies at Oxford: An Intellectual History (1890s–1990s)'. Unpublished doctoral dissertation, University of Oxford, Oxford, England.

Argote, Linda and Henrich R. Greve (2007). '*A Behavioral Theory of the Firm*—40 Years and Counting: Introduction and Impact', *Organization Science*, 18(3) May–June: 337–49.

Arrow, Kenneth J. (1971). 'The Firm in General Equilibrium Theory'. In R. Marris and A. Wood (eds.), *The Corporate Economy: Growth, Competition, and Innovative Potential* (68–110), London: Macmillan.

Aspe, Pedro (1991). 'Thoughts on the Structural Transformation of Mexico: The Case of Privatization of Public Sector Enterprises'. Address to the Los Angeles World Affairs Council, June 21.

Augier, Mie and James G. March (2008). 'A Retrospective Look at *A Behavioral Theory of the Firm*', *Journal of Economic Behavior & Organization*, 66(1) April: 1–6.

Aylen, Jonathan (1988). 'Privatisation of the British Steel Corporation', *Fiscal Studies*, 9(3) August: 1–25.

Babbage, Charles (1832). *On the Economy of Machinery and Manufactures*, London: Charles Knight.

Backhouse, Roger E. (2002). *The Ordinary Business of Life: A History of Economics from the Ancient World to the Twenty-First Century*, Princeton, NJ: Princeton University Press.

Backhouse, Roger E. (2003). 'The Stabilization of Price Theory, 1920–1955'. In Warren J. Samuels, Jeff E. Biddle and John B. Davis (eds.), *A Companion to the History of Economic Thought* (308–24), Oxford: Blackwell Publishing Ltd.

Baker, Dean and Mark Weisbrot (1994). 'The Logic of Contested Exchange', *Journal of Economic Issues*, 28(4) December: 1091–114.

Baker, George, Robert Gibbons and Kevin J. Murphy (2002). 'Relational Contracts and the Theory of the Firm', *Quarterly Journal of Economics*, 117(1) February: 39–84.

Baker, M. H. (1899). 'Water-Works'. In Edward W. Bemis (ed.), *Municipal Monopolies* (3–54), New York: Thomas Y. Crowell and Company.

Baran, Paul A. and Paul M. Sweezy (1966). *Monopoly Capital: An Essay on the American Economic and Social Order*, New York: Monthly Review Press.

Barba Navaretti, Giorgio and Anthony J. Venables with Frank G. Barry, Karolina Ekholm, Anna M. Falzoni, Jan I. Haaland, Karen Helene Midelfart, and Alessandro Turrini (2004). *Multinational Firms in the World Economy*, Princeton, NJ: Princeton University Press.

Barker, Graeme (2006). *The Agricultural Revolution in Prehistory: Why did Forages Become Farmers?*, Oxford: Oxford University Press.

Barney, Jay (1991). 'Firm Resources and Sustained Competitive Advantage', *Journal of Management*, 17(1) March: 99–120.

Barry, P (2002), *The Changing Balance between the Public and Private Sectors*, Wellington: New Zealand Business Roundtable.

Barzel, Yoram (1987). 'Knight's "Moral Hazard" Theory of Organization', *Economic Inquiry*, 25(1) January: 117–20.

Barzel, Yoram (1997). *Economic Analysis of Property Rights*, 2nd edn., Cambridge: Cambridge University Press.

Baumol, William J. (1959). *Business Behavior, Value and Growth*, New York: Macmillan. (Revised edition, 1967).

Baumol, William J. (1962). 'On the Theory of Expansion of the Firm', *American Economic Review*, 52(5) December: 1078–87.

Baumol, William J. (1968). 'Entrepreneurship in Economic Theory', *American Economic Review*, 58(2) May: 64–71.

Beer, M. (1938). *Early British Economics: From the Thirteenth to the Middle of the Eighteenth Century*, London: George Allen and Unwin Ltd.

Beer, M. (1939). *An Inquiry into Physiocracy*, London: George Allen and Unwin Ltd.

Bemis, Edward W. and W. S. Outerbridge, Jr. (1891). 'Municipal Ownership of Gas in the United States', *Publications of the American Economics Association*, 6(4/5) July–September: 9–185.

Berle, Adolf Augustus Jr. and Gardiner C. Means (1932). *The Modern Corporation and Private Property*, New York: Macmillan.

Berry, Arthur (1891). 'The Pure Theory of Distribution'. In *Report of the Sixtieth Meeting of the British Association for the Advancement of Science Held at Leeds September 1890* (923–4), London: John Murray.

Best, Michael H. (2012). 'The Obscure Firm in the *Wealth of Nations*'. In Michael Dietrich and Jackie Kraff (eds.), *Handbook on the Economics and Theory of the Firm* (29–41), Cheltenham, UK: Edward Elgar Publishing Ltd.

Bitran, Eduardo and Raúl E. Sáez (1994). 'Privatization and Regulation in Chile'. In Barry P. Bosworth, Rudiger Dornbusch and Raúl Labán (eds.), *The Chilean Economy: Policy Lessons and Challenges* (329–68), Washington DC: The Brookings Institution.

Blankenburg, Stephanie and Geoffrey Harcourt (2007). 'The Debates on the Representative Firm and Increasing Returns: Then and Now'. In Philip Arestis, Michelle Baddelely and John S. L. McCombie (eds.), *Economic Growth, New Directions in Theory and Policy* (44–64), Cheltenham, UK: Edward Elgar Publishing Ltd.

Blaug, Mark (1958). 'The Classical Economists and the Factory Acts—A Re-Examination', *Quarterly Journal of Economics*, 72(2) May: 211–26.

Blaug, Mark (1997). *Economic Theory in Retrospect*, 5th edn., Cambridge: Cambridge University Press.

Bodenhorn, Diran (1959). 'A Note on the Theory of the Firm', *Journal of Business*, 32(2) April: 164–74.

Böhringer, Christoph, Thomas Rutherford and Wolfgang Wiegard (2003). 'Computable General Equilibrium Analysis: Opening a Black Box', ZEW Discussion Paper No. 03–56, Mannheim, Germany.

Bolton, Patrick and Mathias Dewatripont (1994). 'The Firm as a Communication Network', *Quarterly Journal of Economics*, 109(4) November: 809–40.

Bolton, Patrick and David S. Scharfstein (1998). 'Corporate Finance, the Theory of the Firm, and Organizations', *Journal of Economic Perspectives*, 12(4) Autumn: 95–114.

Bolton, Patrick and Mathias Dewatripont (2005). *Contract Theory*, Cambridge, MA: MIT Press.

Bonar, James (1893). *Philosophy and Political Economy in Some of Their Historical Relations*, London: Swan, Sonnenschein & Co.

Boon, Martin James (1873). *How to Nationalize the Commons & Waste Lands, Railroads, Tramways, Water Works, Gas Works, Public Buildings & Other Works, Throughout England and the Colonies, Without the Burden of Interest, by Means of National Money*, London: Published at F. Farrah's Book Store. Available from JSTOR: www.jstor.org/stable/60219315 [accessed 27 April 2016].

Border, K. C. (2004). 'Moral Hazard in Teams', Lecture Notes, California Institute of Technology, November. Available from www.hss.caltech.edu/~kcb/Notes/MoralHazardTeams.pdf [accessed 27 April 2016].

Borek, T. Christopher, Angelo Frattarelli and Oliver Hart (2013). 'Tax Shelters or Efficient Tax Planning? A Theory of The Firm Perspective on The Economic Substance Doctrine', *National Bureau of Economic Research*, NBER Working Papers No. 19081, May. Available from NBER: www.nber.org/papers/w19081 [accessed 27 April 2016].

Borland, Jeff and Gerald Garvey (1994). 'Recent Developments in the Theory of the Firm', *Australian Economic Review*, issue 105 January–March: 60–82.

Bortolotti, Bernardo and Domenico Siniscalco (2004). *The Challenges of Privatization: An International Analysis*, Oxford: Oxford University Press.

Bös, Dieter (1986). 'A Theory of the Privatization of Public Enterprises', *Journal of Economics-Zeitschrift fur Nationalokonomie*, Supplementum 5: 17–40.

Bös, Dieter (1987). 'Privatization of Public Enterprises', *European Economic Review*, 31(1/2) February/March: 352–60.

Bös, Dieter (1989a). 'Arguments on Privatization'. In Gerhard Fels and George M. von Furstenberg (eds.), *A Supply-Side Agenda for Germany: Sparks from the United States, Great Britain, European Integration* (217–44), Berlin: Springer.

Bös, Dieter (1989b). 'Privatization of Public Firms: A Government-Trade Union-Private Shareholder Cooperative Game'. In M. Neumann and K. W. Roskamp (eds.), *Public Finance and the Performance of Enterprises* (343–63), Detroit: Wayne State University Press.

Bös, Dieter (1991). *Privatization: A Theoretical Treatment*, Oxford: Oxford University Press.

Bös, Dieter (1994). *Pricing and Price Regulation: An Economic Theory for Public Enterprises and Public Utilities*, Amsterdam: Elsevier Science B.V.

Bös, Dieter (2000). 'Privatization under Asymmetric Information', *Indian Journal of Applied Economics*, 8(0) Special Issue Part 3 July/September: 285–326.

Bös, Dieter and Wolfgang Peters (1988). 'Privatization, Internal Control and Internal Regulation', *Journal of Public Economics*, 36(2) July: 231–58.

Bös, Dieter and Wolfgang Peters (1991a). 'A Principal-Agent Approach on Manager Effort and Control in Privatized and Public Firms'. In Attiat F. Ott and Keith Hartley (eds.), *Privatization and Economic Efficiency: A Comparative Analysis of Developed and Developing Countries* (26–52), Aldershot, UK: Edward Elgar Publishing Ltd.

Bös, Dieter and Wolfgang Peters (1991b). 'Privatization of Public Enterprises: A Principal-Agent Approach Comparing Efficiency in Private and Public Sectors', *Empirica–Austrian Economic Papers*, 18(1): 5–16.

Boudreaux, Donald J. and Randell G. Holcombe (1989). 'The Coasian and Knightian Theories of the Firm', *Managerial and Decision Economics*, 10(2) June: 147–54.

Boulding, Kenneth E. (1942). 'The Theory of the Firm in the Last Ten Years', *American Economic Review*, 32(4) December: 791–802.

Boulding, Kenneth E. (1960). 'The Present Position of the Theory of the Firm'. In Kenneth E. Boulding and W. Allen Spivey (eds.), *Linear programming and the theory of the firm* (1–17), New York: The Macmillan Company.

Bowen, Howard R. (1955). *The Business Enterprise as a Subject for Research: Prepared for the Committee on Business Enterprise Research*, Social Science Research Council, Pamphlet No. 11, New York: Social Science Research Council.

Boycko, Maxim, Andrei Shleifer and Robert W. Vishny (1995). *Privatizing Russia*, Cambridge, MA: MIT Press.

Boycko, Maxim, Andrei Shleifer and Robert W. Vishny (1996). 'A Theory of Privatisation', *Economic Journal*, 106(435) March: 309–19.

Bresson, Alain (2014). 'Capitalism and the Ancient Greek Economy'. In Larry Neal and Jeffrey G. Williamson (eds.), *The Cambridge History of Capitalism* (vol. I The Rise of Capitalism: From Ancient Origins to 1848, 43–74), Cambridge: Cambridge University Press.

Bresson, Alain (2016). *The Making of the Ancient Greek Economy: Institutions, Markets, and Growth in the City-States*, Princeton, NJ: Princeton University Press.

Brittan, Samuel (1989). 'The Thatcher Government's Economic Policy'. In Dennis Kavanaugh and Anthony Seldon (eds.), *The Thatcher Effect* (1–37), Oxford: Oxford University Press.

Brown, J. David, John S. Earle, and Scott Gelbach (2013). 'Privatization'. In Michael Alexeev and Shlomo Weber (eds.), *The Oxford Handbook of the Russian Economy* (161–88), Oxford: Oxford University Press.

Brynjolfsson, Erik (1994). 'Information Assets, Technology, and Organization', *Management Science*, 40(12): 1645–62.

Buhai, Sebastian (2003). 'Incomplete Contracts and the Theory of the Firm', Notes, 20th January. Available from www.sebastianbuhai.com/papers/others/incomplete_contracts.pdf [accessed 27 April 2016].

Butler, Eamonn (2007). *Adam Smith—A Primer*, London: Institute of Economic Affairs.

Butterfield, Herbert (1931). *The Whig Interpretation of History*, London: G. Bell and Sons.

Bylund, Per L. (2011). 'Division of Labor and the Firm: An Austrian Attempt at Explaining the Firm in the Market', *Quarterly Journal of Austrian Economics*, 14(2): 188–215.

Bylund, Per L. (2014a). 'Ronald Coase's "Nature of The Firm" and the Argument for Economic Planning', *Journal of the History of Economic Thought*, 36(3) September: 305–29.

Bylund, Per L. (2014b). 'The Firm and the Authority Relation: Hierarchy vs. Organization'. In Guinevere Liberty Nell (ed.), *Austrian Theory and Economic Organization: Reaching Beyond Free Market Boundaries* (97–120), New York: Palgrave Macmillan.

Bylund, Per L. (2016). *The Problem of Production: A New Theory of the Firm*, London: Routledge.

Cannan, Edwin (1902). 'The Practical Utility of Economic Science', *Economic Journal*, 12(8) December: 459–71.

Cannan, Edwin (1917). *A History of the Theories of Production and Distribution in English Political Economy from 1776 to 1848*, 3rd edn., London: P. S. King & Son.

Cantillon, Richard (1755). *Essai sur la Nature du Commerce en Général* edited and with an English translation by Henry Higgs, London: Frank Cass and Company, 1931.

Carlos, Ann M. and Stephen Nicholas (1996). 'Theory and History: Seventeenth-Century Joint-Stock Chartered Trading Companies', *Journal of Economic History*, 56(4) December: 916–24.

Carlson, Benny (1994). *The State as a Monster: Gustav Cassel and Eli Heckscher on the Role and Growth of the State*, Lanham, MD: University Press of America.

Carlson, S. (1939). *A Study on the Pure Theory of Production*, London: P. S. King.

Carson, Kevin (2014). 'Economic Calculation Under Capitalist Central Planning'. In Guinevere Liberty Nell (ed.), *Austrian Theory and Economic Organization: Reaching Beyond Free Market Boundaries* (57–95), New York: Palgrave Macmillan.

Cawston, George and A. H. Keane (1896). *The Early Chartered Companies (A.D. 1296–1858)*, London: Edward Arnold.

CESifo (2005). Forum on Privatisation. *CESifo DICE Report*, 3(1) Spring: 3–40.

Chamberlin, Edward H. (1933). *The Theory of Monopolistic Competition*, Cambridge, MA: Harvard University Press.

Chamberlin, Edward H. (1937). 'Monopolistic or Imperfect Competition?', *Quarterly Journal of Economics*, 51(4) August: 557–80.

Chandler, Alfred D., Jr. (1962). *Strategy and Structure: Chapters in the History of the American Industrial Enterprise*, Cambridge, MA: MIT Press.

Chandler, Alfred D., Jr. (1977). *The Visible Hand: The Managerial Revolution in American Business*, Cambridge, MA: Harvard University Press.

Chandler, Alfred D., Jr. (1990). *Scale and Scope: The Dynamics of Industrial Capitalism*, Cambridge, MA: Harvard University Press, Belknap Press.

Chapman, Stanley D. (1974). 'The Textile Factory before Arkwright: A Typology of Factory Development', *Business History Review*, 48(4) Winter: 451–78.

Cheung, Steven N.S. (1983). 'The Contractual Nature of the Firm', *Journal of Law and Economics*, 26(1) April: 1–21.

Cho, Dong-Sung and Se-Yeon Ahn (2009). 'Exploring the Characteristics of the Founder and CEO Succession as Causes of Corporate Longevity: Findings from Korean Long-Lived Companies', *Journal of International Business and Economy*, 10(2) Fall: 157–87.

Chong, Alberto and Florencio López-de-Silanes (2003). 'The Truth about Privatization in Latin America', memo, October.

Chong, Alberto and Florencio López-de-Silanes (eds.) (2005). *Privatization in Latin America: Myths And Reality*, Palo Alto, CA: Stanford University Press.

Claessens, Stijn and Simeon Djankov (2002). 'Privatization Benefits in Eastern Europe', *Journal of Public Economics*, 83(3) March: 307–24.

Clapham, J. H. (1922). 'Of Empty Economic Boxes', *Economic Journal*, 32(127) September: 305–4.

Coad, Alexander (2007). 'Firm Growth: A Survey', Evolutionary Economics Group, Max Planck Institute of Economics, Jena, Papers on Economics and Evolution # 0703, May 14.

Coad, Alexander (2009). *The Growth of Firms: A Survey of Theories and Empirical Evidence*, Cheltenham, UK: Edward Elgar Publishing Ltd.

Coase, Ronald Harry (1937). 'The Nature of the Firm', *Economica*, n.s. 4(16) November: 386–405.

Coase, Ronald Harry (1955). 'Comment' (on Heflebower (1955)). In Universities-National Bureau Committee for Economic Research, *Business Concentration and Price Policy* (392–4), Princeton, NJ: Princeton University Press.

Coase, Ronald Harry (1960). 'The Problem of Social Cost', *Journal of Law and Economics*, 3 October: 1–44.

Coase, Ronald Harry (1972). 'Industrial Organization: A Proposal for Research'. In Victor R. Fuchs (ed.), *Economic Research: Retrospect and Prospect* (vol. 3: Policy Issues and Research Opportunities in Industrial Organization, 59–73), Cambridge, MA: National Bureau of Economic Research.

Coase, Ronald Harry (1988a). 'The Nature of the Firm: Meaning', *Journal of Law, Economics & Organization*, 4(1) Spring: 19–32.

Coase, Ronald Harry (1988b). 'The Nature of the Firm: Influence', *Journal of Law, Economics & Organization*, 4(1) Spring: 33–47.

Coase, Ronald Henry and Wang Ning (2011). 'The Industrial Structure of Production: A Research Agenda for Innovation in an Entrepreneurial Economy', *Entrepreneurship Research Journal*, 1(2): Article 1.

Colander, David, Richard Holt and J. Barkley Rosser Jr. (2004). 'The Changing Face of Mainstream Economics', *Review of Political Economy*, 16(4): 485–99.

Colander, David, Richard Holt and J. Barkley Rosser Jr. (2005). *The Changing Face of Economics: Conversations with Cutting Edge Economists*, Ann Arbor, MI: University of Michigan Press.

Conner, K. R. (1991). 'A Historical Comparison of Resource-Based Theory and Five Schools of Thought Within Industrial Organization: Do We Have a New Theory of the Firm?', *Journal of Management*, 17: 121–54.

Conner, K. R. and C. K. Prahalad (1996). 'A Resource-Based Theory of the Firm: Knowledge versus Opportunism', *Organization Science*, 7(5) September–October: 477–501.

Cooper, W. W. (1949a). 'Theory of the Firm: Some Suggestions for Revision', *American Economic Review*, 39(6) December: 1202–22.

Cooper, W. W. (1949b). 'Theory of the Firm: Some Suggestions for Revision, II', Commission Discussion Papers: Economics: No. 255, March 29.

Cooper, W. W. (1951). 'A Proposal for Extending the Theory of the Firm', *Quarterly Journal of Economics*, 65(1) February: 87–109.

Copp, Stephen F. (2008). 'Limited Liability and Freedom'. In Stephen F. Copp (ed.), *The Legal Foundations of Free Markets* (158–90), London: Institute of Economic Affairs.

Cowell, Frank (2006). *Microeconomics: Principles and Analysis*, Oxford: Oxford University Press.

Cowen, Tyler and David Parker (1997). *Markets in the Firm: A Market-Process Approach to Management*, Hobart Paper No. 134, London: Institute of Economic Affairs.

Creedy, John (1997). 'Taxation in General Equilibrium: an Introduction', *Bulletin of Economic Research*, 49(3) July: 177–203.

Crew, Michael A. (1975). *Theory of the Firm*, London: Longman.

Cyert, Richard M. and Charles L. Hedrick (1972). 'Theory of the Firm: Past, Present, and Future; An Interpretation', *Journal of Economic Literature*, 10(2) June: 398–412.

Cyert, Richard M. and James G. March (1963). *A Behavioral Theory of the Firm*, Englewood Cliffs, NJ: Prentice-Hall, Inc.

Dano, Sven (1966). *Industrial Production Models: A Theoretical Study*, Wien, Austria: Springer-Verlag.

Davies, Ernst (1952). *Problems of Public Ownership*, London: Labour Party.

Davies, John K. (2007). 'Classical Greece: Production'. In Walter Scheidel, Ian Morris and Richard P. Saller (eds.), *The Cambridge Economic History of the Greco-Roman World* (331–61), Cambridge: Cambridge University Press.

Debreu, Gerard (1959). *Theory of Value*, New York: Wiley.

Demsetz, Harold (1967). 'Toward a Theory of Property Rights', *American Economic Review*, 57(0) May: 347–59.

Demsetz, Harold (1982). *Economic, Legal, and Political Dimensions of Competition*, Amsterdam: North-Holland Publishing Company.

Demsetz, Harold (1988a). 'The Theory of the Firm Revisited', *Journal of Law, Economics, & Organization*, 4(1) Spring: 141–61.

Demsetz, Harold (1988b). 'Profit as a Functional Return: Reconsidering Knight's Views'. In Harold Demsetz, *Ownership, Control, and the Firm: The Organization of Economic Activity*, (vol. I, 236–47), Oxford: Basil Blackwell.

Demsetz, Harold (1995). *The Economics of the Business Firm: Seven Critical Commentaries*, Cambridge: Cambridge University Press.

Demsetz, Harold (1996). 'The Core Disagreement Between Pigou, the Profession, and Coase in the Analyses of the Externality Question', *European Journal of Political Economy*, 12(4) December: 565–79.

Demsetz, Harold (1997). 'The Firm in Economic Theory: A Quiet Revolution', *American Economic Review*, 87(2) May: 426–9.
Dequech, David (2007). 'Neoclassical, Mainstream, Orthodox, and Heterodox Economics', *Journal of Post Keynesian Economics*, 30(2): 279–302.
De Scitovsky, T. (1943). 'A Note on Profit Maximisation and its Implications', *Review of Economic Studies*, 11(1) Winter: 57–60.
Dietrich, Michael and Jackie Krafft (eds.) (2012). *Handbook on the Economics and Theory of the Firm*, Cheltenham, UK: Edward Elgar Publishing Ltd.
Domberger, Simon and John Piggott (1986). 'Privatization Policies and Public Enterprise: A Survey', *Economic Record*, 62 Issue 177 June: 145–62.
Dreze, Jacques H. (1985). '(Uncertainty and) The Firm in General Equilibrium Theory', *Economic Journal*, 95(Suppl.: Conference Papers): 1–20.
Drucker, Peter (1958). 'Business Objectives and Survival Needs: Notes on a Discipline of Business Enterprise', *Journal of Business*, 31(2) April: 81–90.
Drucker, Peter (1969). *The Age of Discontinuity*, New York: Harper & Row.
Dulbecco, Philippe and Pierre Garrouste (1999). 'Towards an Austrian Theory of the Firm', *Review of Austrian Economics*, 12(1): 43–64.
Dumez, Hervé and Alain Jeunemaitre (1994). 'Privatization in France: 1983–1993'. In Vincent Wright (ed.), *Privatization in Western Europe: Pressures, Problems and Paradoxes* (83–104), London: Pinter Publishers.
Duncan, Ian (1996). 'Public Enterprises'. In Brian Silverstone, Alan Bollard and Ralph Lattimore (eds.), *A Study of Economic Reform: The Case of New Zealand* (389–424), Amsterdam: North-Holland.
Duncan, Ian and Alan Bollard (1992). *Corporatization and Privatization: Lessons from New Zealand*, Auckland and New York: Oxford University Press.
Düppe, Till (2010). 'Debreu's Apologies for Mathematical Economics after 1983', *Erasmus Journal for Philosophy and Economics*, 3(1) Spring: 1–32.
Earley, James S. (1955). 'Recent Developments in Cost Accounting and the "Marginal Analysis"', *Journal of Political Economy*, 63(3) June: 227–42.
Earley, James S. (1956). 'Marginal Policies of "Excellently Managed" Companies', *American Economic Review*, 46(1) March: 44–70.
Economist (1994). 'European Privatisation: Two Half Revolutions', 330(7847) January 22: 55–58.
Economist (1997). 'Banking's Biggest Disaster', 344(8024) July 5: 69–71.
Edgeworth, Francis Y. (1889). 'On the Application of Mathematics to Political Economy', *Journal of the Royal Statistical Society*, 52(4) December: 538–76.
Ekelund, Robert Jr. and Robert D. Tollison (1997). *Politicized Economies: Monarchy, Monopoly, and Mercantilism*, College Station: Texas A&M University Press.
Ekelund, Robert Jr. and Robert D. Tollison (2011). *Economic Origins of Roman Christianity*, Chicago: University of Chicago Press.
Ekelund, Robert Jr., Robert F. Hébert, Robert D. Tollison, Gary M. Anderson and Audrey B. Davidson (1996). *Sacred Trust: The Medieval Church as a Firm*, New York: Oxford University Press.
Ekman, Elan V. (1978). *Some Dynamic Economic Models of the Firm: A Microeconomic Analysis with Emphasis on Firms that Maximize Other Goals Than Profit Alone*, Stockholm: Economic Research Institute at the Stockholm School of Economics.
Ely, Richard T. (1894). *Socialism: An Examination of Its Nature, Its Strength and Its Weakness, with Suggestions for Social Reform*, New York: Thomas Y. Crowell & Co.

Evensky, J. (2005). *Adam Smith's Moral Philosophy: A Historical and Contemporary Perspective on Markets, Law, Ethics, and Culture*, Cambridge: Cambridge University Press.

Fama, Eugene F. (1980). 'Agency Problems and the Theory of the Firm', *Journal of Political Economy*, 88(2) April: 288–307.

Fehr, Ernst, Oliver D. Hart and Christian Zehnder (2009). 'Contracts, Reference Points, and Competition—Behavior Effects of the Fundamental Transformation', *Journal of the European Economic Association*, 7(2) April–May: 561–72.

Fehr, Ernst, Oliver D. Hart and Christian Zehnder (2011). 'Contracts as Reference Points—Experimental Evidence', *American Economic Review*, 101(2) May: 493–525.

Ferguson, C. E. (1969). *The Neoclassical Theory of Production & Distribution*, Cambridge: Cambridge University Press.

Fleckner, Andreas Martin (2015). 'Roman Business Associations', Max Planck Institute for Tax Law and Public Finance Working Paper 2015-10 October.

Fleckner, Andreas Martin (2016). 'Adam Smith on the Joint Stock Company', Max Planck Institute for Tax Law and Public Finance Working Paper, 1 January 2016.

Forum (2015). 'A forum on the judgment-based approach to entrepreneurship', *Journal of Institutional Economics*, 11(3) September: 585–681.

Foss, Kirsten and Nicolai J. Foss (2001). 'Assets, Attributes and Ownership', *International Journal of the Economics of Business*, 8(1) February: 19–37.

Foss, Kirsten and Nicolai J. Foss (2006). 'Entrepreneurship, Transaction Costs, and Resource Attributes', *International Journal of Strategic Change Management*, 1(1/2): 53–60.

Foss, Kirsten and Nicolai J. Foss (2015). 'Coasian and Modern Property Rights Economics', *Journal of Institutional Economics*, 11(2) June: 391–411.

Foss, Kirsten, Nicolai J. Foss and Peter G. Klein (2016). 'Managerial Authority in the Coasean Firm: An Entrepreneurial Perspective'. In Claude Ménard and Elodie Bertrand (eds.), *The Elgar Companion to Ronald H. Coase* (160–72), Cheltenham, UK: Edward Elgar Publishing Ltd.

Foss, Nicolai J. (1993). 'More on Knight and the Theory of the Firm', *Managerial and Decision Economics*, 14(3) May–June: 269–76.

Foss, Nicolai J. (1994). 'The Theory of the Firm: The Austrians as Precursors and Critics of Contemporary Theory', *Review of Austrian Economics*, 7: 31–64.

Foss, Nicolai J. (1994a). 'The Biological Analogy and the Theory of the Firm: Marshall and Monopolistic Competition', *Journal of Economic Issues*, 28(4) December: 1115–36.

Foss, Nicolai J. (1996a). 'Knowledge-Based Approaches to the Theory of the Firm: Some Critical Comments', *Organization Science*, 7(5) September–October: 470–6.

Foss, Nicolai J. (1996b). 'More Critical Comments on Knowledge-Based Theories of the Firm', *Organization Science*, 7(5) September–October: 519–23.

Foss, Nicolai J. (1996c). 'Harald B. Malmgren's Analysis of the Firm: Lessons for Modern Theorists?', *Review of Political Economy*, 8(4): 349–66.

Foss, Nicolai J. (1996d). 'The "Alternative" Theories of Knight and Coase, and the Modern Theory of the Firm', *Journal of the History of Economic Thought*, 18(1): Spring: 76–95.

Foss, Nicolai J. (1997). 'Austrian Insights and the Theory of the Firm', *Advances in Austrian Economics*, 4: 175–98.

Foss, Nicolai J. (2000). 'The Theory of the Firm: An Introduction to Themes and Contributions'. In Nicolai Foss (ed.), *The Theory of the Firm: Critical Perspectives on Business and Management* (xv–lxi), London: Routledge.

Foss, Nicolai J. and Peter G. Klein (2005). 'Entrepreneurship and the Economic Theory of the Firm: Any Gains from Trade?'. In Sharon A. Alvarez, Rajshree Agarwal and Olav Sorenson (eds.), *Handbook of Entrepreneurship Research: Disciplinary Perspectives* (55–80), New York: Springer.

Foss, Nicolai J. and Peter G. Klein (2006). 'The Emergence of the Modern Theory of the Firm', Center for Strategic Management and Globalization, Copenhagen Business School, SMG Working Paper 1/2006, January.

Foss, Nicolai J. and Peter G. Klein (2008). 'The Theory of the Firm and Its Critics: a Stock-taking and an Assessment'. In Eric Brousseau and Jean-Michel Glachant (eds.), *New Institutional Economics: A Guidebook* (425–42), Cambridge: Cambridge University Press.

Foss, Nicolai J. and Peter G. Klein (2009). 'Austrian Economics and the Transaction Cost Approach to the Firm', *Libertarian Papers*, 1(39), 1.

Foss, Nicolai J. and Peter G. Klein (2010). 'Austrian Economics and the Theory of the Firm'. In Peter G. Klein and Michael E. Sykuta (eds.), *The Elgar Companion to Transaction Cost Economics* (281–96), Cheltenham, UK: Edward Elgar Publishing Ltd.

Foss, Nicolai J and Nils Stieglitz (2010). 'Modern Resource-Based Theory(ies)', Center for Strategic Management and Globalization, Copenhagen Business School, SMG Working Paper 7/2010, September.

Foss, Nicolai J. and Peter G. Klein (2012). *Organizing Entrepreneurial Judgment: A New Approach to the Firm*, Cambridge: Cambridge University Press.

Foss, Nicolai J., Henrik Lando and Steen Thomsen (2000). 'The Theory of the Firm'. In Boudewijn Bouckaert and Gerrit De Geest (eds.), *Encyclopedia of Law and Economics* (vol. III, 631–58), Cheltenham, UK: Edward Elgar Publishing Ltd.

Foss, Nicolai J., Peter G. Klein and Per L. Bylund (2012). 'Entrepreneurship and the Economics of the Firm'. In Daniel Hjorth (ed.), *Handbook of Organisational Entrepreneurship* (49–63), Cheltenham, UK: Edward Elgar Publishing Ltd.

Foss, Nicolai J., Peter G. Klein and Stefan Linder (2015). 'Organizations and Markets'. In Peter Boettke and Christopher Coyne (eds.), *The Oxford Handbook of Austrian Economics* (272–95), Oxford: Oxford University Press.

Freeland, Robert F. (2016). 'The Employment Relation and Coase's Theory of the Firm'. In Claude Ménard and Elodie Bertrand (eds.), *The Elgar Companion to Ronald H. Coase* (148–59), Cheltenham, UK: Edward Elgar Publishing Ltd.

Friedman, Milton (1955). 'Leon Walras and His Economic System', *American Economic Review*, 45(5) December: 900–9.

Friedman, Milton (1962). *Capitalism and Freedom*, Chicago: University of Chicago Press.

Frisch, Ragnar (1965). *The Theory of Production*, Dordrecht, Netherlands: D. Reidel Publishing Company. (First Norwegian edition 1927).

Furubotn, Eirik G. and Rudolf Richter (2005). *Institutions and Economic Theory: The Contribution of the New Institutional Economics*, 2nd edn., Ann Arbor, MI: The University of Michigan Press.

Galbraith, John Kenneth (1963). *American Capitalism: The Concept of Countervailing Power*, New York: Penguin Books.

Galbraith, John Kenneth (1969). *The New Industrial State*, New York: Penguin Books.

Gale, Douglas (2000). *Strategic Foundations of General Equilibrium: Dynamic Matching and Bargaining Games* (Churchill Lectures in Economic Theory), Cambridge: Cambridge University Press.

Garicano, Luis (2000). 'Hierarchies and the Organization of Knowledge in Production', *Journal of Political Economy*, 108(5) October: 874–904.

Garrouste, Pierre (2004). 'The New Property Rights Theory of the Firm'. In E. Colombatto (ed.), *The Edward Elgar Companion to the Economics of Property Rights* (370–82), Cheltenham, UK: Edward Elgar Publishing Ltd.

Garrouste, Pierre and Stéphane Saussier (2008). 'The Theories of the Firm'. In Eric Brousseau and Jean-Michel Glachant (eds.), *New Institutional Economics: A Guidebook* (23–36), Cambridge: Cambridge University Press.

Gattai, Valeria (2006). 'From the Theory of the Firm to FDI and Internalisation: a Survey', *Giornale degli Economisti e Annali di Economia*, 65(2) November 2006: 225–62.

Gattai, Valeria and Piergiovanna Natale (forthcoming). 'A New Cinderella Story: Joint Ventures and the Property Rights Theory of the Firm', *Journal of Economic Surveys*.

Gelderblom, Oscar, Abe De Jong and Joost Jonker (2013). 'The Formative Years of the Modern Corporation: The Dutch East India Company VOC, 1602–1623', *Journal of Economic History*, 73(4) December: 1050–76.

Gibbons, Robert (2005). 'Four formal(izable) Theories of the Firm?', *Journal of Economic Behavior & Organization*, 58(2): 200–45.

Gibbons, Robert (2010). 'Transaction-Cost Economics: Past, Present, and Future?', *Scandinavian Journal of Economics*, 112(2): 263–88.

Gibbons, Robert (2013). 'Cyert and March (1963) at Fifty: A Perspective from Organizational Economics', Working Paper, April 7. Available from http://web.mit.edu/rgibbons/www/ [accessed 27 April 2016].

Gibbons, Robert and John Roberts (2013). *The Handbook of Organizational Economics*, Princeton, NJ: Princeton University Press.

Gökgür, Nilgün (2006). 'Turkish Privatization Proceeds Apace', *The PB Newsletter*, Issue 4 January: 31–46.

Gordon, R. A. (1948). 'Short–Period Price Determination in Theory and Practice', *American Economic Review*, 38(3) June: 265–88.

Gravelle, Hugh and Ray Rees (2004). *Microeconomics*, 3rd edn., Harlow: Pearson Education Limited.

Griffiths, Percival (1974). *A Licence to Trade: A History of the English Chartered Companies*, London: Ernest Benn Limited.

Grossman, Sanford J. and Oliver D. Hart (1986). 'The Costs and Benefits of Ownership: A Theory of Vertical and Lateral Integration', *Journal of Political Economy*, 94(4): 691–719.

Grossman, Sanford J. and Oliver D. Hart (1987). 'Vertical Integration and the Distribution of Property Rights'. In Assaf Razin and Efraim Sadka (eds.), *Economic Policy in Theory and Practice* (504–48), London: Macmillan Press.

Guelzo, Carl M. (1976). 'John R. Commons and the Theory of the Firm', *The American Economist*, 20(2) Fall: 40–6.

Guesnerie, Roger (1992). 'The Arrow-Debreu Paradigm Faced with Modern Theories of Contracting: a Discussion of Selected Issues Involving Information and Time'. In Lars Werin and Hans Wijkander (eds.), *Contract Economics* (12–41), Oxford: Basil Blackwell Ltd.

Gupta, Sanjeev, Christian Shiller, Henry Ma and Erwin Tiongson (2001). 'Privatization, Labor and Social Safety Nets', *Journal of Economic Surveys*, 15(5) December: 647–69.

Hachette, Dominique and Rolf Luders (1993). *Privatization in Chile: An Economic Appraisal*, San Francisco: ICS Press.

Hagendorf, Klaus (2009). 'Labour Values and the Theory of the Firm, Part I: The Competitive Firm', October 15. Available from SSRN: http://ssrn.com/abstract=1489383 [accessed 27 April 2016].

Haley, Bernard F. (1948). 'Value and Distribution'. In Howard S. Ellis (ed.), *A Survey of Contemporary Economics* (vol. I, 1–48), Homewood, IL: Richard D. Irwin.

Hall, R. L. and C. J. Hitch (1939). 'Price Theory and Business Behaviour', *Oxford Economic Papers*, 1939(2) May: 12–45.

Halonen-Akatwijuka, Maiji and Oliver D. Hart (2013). 'More is Less: Why Parties May Deliberately Writes Incomplete Contracts', *National Bureau of Economic Research*, NBER Working Papers No. 19001, April. Available from NBER: www.nber.org/papers/w19001 [accessed 27 April 2016].

Hanappi, Gerhard (2012). 'Schumpeter'. In Michael Dietrich and Jackie Kraff (eds.), *Handbook on the Economics and Theory of the Firm* (62–9), Cheltenham, UK: Edward Elgar Publishing Ltd.

Hansmann, Henry (1996). *The Ownership of Enterprise*, Cambridge, MA: Harvard University Press.

Hansmann, Henry (2013) 'Ownership and Organizational Form'. In Robert Gibbons and John Roberts (eds.), *The Handbook of Organizational Economics* (891–917), Princeton, NJ: Princeton University Press.

Hansmann, Henry and Reinier Kraakman (2000a). 'The Essential Role of Organizational Law', *Yale Law Journal*, 110(3) December: 387–440.

Hansmann, Henry and Reinier Kraakman (2000b). 'Organizational Law as Asset Partitioning', *European Economic Review*, 44: 807–17.

Hansmann, Henry, Reinier Kraakman and Richard Squire (2005). 'The New Business Entities in Evolutionary Perspective', *University of Illinois Law Review*, 2005(1): 5–14.

Hansmann, Henry, Reinier Kraakman and Richard Squire (2006). 'Law and the Rise of the Firm', *Harvard Law Review*, 119(5) March: 1333–403.

Harper, Robert (1886). *The Nationalisation of British Industry; or, Compound Profits, Interest and Rent*, London: E. W. Allen.

Hart, Neil (2003). 'Marshall's Dilemma: Equilibrium versus Evolution', *Journal of Economic Issues*, 37(4) December: 1139–60.

Hart, Oliver D. (1985). 'Imperfect Competition in General Equilibrium: An Overview of Recent Work'. In Kenneth J. Arrow and Seppo Honkapohja (eds.), *Frontiers of Economics* (100–49), Oxford: Basil Blackwell.

Hart, Oliver D. (1989). 'An Economist's Perspective on the Theory of the Firm', *Columbia Law Review*, 89(7) November: 1757–74.

Hart, Oliver D. (1995). *Firms, Contracts, and Financial Structure*, Oxford: Oxford University Press.

Hart, Oliver D. (2003). 'Incomplete Contracts and Public Ownership: Remarks, and an Application to Public-Private Partnerships', *Economic Journal*, 113 No. 486 Conference Papers March: C69–C76.

Hart, Oliver D. (2008). 'Economica Coase Lecture: Reference Points and the Theory of the Firm', *Economica*, 75(299) August: 404–11.

Hart, Oliver D. (2009). 'Hold-up, Asset Ownership, and Reference Points', *Quarterly Journal of Economics*, 124(1) February: 267–300.

Hart, Oliver D. (2011). 'Thinking about the Firm: A Review of Daniel Spulber's The Theory of the Firm', *Journal of Economic Literature*, 49(1) March: 101–13.

Hart, Oliver D. (2013) 'Noncontractible Investments and Reference Points', *Games*, 4(3) September: 437–456.

Hart, Oliver D. and John Moore (1990). 'Property Rights and the Nature of the Firm', *Journal of Political Economy*, 98(6): 1119–58.

Hart, Oliver D. and John Moore (2007). 'Incomplete Contracts and Ownership: Some New Thoughts, *American Economic Review*, 97(2) May: 182–6.

Hart, Oliver D. and John Moore (2008). 'Contracts as Reference Points' *Quarterly Journal of Economics*, 123(1) February: 1–48.

Hart, Oliver D. and Bengt Holmström (2010). 'A Theory of Firm Scope', *Quarterly Journal of Economics*, 125(2) May: 483–513.

Hart, Oliver D., Andrei Shleifer and Robert W. Vishny (1997). 'The Proper Scope of Government: Theory and an Application to Prisons', *Quarterly Journal of Economics*, 112(4) November: 1127–61.

Hartley, James E. (1996). 'The Origins of the Representative Agent', *Journal of Economic Perspectives*, 10(2) Spring: 169–77.

Haskel, Jonathan and Stefan Szymanski (1992). 'A Bargaining Theory of Privatisation', *Annals of Public and Cooperative Economics*, 63(2): 207–27.

Havrylyshyn, Oleh and Donal MacGettigan (1999). 'Privatization in Transition Countries: A Sampling of the Literature', IMF Working Paper WP/99/6, International Monetary Fund, Washington DC, January.

Hawkins, C. J. (1973). *Theory of the Firm*, London: The Macmillan Press.

Hayek, F. von (1944). *The Road to Serfdom*, London: Routledge & Kegan Paul.

Heckscher, Eli F. (1918). 'Staten och det enskilda initiativet efter kriget', Föredrag vid Sveriges Industriförbunds årsmöte den 23 April. ('The State and Private Initiative after the War', Address to the annual meeting of the Federation of Swedish Industries, 23 April).

Heckscher, Eli F. (1934). *Mercantilism*, 2 vols., London: George Allen & Unwin.

Heflebower, Richard B. (1955). 'Full Costs, Cost Changes, and Prices'. In Universities-National Bureau, *Business Concentration and Price Policy* (359–92), Princeton, NJ: Princeton University Press.

Heilbroner, Robert L. (1999). *The Worldly Philosophers: The Lives, Times, and Ideas of the Great Economic Thinkers*, 7th edn., New York: Simon & Schuster.

Heldman, Herbert (1951). 'The Economic Problems of Denationalization', *Political Science Quarterly*, 66(4) December: 576–97.

Hermalin, Benjamin E. (2013). 'Corporate Governance: A Critical Assessment'. In Robert Gibbons and John Roberts (eds.), *The Handbook of Organizational Economics* (32–63), Princeton, NJ: Princeton University Press.

Hicks, John R. (1946). *Value and Capital: An Inquiry into Some Fundamental Principles of Economic Theory*, 2nd edn., Oxford: Clarendon Press.

Hickson, Charles R. and John D. Turner (2006). 'Corporation or Limited Liability Company'. In John J. McCusker (ed.), *History of World Trade since 1450* (vol. 1 A-K, 163–6), New York: Macmillan Reference USA.

Higgs, Henry (1897). *The Physiocrats: Six Lectures on the French Economistes of the 18th Century*, London: Macmillan and Co., Limited.

Hill, Christopher (1961). *The Century of Revolution, 1602–1715*, Edinburgh: Edinburgh University Press.

Hodge, Graeme A. (2003). 'Privatization: The Australia Experience'. In David Parker and David Saal (eds.), *International Handbook on Privatization* (161–86), Cheltenham, UK: Edward Elgar Publishing.

Hodgson, Geoffrey M. (2012). 'Veblen, Commons and the Theory of the Firm'. In Michael Dietrich and Jackie Kraff (eds.), *Handbook on the Economics and Theory of the Firm* (55–61), Cheltenham, UK: Edward Elgar Publishing Ltd.

Holmström, Bengt (1982). 'Moral Hazard in Teams', *Bell Journal of Economics*, 13(2) Autumn: 324–40.

Holmstrom, Bengt (1999). 'The Firm as a Subeconomy', *Journal of Law, Economics, and Organization*, 15(1) April: 74–102.
Holmström, Bengt and Jean Tirole (1989). 'The Theory of the Firm'. In Richard Schmalensee and Robert D. Willig (eds.), *Handbook of Industrial Organization* (vol. I, 61–133), Amsterdam: North-Holland.
Holmström, Bengt and Paul Milgrom (1991). 'Multitask Principal-Agent Analyses: Incentive Contracts, Asset Ownership, and Job Design', *Journal of Law, Economics, & Organization*, 7(Special Issue): 24–52.
Holmström, Bengt and Paul Milgrom (1994). 'The Firm as an Incentive System', *American Economic Review*, 84(4) September: 972–91.
Holmström, Bengt and John Roberts (1998). 'Boundaries of the Firm Revisited', *Journal of Economic Perspectives*, 12(4) Fall: 73–94.
Hoppe, Eva I. and Patrick W. Schmitz (2010). 'Public versus Private Ownership: Quantity Contracts and the Allocation of Investment Tasks', *Journal of Public Economics*, 94(3–4) April: 258–68.
Hoppe, Eva I. and Patrick W. Schmitz (2011). 'Can Contracts Solve the Hold-up Problem? Experimental Evidence', *Games and Economic Behavior*, 73(1) September: 186–99.
Horn, Murray J. (1995). *The Political Economy of Public Administration: Institutional Choice in the Public Sector*, Cambridge: Cambridge University Press.
Howell, David (1970). *A New Style of Government: A Conservative View of the Tasks of Administrative, Financial and Parliamentary Reform Facing an Incoming Government*, London: Conservative Political Centre.
Hubbard, Thomas N. (2008). 'Viewpoint: Empirical Research on Firms' Boundaries', *Canadian Journal of Economics*, 41(2) May: 341–59.
Humphrey, Thomas M. (1997). 'Algebraic Production Functions and Their Uses Before Cobb-Douglas', *Federal Reserve Bank of Richmond Economic Quarterly*, 83(1) Winter: 51–83.
Hunt, Edwin S. and James M. Murray (1999). *A History of Business in Medieval Europe 1200–1550*, Cambridge: Cambridge University Press.
Hutchison, T. W. (1953). *A Review of Economic Doctrines 1870–1929*, Oxford: Oxford University Press.
Ioannides, Stavros (1999). 'Towards an Austrian Perspective on the Firm', *Review of Austrian Economics*, 11(1–2): 77–97.
Jackson, Peter M. and Catherine M. Price (1994). 'Privatisation and Regulation: A Review of the Issues'. In Peter M. Jackson and Catherine M. Price (eds.), *Privatisation and Regulation: A Review of the Issues* (1–34), London: Longman.
Jacobides, M. and S. Winter (2005). The Co-evolution of Capabilities and Transaction Costs: Explaining the Institutional Structure of Production. *Strategic Management Journal*, 26(5) May: 395–413.
Jacobsen, Lowell (2008). 'On Robinson, Coase, and "The Nature of the Firm"', *Journal of the History of Economic Thought*, 30(1) March: 65–80.
Jacobsen, Lowell (2013). 'On Robinson, Penrose, and the Resource-based View', *European Journal History of Economic Thought*, 20(1): 125–47.
Jacobsen, Lowell (2015a). 'On Robinson, Robertson, and the Industrial Organization View', *History of Political Economy*, 47(1): 41–89.
Jacobsen, Lowell (2015b). 'Coase and the Theory of the Firm: Guest Editor's Introduction', *Managerial and Decision Economics*, 36(1): 2–5.
Jankovic, Ivan (2010). 'Firm as a Nexus of Markets', *Journal des Economistes et des Etudes Humaines*, 16(1): October. Available from: www.degruyter.com/view/j/jeeh.

2010.16.1/jeeh.2010.16.1.1241/jeeh.2010.16.1.1241.xml?format=INT [accessed 27 April 2016].

Jensen, Michael C. and William H. Meckling (1976). 'Theory of the Firm: Managerial Behaviour, Agency Costs, and Ownership Structure', *Journal of Financial Economics*, 3(4) October: 305–60.

Jewkes, John (1948). *Ordeal by Planning*, London: Macmillan & Co. Ltd.

Jewkes, John (1953). 'The Nationalisation of Industry', *University of Chicago Law Review*, 20(4) Summer: 615–45.

Jewkes, John (1965). *Public and Private Enterprise: The Lindsay Memorial Lectures given at the University of Keele 1964*, London: Routledge & Kegan Paul.

Johnson, William E. (1891). 'Exchange and Distribution', *Cambridge Economic Club*. Reprinted, with brief commentary, in William J. Baumol and Stephen N. Goldfeld (eds.), *Precursors in Mathematical Economics*: An Anthology (316–20), London: The London School of Economics and Political Science, 1968 and in A. C. Darnell (ed.), *Early Mathematical Economics* (vol. 2, 67–71) London: Pickering & Chatto, 1991.

Jones, Eliot (1921). *The Trust Problem in the United States*, New York: Macmillan Co.

Jones, Ronald W. (2011). 'General Equilibrium Theory and Competitive Trade Models', paper given at the European Trade Study Group (ETSG), Thirteenth Annual Conference, Copenhagen Business School, University of Copenhagen, 8–10 September.

Jones, S. R. H. and Simon P. Ville (1996a). 'Efficient Transactors or Rent-Seeking Monopolists? The Rationale for Early Chartered Trading Companies', *Journal of Economic History*, 56(4) December: 898–915.

Jones, S. R. H. and Simon P. Ville (1996b). 'Theory and Evidence: Understanding Chartered Trading Companies', *Journal of Economic History*, 56(4) December: 925–6.

Joskow, Paul L. (1988). 'Asset Specificity and the Structure of Vertical Relationships: Empirical Evidence', *Journal of Law, Economics, & Organization*, 4(1) Spring: 95–117.

Jursa, Michael (2010). 'Business Companies in Babylonia in the First Millennium BC: Structure, Economic Strategies, Social Setting'. In Myriam Wissa (ed.), *The Knowledge Economy and Technological Capabilities Egypt, the Near East and the Mediterranean 2nd Millennium B.C.—1st Millennium A.D.* (53–68), Sabadell: Editorial AUSA.

Jursa, Michael (2014). 'Babylonia in the First Millennium BC—Economic Growth in Times of Empire'. In Larry Neal and Jeffrey G. Williamson (eds.), *The Cambridge History of Capitalism* (vol. 1, 24–42), Cambridge: Cambridge University Press.

Kállay, Balázs (2012). 'Contract Theory of the Firm', *Economics and Sociology*, 5(1): 39–50.

Kay, J. A. and D. J. Thompson (1986). 'Privatisation: A Policy in Search of a Rationale', *Economic Journal*, 96 No. 381 March: 18–32.

Kennedy, Gavin (2005). *Adam Smith's Lost Legacy*, Houndmills, Basingstoke, Hampshire: Palgrave Macmillan.

Kennedy, Gavin (2010). *Adam Smith: A Moral Philosopher and His Political Economy*, 2nd edn., Houndmills, Basingstoke, Hampshire: Palgrave Macmillan.

Keynes, John Maynard (1926). *The End of Laissez-Faire*, London: Hogarth Press.

Khachatrian, Arman (2003). 'Theory of the Firm: A Critical Survey', Siena Memos and Papers in Law and Economics (SIMPLE) 4/03, March.

Khanna, Vikramaditya S. (2005). 'The Economic History of Organizational Entities in Ancient India', University of Michigan Law School Program in Law & Economics Working Paper No. 14 (updated version February 2006).

Kihlstrom, Richard E. and Jean-Jacques Laffont (1979). 'A General Equilibrium Entrepreneurial Theory of Firm Formation Based on Risk Aversion', *Journal of Political Economy*, 87(4) August: 719–48.

Kikeri, Sunita and John Nellis (2004). 'An Assessment of Privatization', *World Bank Research Observer*, 19(1) Spring: 87–118.

Kikeri, Sunita, John Nellis and Mary Shirley (1992). *Privatization: The Lessons of Experience*, Washington, DC: The World Bank.

Kikuchi, Tomoo, Kazuo Nishimura and John Stachurski (2012). 'Coase meets Tarski: New Insights from Coase's Theory of the Firm', Working Paper, November 1.

King, Stephen and Rohan Pitchford (1998). 'Privatisation in Australia: Understanding the Incentives in Public and Private Firms', *Australian Economic Review*, 31(4) December: 313–28.

Klein, Benjamin, Robert G. Crawford and Armen A. Alchian (1978). 'Vertical Integration, Appropriable Rents, and the Competitive Contracting Process', *Journal of Law and Economics*, 21(2) October: 297–326.

Klein, Peter G. (1996). 'Economic Calculation and the Limits of Organization', *Review of Austrian Economics*, 9(2): 3–28.

Klein, Peter G. (2005). 'The Make-or-Buy Decision: Lessons from Empirical Studies'. In Claude Menard and Mary M. Shirley (eds.), *Handbook of New Institutional Economics* (435–64), Dordrecht and New York: Springer.

Klein, Peter G. (2010). *The Capitalist and The Entrepreneur: Essays on Organizations and Markets*, Auburn: Ludwig von Mises Institute.

Knight, Frank H. (1921a). 'Cost of Production and Price over Long and Short Periods', *Journal of Political Economy*, 29 April: 304–35.

Knight, Frank H. (1921b). *Risk, Uncertainty and Profit*, Boston: Houghton Mifflin Company.

Kogut, B. and U. Zander (1992). 'Knowledge of the Firm, Combinative Capabilities, and the Replication of Technology', *Organization Science*, 3(3) August: 383–97.

Kogut, B. and U. Zander (1996). 'What Firms Do? Coordination, Identity, and Learning', *Organization Science*, 7(5) September–October: 502–18.

Kokh, Alfred (1998). *The Selling of the Soviet Empire: Politics & Economics of Russia's Privatization—Revelations of the Principal Insider*, New York: S.P.I. Books.

Köthenbürger, Marko, Hans-Werner Sin and J. Whalley (eds.) (2006). *Privatization Experiences in the European Union*, Cambridge, MA: MIT Press.

Koutsoyiannis, A. (1979). *Modern Microeconomics*, 2nd edn., London: The Macmillan Press Ltd.

Kuran, Timur (2005). 'The Absence of the Corporation in Islamic Law: Origins and Persistence', *American Journal of Comparative Law*, 53(4) Fall: 785–834.

Laffont, Jean-Jacques and Jean Tirole (1991). 'Privatization and Incentives', *Journal of Law, Economics, & Organization*, 7(Special Issue) [Papers from the Conference on the New Science of Organization, January 1991]: 84–105.

Lafontaine, Francine and Margaret Slade (2007). 'Vertical Integration and Firm Boundaries: The Evidence', *Journal of Economic Literature*, 45(3) September: 629–85.

Lal, Deepak (2006). 'The Contemporary Relevance of Heckscher's *Mercantilism*'. In Ronald Findlay, Rolf G. H. Henriksson, Håkan Lindgren and Mats Lundahl (eds.), *Eli Heckscher, International Trade, and Economic History* (305–19), Cambridge, MA: MIT Press.

Langlois, Richard N. (1981). 'Why are there Firms?', C. V. Starr Center for Applied Economics, New York University, D.P. 81–30, March.

Langlois, Richard N. (2013). 'The Austrian Theory of the Firm: Retrospect and Prospect', *Review of Austrian Economics*, 26(3) September: 247–58.

Langlois, Richard N. and Metin M. Cosgel (1993). 'Frank Knight on Risk, Uncertainty, and the Firm: A New Interpretation', *Economic Inquiry*, 31(3) July: 435–65.

La Porta, Rafael and Florencio López-de-Silanes (1999). 'The Benefits of Privatization: Evidence From Mexico', *Quarterly Journal of Economics*, 114(4) November: 1193–242.

Larsen, Mogens Trolle (2015). *Ancient Kanesh: A Merchant Colony in Bronze Age Anatolia*, Cambridge: Cambridge University Press.

Lawson, Colin (1994). 'The Theory of State-Owned Enterprises in Market Economics', *Journal of Economics Surveys*, 8(3) September: 283–309.

Lawson, Nigel (1993). *The View from No. 11*, New York: Doubleday.

Lee, F. S. (1984). 'The Marginalist Controversy and the Demise of Full-Cost Pricing', *Journal of Economic Issues*, 18(4) December: 1107–32.

Leibenstein, Harvey (1966). 'Allocative Efficiency vs. X-Efficiency', *American Economic Review*, 56(3) June: 392–415.

Lester, Richard A. (1946). 'Shortcomings of Marginal Analysis for Wage-Employment Problems', *American Economic Review*, 36(1) March: 63–82.

Le Texier, Thibault (2013). 'Veblen, Commons, and the Modern Corporation: Why Management Does Not Fit Economics', *Homo Oeconomicus*, 30(1) March: 79–98.

Lewin, Peter and Steven E. Phelan (2000). 'An Austrian Theory of the Firm', *Review of Austrian Economics*, 13(1): 59–79.

Lewis, W. Arthur (1949). *The Principles of Economic Planning*, London: George Allen & Unwin.

Liebhafsky, H. H. (1955). 'A Curious Case of Neglect: Marshall's Industry and Trade', *Canadian Journal of Economics and Political Science*, 21(3) August: 339–53.

Loasby, Brian J. (2015). 'Ronald Coase's Theory of the Firm and the Scope of Economics', *Journal of Institutional Economics*, 11(2) (Ronald H. Coase Memorial Issue) June: 245–64.

Lockett, Andy, Rory P. O'Shea and Mike Wright (2008). 'The Development of the Resource-based View: Reflections from Birger Wernerfelt', *Organization Studies*, 29(8–9) August: 1125–41.

López-de-Silanes, Florencio, Andrei Shleifer and Robert W Vishny (1997). 'Privatization in the United States'. *RAND Journal of Economics*, 28(3) Autumn: 447–71.

Lowry, S. Todd (1987). *The Archaeology of Economic Ideas: The Classical Greek Tradition*, Durham, NC: Duke University Press.

Luders, Rolf J. (1991). 'Massive Divestiture and Privatization: Lessons from Chile'. *Contemporary Economic Policy*, 9(4) October: 1–19.

McAfee, R Preston and John McMillan (1991). 'Optimal Contracts for Teams', *International Economic Review*, 32(3) August: 561–77.

McDonald, Hamish (1991). 'Key to the Door: New Delhi Starts to Dismantle Apparatus of Economic Nationalism'. *Far Eastern Economic Review*, 153(32) August 8: 48.

McDonald, John and G. D. Snooks (1986). *Domesday Economy: A New Approach to Anglo-Norman History*, Oxford: Oxford University Press.

Macgregor, D. H. (1906). *Industrial Combination*, Kitchener, Ontario: Baroche Books, 2001.

Macgregor, D. H. (1949). *Economic Thought and Policy*, Oxford: Oxford University Press.

Machlup, Fritz (1946). 'Marginal Analysis and Empirical Research', *American Economic Review*, 36(4) September: 519–54.

Machlup, Fritz (1967). 'Theories of the Firm: Marginalist, Behavioral, Managerial', *American Economic Review*, 57(1) March: 1–33.

McManus, John C. (1975). 'The Costs of Alternative Economic Organizations', *Canadian Journal of Economics*, 8(3) August: 334–50.

McMillan, John (2002). *Reinventing the Bazaar: A Natural history of Markets*, New York: W.W. Norton and Company.

McNulty, Paul J. (1984). 'On the Nature and Theory of Economic Organization: the Role of the Firm Reconsidered', *History of Political Economy*, 16(2) Summer: 233–53.

Maekawa, Kazuya (1980). 'Female Weavers and Their Children in Lagash: Pre-Sargonic and Ur III', *Acta Sumerologica*, 21: 81–125.

Magnusson, Lars G. (1994). *Mercantilism: The Shaping of Economic Language*, London: Routledge.

Magnusson, Lars G. (2003). 'Mercantilism'. In Warren J. Samuels, Jeff E. Biddle and John B. Davis (eds.), *A Companion to the History of Economic Thought* (46–60), Oxford: Blackwell Publishing Ltd.

Magnusson, Lars G. (2015). *The Political Economy of Mercantilism*, London: Routledge.

Mahoney, Joseph T. (2005). *Economic Foundations of Strategy*, London: Sage Publication.

Malmgren, H. B. (1961). 'Information, Expectations and the Theory of the Firm', *Quarterly Journal of Economics*, 75(3) August: 399–421.

Marchionatti, Roberto (2003). 'On the Methodological Foundations of Modern Microeconomics: Frank Knight and the "Cost Controversy" in the 1920s', *History of Political Economy*, 35(1): 49–75.

Margolis, Julius (1958). 'The Analysis of the Firm: Rationalism, Conventionalism, and Behaviorism', *Journal of Business*, 31(3) July: 187–99.

Margolis, Julius (1959). 'Traditional and Revisionist Theories of the Firm: A Comment', *Journal of Business*, 32(2) April: 178–82.

Markusen, James R. (1995). 'The Boundaries of Multinational Enterprises and the Theory of International Trade', *Journal of Economic Perspectives*, 9(2) Spring: 169–89.

Markusen, James R. and Keith E. Maskus (2001). 'General-Equilibrium Approaches to the Multinational Firm: A Review of Theory and Evidence', *National Bureau of Economic Research*, NBER Working Papers No. 8334, June. Available from NBER: www.nber.org/papers/w8334 [accessed 27 April 2016].

Marris, Robin L. (1964). *The Economic Theory of Managerial Capitalism*, London: Macmillan.

Marschak, Jacob and Roy Radner (1972). *Economic Theory of Teams*, New Haven, CT: Yale University Press.

Marshall, Alfred (1907). 'The Social Possibilities of Economic Chivalry', *Economic Journal*, 17 No. 65 March: 7–29.

Marshall, Alfred (1920a). *Industry and Trade: A Study of Industrial Technique and Business Organization; and of Their Influences on the Conditions of Various Classes and Nations*, 2 vols., Honolulu, HI: University Press of the Pacific, 2003.

Marshall, Alfred (1920b). *Principles of Economics: An Introductory Volume*, 8th edn., London: Macmillan and Co., Limited. (First published: 1890).

Martimort, David (2006). 'An Agency Perspective on the Costs and Benefits of Privatization', *Journal of Regulatory Economics*, 30(1) July: 5–44.

Mas-Colell, A., M. D. Whinton and J. R. Green (1995). *Microeconomic Theory*, New York: Oxford University Press.

Maskin, Eric (2002). 'On Indescribable Contingencies and Incomplete Contracts', *European Economic Review*, 46(4–5) May: 725–33.

Maskin, Eric and Jean Tirole (1999). 'Unforeseen Contingencies and Incomplete Contracts', *Review of Economic Studies*, 66(1) January: 83–114.

Maude, Francis (1991). House of Commons, Friday 7 June, Hansard Volume 192, Column 507.

Mead, Margaret and Glenn Withers (eds.) (2002). *Privatisation: A review of the Australian experience* (CEDA Growth Report 50), Melbourne: Committee for Economic Development of Australia.

Meade, James Edward (1948). *Planning and the Price Mechanism: The Liberal Socialist Solution*, London: George Allen & Unwin.

Means, G. C. (1958). 'Looking Around', *Harvard Business Review*, 36(3) May–June: 27–180.

Megginson, William L. (2005). *The Financial Economics of Privatization*, New York: Oxford University Press.

Megginson, William L. and Jeffry M. Netter (2001). 'From State to Market: A Survey of Empirical Studies on Privatization', *Journal of Economic Literature*, 39(2) June: 321–89.

Menard, Claude (2005). 'A New Institutional Approach to Organization'. In Claude Menard and Mary Shirley (eds.), *Handbook of New Institutional Economics* (281–318), Dordrecht and New York: Springer.

Michel, Cécile (2008). 'The Old Assyrian Trade in the light of Recent Kültepe Archives', *Journal of the Canadian Society for Mesopotamian Studies*, 3: 71–82.

Micklethwait, John and Adrian Wooldridge (2003). *The Company: A Short History of a Revolutionary Idea*, New York: The Modern Library.

Milgrom, Paul and John Roberts (1988). 'Economic Theories of the Firm: Past, Present, and Future', *Canadian Journal of Economics*, 21(3) August: 444–58.

Milgrom, Paul and Chris Shannon (1994). 'Monotone Comparative Statics', *Econometrica*, 62(1) January: 157–80.

Mill, John Stuart (1909). *Principles of Political Economy with Some of Their Applications to Social Philosophy*, Seventh Edition, William J. Ashley (ed.), London: Longmans, Green and Co. First published: 1848.

Millward, Robert (1997). 'The 1940s Nationalizations in Britain: Means to an End or the Means of Production?', *Economic History Review*, 50(2) May: 209–234.

Mokyr, Joel (2002). *The Gifts of Athena: Historical Origins of the Knowledge Economy*, Princeton, NJ: Princeton University Press.

Mokyr, Joel (2009). *The Enlightened Economy: An Economic History of Britain 1700–1850*, New Haven, CT: Yale University Press.

Mongin, Philippe (1992). 'The Full-Cost Controversy of the 1940s and 1950s: A Methodological Assessment', *History of Political Economy*, 24(2) Summer: 311–56.

Mongin, Philippe (1998). 'The Marginalist Controversy'. In John B. Davis, D. Wade Hands and Uskali Mäki (eds.), *Handbook of Economic Methodology* (277–81), Cheltenham, UK: Edward Elgar Publishing Ltd.

Moore, John H. (1992). 'The Firm as a Collection of Assets', *European Economic Review*, 36(2–3) April: 493–507.

Morck, Randall and Masao Nakamura (2007). 'Business Groups and the Big Push: Meiji Japan's Mass Privatization and Subsequent Growth', *Enterprise & Society*, 8(3) September: 543–601.

Moss, Scott (1984a). 'The History of the Theory of the Firm from Marshall to Robinson and Chamberlin: the Source of Positivism in Economics', *Economica*, n.s. 51(203) August: 307–18.

Moss, Scott (1984b). 'O'Brien's "The Evolution of the Theory of the Firm": a Discussion'. In Frank H. Stephen (ed.), *Firms, Organization and Labour: Approaches to the Economics of Work Organization* (63–8), London: Macmillan Press.

Müller, Alberto (2009). 'Teoria de la firma, teoria del mercado y teoria economica: Una reflexion', *Desarrollo Economico*, 49 issue 194 July-September: 335–50.

Nellis, John (1999). 'Time to Rethink Privatization in Transition Economies?', Discussion Paper Number 38, World Bank, International Finance Corporation, Washington, DC.

Nellis, John (2003a). 'Privatization in Africa: What has happened? What is to be done?', Working Paper Number 25, Center for Global Development, Washington, DC, February.

Nellis, John (2003b). 'Privatization in Latin America', Working Paper 31, Center for Global Development, Washington, DC, August.

Nelson, Richard R. and Sidney G. Winter (1982). *An Evolutionary Theory of Economic Change*, Cambridge, MA: The Belknap Press.

Newbery, David M. G. (2006). 'Privatising Network Industries'. In Marko Köthenbürger, Hans-Werner Sin and John Whalley (eds.), *Privatization Experiences in the European Union* (3–49), Cambridge, MA: MIT Press.

O'Brien, Denis P. (1984). 'The Evolution of the Theory of the Firm'. In Frank H. Stephen (ed.), *Firms, Organization and Labour: Approaches to the Economics of Work Organization* (25–62), London: Macmillan Press.

O'Brien, Denis P. (2003). 'Classical Economics'. In Warren J. Samuels, Jeff E. Biddle and John B. Davis (eds.), *A Companion to the History of Economic Thought* (112–29), Oxford: Blackwell Publishing Ltd.

O'Brien, Denis P. (2004). *The Classical Economists Revisited*, Princeton, NJ: Princeton University Press.

Ofek, Haim (2001). *Second Nature: Economic Origins of Human Evolution*, Cambridge: Cambridge University Press.

Ogilvie, Sheilagh (2011). *Institutions and European Trade: Merchant Guilds, 1000–1800*, Cambridge: Cambridge University Press.

Ogus, Anthony I. (1994). *Regulation: Legal Form and Economic Theory*, Oxford: Clarendon Press.

Olson, Mancur (1974). 'On the Priority of Public Problems'. In R. Marris (ed.), *The Corporate Society* (294–336), London: Macmillan.

Otteson, J. R. (2002). *Adam Smith's Market Place of Life*, Cambridge: Cambridge University Press.

Otteson, J. R. (2011). *Adam Smith* (Major Conservative and Libertarian Thinkers vol. 16), John Meadowcroft (series ed.), New York: Continuum.

Otteson, J. R. (2014). *The End of Socialism*, Cambridge: Cambridge University Press.

Papandreou, Andreas G. (1952). 'Some Basic Problems in the Theory of the Firm'. In Bernard F. Haley (ed.), *A Survey of Contemporary Economics* (vol. II, 183–222), Homewood, IL: Richard D. Irwin, Inc.

Parker, David (1999). 'Privatization in the European Union: A Critical Assessment of its Development, Rational and Consequences', *Economic and Industrial Democracy*, 20(1): 9–28.

Parker, David (2004). 'Editorial: Lessons From Privatisation', *Economic Affairs*, 24(3) September: 2–8.

Parker, David and Colin Kirkpatrick (2003). 'Privatisation in Developing Countries: A Review of The Evidence and the Policy Lessons', Centre on Regulation and Competition, University of Manchester, Working Paper Series Paper No. 55 July, Manchester.

Peaucelle, Jean-Louis (2006). 'Adam Smith's Use of Multiple References for His Pin Making Example', *European Journal of the History of Economic Thought*, 13(4) December: 489–512.

Peaucelle, Jean-Louis and Cameron Guthrie (2011). 'How Adam Smith Found Inspiration in French Texts on Pin Making in the Eighteenth Century', *History of Economic Ideas*, 19(3): 41–67.

Penrose, E. T. (1959). *The Theory of the Growth of the Firm*, New York: Wiley.

Pigou, A. C. (1922). 'Empty Economic Boxes: A Reply', *Economic Journal*, 32(128) December: 458–65.

Pigou, A. C. (1928). 'An Analysis of Supply', *Economic Journal*, 38(150) June: 238–57.

Pigou, A. C. (1937). *Socialism versus Capitalism*, London: The Macmillan Press.

Pirie, Madsen (1988). *Privatization: Theory, Practice and Choice*, Aldershot, UK: Wildwood House.

Pollard, Sidney (1968). *The Genesis of Modern Management*, London: Penguin.

Pollitt, Michael G. (1999). 'A Survey of the Liberalisation of Public Enterprises in the UK since 1979', Department of Applied Economics, University of Cambridge, Working Papers Amalgamated Series: 9901 January, Cambridge.

Puu, T. (1970). 'Ferguson, C. E.: "The Neoclassical Theory of Production and Distribution." Some Comments on Part I', *Swedish Journal of Economics*, 72(3) September: 230–40.

Quéré, Michel (2006). 'The Representative Firm'. In Tiziano Raffaelli, Giacomo Becattini and Marco Dardi (eds.), *The Elgar Companion to Alfred Marshall* (412–7), Cheltenham, UK: Edward Elgar.

Rabin, Matthew (1993). 'Information and the Control of Productive Assets', *Journal of Law, Economics and Organization*, 9(1) Spring: 51–76.

Radner, Roy (1992). 'Hierarchy: The Economics of Managing', *Journal of Economic Literature*, 30(3) September: 1382–1415.

Radygin, Alexander (2003). 'Privatization, Ownership Redistribution, and Formation of the Institutional Basis for Economic Reforms'. In Yegor Gaidar (ed.), *The Economics of Transition* (395–459), Cambridge, MA: MIT Press.

Rajan, Raghuram G. and Luigi Zingales (1998). 'Power in a Theory of the Firm', *Quarterly Journal of Economics*, 113(2) May: 387–432.

Rajan, Raghuram G. and Luigi Zingales (2001a). 'The Firm as a Dedicated Hierarchy: A Theory of the Origins and Growth of Firms', *Quarterly Journal of Economics*, 116(3) August: 805–51.

Rajan, Raghuram G. and Luigi Zingales (2001b). 'The Influence of the Financial Revolution on the Nature of Firms', *American Economic Review*, 91(2) May: 206–12.

Rees, Ray. (1974). 'A Reconsideration of the Expense Preference Theory of the Firm', *Economica*, 41(163) August: 295–307.

Rees, Ray (1994). 'Economic Aspects of Privatization in Britain'. In Vincent Wright (ed.), *Privatization in Western Europe: Pressures, Problems and Paradoxes* (44–56), London: Pinter Publishers.

Richardson, G. B. (1972). 'The Organization of Industry', *Economic Journal*, 82(327) September: 883–96.

Ricketts, Martin (2002). *The Economics of Business Enterprise: An Introduction to Economic Organisation and the Theory of the Firm*, 3rd edn., Cheltenham, UK: Edward Elgar.

Ricketts, Martin (2015). 'Ownership, Governance and the Coasian Firm'. In Cento Veljanovski (ed.), *Forever Contemporary: The Economics of Ronald Coase* (46–69), London: Institute of Economic Affairs.

Ridley, Matt (2010). *The Rational Optimist: How Prosperity Evolves*, New York: Harper-Collins Publishers.
Rizvi, S. Abu Turab (2006). 'The Sonnenschein-Mantel-Debreu Results after Thirty Years', *History of Political Economy*, 38(Suppl. 1): 228–45.
Robbins, Lionel (1928). 'The Representative Firm', *Economic Journal*, 38(151) September: 387–404.
Robbins, Lionel (1935). *An Essay on the Nature & Significance of Economic Science*, 2nd edn., Revised and Extended, London: Macmillan and Co. Limited.
Robbins, Lionel (1998). *A History of Economic Thought: The LSE Lectures*, Steven G. Medema and Warren J. Samuels (eds.), Princeton, NJ: Princeton University Press.
Roberts, John (2004). *The Modern Firm: Organizational Design for Performance and Growth*, Oxford: Oxford University Press.
Robinson, E. A. G. (1931). *The Structure of Competitive Industry*, London: Nisbet & Co.
Robinson, Joan (1933). *The Economics of Imperfect Competition*, London: Macmillan and Co., Ltd.
Robinson, Joan (1969). *The Economics of Imperfect Competition*, 2nd edn., London: The Macmillan Press Ltd.
Robinson, Romney (1971). *Edward H. Chamberlin*, New York: Columbia University Press.
Roe, Mark J. (1994). *Strong Managers, Weak Owners: The Political Roots of American Corporate Finance*, Princeton, NJ: Princeton University Press.
Roemer, John E. (1989). 'Public Ownership and Private Property Externalities'. In Jon Elster and Karl Ove Moene (eds.), *Alternatives to Capitalism* (159–79), Cambridge: Cambridge University Press.
Roemer, John E. (1994). *Egalitarian Perspectives: Essays in Philosophical Economics*, Cambridge: Cambridge University Press.
Rosenberg, Nathan and L. E. Birdzell, Jr. (1986). *How the West Grew Rich: The Economic Transformation of the Industrial World*, New York: Basic Books.
Rothchild, K. W. (1947). 'Price Theory and Oligopoly', *Economic Journal*, 57(227) September: 299–320.
Salanié, Bernard (2005). *The Economics of Contracts: A Primer*, 2nd edn., Cambridge, MA: The MIT Press.
Samuels, Warren J., Jeff E. Biddle and John B. Davis (eds.) (2003). *A Companion to the History of Economic Thought*, Oxford: Blackwell Publishing Ltd.
Samuelson, Paul A. (1947). *Foundations of Economic Analysis*, Cambridge, MA: Harvard University Press.
Sandmo, Agnar (2011). *Economics Evolving—A History of Economic Thought*, Princeton, NJ: Princeton University Press.
Sappington, David E. and Joseph E. Stiglitz (1987). 'Privatization, Information and Incentives', *Journal of Policy Analysis & Management*, 6(4) Summer: 567–85.
Sautet, Frederic E. (2000). *An Entrepreneurial Theory of the Firm*, London and New York: Routledge.
Sawyer, Malcolm C. (1979). *Theories of the Firm*, London: Weidenfeld and Nicolson.
Schmidt, Klaus (1996a). 'Incomplete Contracts and Privatization', *European Economic Review*, 40(3–5): 569–79.
Schmidt, Klaus (1996b). 'The Costs and Benefits of Privatization: An Incomplete Contracts Approach', *Journal of Law, Economics & Organization*, 12(1): 1–24.
Schmidt, Vivien A. (1999). 'Privatization in France: The Transformation of French Capitalism', *Environment and Planning C: Government and Policy*, 17(4): 445–61.

Schultz, T. W. (1939). 'Theory of the Firm and Farm Management Research', *Journal of Farm Economics*, 21(3, Part 1) August: 570–86.

Schumpeter, Joseph A. (1950). *Capitalism, Socialism and Democracy*, Third Edition, New York: Harper Torchbooks.

Scitovsky, Tibor (1952). *Welfare and Competition: The Economics of a Fully Employed Economy*, London: George Allen & Unwin.

Shackle, G. L. S. (1967). *The Years of High Theory: Invention and Tradition in Economic Thought 1926–1939*, Cambridge: Cambridge University Press.

Shafer, W. and H. Sonnenschein (1982). 'Market Demand and Excess Demand Functions'. In K. Arrow and M. Intriligator (eds.), *Handbook of Mathematical Economics* (vol. 2, 671–93), Amsterdam: North-Holland.

Shapiro, Carl and Robert D. Willig (1990). 'Economic Rationales for Privatization in Industrial and Developing Countries'. In Ezra N. Suleiman and John Waterbury (eds.), *The Political Economy of Public-Sector Reform and Privatization* (55–87), Boulder, CO: Westview Press.

Sharkey, William W. (1982). *The Theory of Natural Monopoly*, Cambridge: Cambridge University Press.

Shelanski, Howard A. and Peter G. Klein (1995). 'Empirical Research in Transaction Cost Economics: A Review and Assessment', *Journal of Law, Economics & Organization*, 11(2) October: 335–61.

Sheshinski, Eytan and Luis F. López-Calva (2003). 'Privatization and Its Benefits: Theory and Evidence', *CESifo Economic Studies*, 49(3): 429–59.

Shirley, Mary M. and Patrick Walsh (2000). 'Public versus Private Ownership: The Current State of the Debate', Policy Research Working Paper 2420, World Bank, Development Research Group, Washington DC, August.

Shleifer, Andrei (1998). 'State versus Private Ownership', *Journal of Economic Perspectives*, 12(4) Autumn: 133–50.

Shleifer, Andrei and Robert W. Vishny (1994). 'Politicians and Firms', *Quarterly Journal of Economics*, 109(4) November: 995–1025.

Shleifer, Andrei and Robert W. Vishny (1997). 'A Survey of Corporate Governance', *Journal of Finance*, 52(2) June: 737–83.

Shoven, John B. and John Whalley (1984). 'Applied General-Equilibrium Models of Taxation and International Trade: An Introduction and Survey', *Journal of Economic Literature*, 22(3) September: 1007–51.

Silver, Morris (1984). *Enterprise and the Scope of the Firm: The role of vertical integration*, Oxford: Martin Robertson.

Silver, Morris (1995). *Economic Structures of Antiquity*, Westport Connecticut: Greenwood Press.

Simon, Herbert A. (1951). 'A Formal Theory of the Employment Relationship', *Econometrica*, 9(3) July: 293–305.

Simon, Herbert A. (1955). 'A Behavioral Model of Rational Choice', *Quarterly Journal of Economics*, 69(1) February: 99–118.

Simon, Herbert A. (1962). 'New Developments in the Theory of the Firm', *American Economic Review*, 52(2) May: 1–15.

Smith, Adam (1776). *An Inquiry into the Nature and Causes of the Wealth of Nations*, Vols. I and II, R. H. Campbell and A. S. Skinner (general eds.), W. B. Todd (textual ed.), Indianapolis: Liberty Classics, 1981.

Sobel, Robert (1999). *The Pursuit of Wealth: The Incredible Story of Money Throughout the Ages*, New York: McGraw-Hill.

Sobel, Russell S. (2007). 'Entrepreneurship'. In David Henderson (ed.), *The Concise Encyclopedia of Economics*, 2nd edn. (154–7), Indianapolis, Ind.: Liberty Fund.

Solow, Robert (1971). 'Some Implications of Alternative Criteria for the Firm'. In R. Marris and A. Wood, (eds.), *The Corporate Economy: Growth, Competition, and Innovative Potential* (318–42), London: Macmillan.

Sowell, Thomas (2006). *On Classical Economics*, New Haven, CT: Yale University Press.

Spulber, Daniel F. (2008). 'Discovering the Role of the Firm: The Separation Criterion and Corporate Law', Northwestern Law & Economics Research Paper No. 08–23, December 6.

Spulber, Daniel F. (2009). *The Theory of the Firm: Microeconomics with Endogenous Entrepreneurs, Firms, Markets, and Organizations*, Cambridge: Cambridge University Press.

Sraffa, Piero (1925). 'Sulle relazioni fra costo e quantità prodotta', *Annali di Economia*, 2: 277–328.

Sraffa, Piero (1926). 'The Laws of Returns under Competitive Conditions', *Economic Journal*, 36(144) December: 535–50.

Sraffa, Piero (1998), 'On the Relations Between Cost and Quantity Produced'. English translation by John Eatwell and Alessandro Roncaglia. In L.L. Pasinetti (ed.), *Italian Economic Papers* (vol. 3, 323–63), Bologna: Il Mulino and Oxford: Oxford University Press.

Stigler, George J. (1941). *Production and Distribution Theories: The Formative Period*, New York: The Macmillan Company.

Stigler, George J. (1951). 'The Division of Labor is Limited by the Extent of the Market', *Journal of Political Economy*, 59(3) June: 185–93.

Sue Wing, Ian (2004). 'Computable General Equilibrium Models and Their Use in Economy-Wide Policy Analysis: Everything You Ever Wanted to Know (But Were Afraid to Ask)', MIT Joint Program on the Science and Policy of Global Change, Technical Note No. 6, September.

Suleiman, Ezra N. (1990). 'The Politics of Privatization in Britain and France'. In Ezra Suleiman and John Waterbury (eds.), *The Political Economy of Public Sector Reform and Privatization* (113–36), Boulder, CO: Westview Press.

Sun, Qian and Wilson H. S. Tong (2002). 'Malaysia Privatization: A Comprehensive Study', *Financial Management*, 31(4) Winter: 79–105.

Svensk Tidskrift (SvT) (1918). 'Statsmonopol', vol. 8: 520–3.

Sweezy, Paul M. (1939). 'Demand Under Conditions of Oligopoly', *Journal of Political Economy*, 47(4) August: 568–73.

Tadelis, Steven and Oliver E. Williamson (2013). 'Transaction Cost Economics'. In Robert Gibbons and John Roberts (eds.), *The Handbook of Organizational Economics* (159–89), Princeton, NJ: Princeton University Press.

Tirole, Jean (1988). *The Theory of Industrial Organization*, Cambridge, MA: MIT Press.

Tirole, Jean (2001). 'Corporate Governance', *Econometrica*, 69(1) January: 1–35.

Tirole, Jean (2006). *The Theory of Corporate Finance*, Princeton, NJ: Princeton University Press.

Todd, S. C., trans. (2000). *Lysians (The Oratory of Classical Greece)*, Austin, TX: University of Texas Press.

Topkis, D. M. (1998). *Supermodularity and Complementarity*, Princeton, NJ: Princeton University Press.

Troesken, Werner (1997). 'The Sources of Public Ownership: Historical Evidence from the Gas Industry', *Journal of Law, Economics & Organization*, 13(1): 1–25.

Troesken, Werner and Rick Geddes (2003). 'Municipalizing American Waterworks, 1897–1915', *Journal of Law, Economics & Organization*, 19(2): 373–400.

Tudge, Colin (1998). *Neanderthals, Bandits and Farmers: How Agriculture Really Began*, New Haven, CT: Yale University Press.

Vannoni, Davide (2002). 'Empirical Studies of Vertical Integration: The Transaction Cost Orthodoxy', *RISEC: International Review of Economics and Business*, 49(1) March: 113–41.

Van Zandt, Timothy (2002). 'An Introduction to Monotone Comparative Statics', Notes, INSEAD, 14 November. Available from http://faculty.insead.edu/vanzandt/teaching/CompStatics.pdf [accessed 27 April 2016].

Varian, Hal R. (2014). *Intermediate Microeconomics: A Modern Approach*, 9th edn., New York: W. W. Norton and Company.

Veenhof, K. R. (2010). 'Ancient Assur: The City, its Traders, and its Commercial Network', *Journal of the Economic and Social History of the Orient*, 53(1/2): 39–82.

Veljanovski, Cento (1989). 'Foreword'. In Cento Veljanovski (ed.), *Privatisation and Competition: A Market Prospectus* (vii–x), London: Institute of Economic Affairs.

Veljanovski, Cento (2015a). 'The Economics of Ronald Coase'. In Cento Veljanovski (ed.), *Forever Contemporary: The Economics of Ronald Coase* (14–45), London: Institute of Economic Affairs.

Veljanovski, Cento (ed.) (2015b). *Forever Contemporary: The Economics of Ronald Coase*, London: Institute of Economic Affairs.

Vickers, John and George Yarrow (1988). *Privatization: An Economic Analysis*, Cambridge, MA: MIT Press.

Viner, Jacob (1932). 'Cost Curves and Supply Curves', *Journal of Economics*, 3(1): 23–46.

Viner, Jacob (1937). *Studies in the Theory of International Trade*, New York: Harper and Brothers Publishers.

Vives, Xavier (1999). *Oligopoly Pricing: Old Ideas and New Tools*, Cambridge, MA: MIT Press.

Vogelsang, Ingo (1990). *Public Enterprise in Monopolistic and Oligopolistic Industries*, Chur, Switzerland: Harwood Academic Publishers.

Walker, Paul (2013). 'The 'Reference Point' Approach to the Theory of the Firm: An Introduction', *Journal of Economic Surveys*, 27(4) September: 670–95.

Walsh, Aidan (2009). 'A Mengerian Theory of the Origins of the Business Firm', *Studies in Emergent Order*, 2: 54–75.

Wang, Ning (2014). 'A Life in Pursuit of "Good Economics": Interview with Ronald Coase by Ning Wang', *Man and the Economy*, 1(1) June: 99–120.

Wei, Zuobao, Oscar Varela, Juliet D'Souza and M Kabir Hassan (2003). 'The Financial and Operating Performance of China's Newly Privatized Firms', *Financial Management*, 32(2) Summer: 107–26.

Wernerfelt, Birger (1984). 'A Resource-based View of the Firm', *Strategic Management Journal*, 5(2) April–June: 171–80.

Wernerfelt, Birger (1997). 'On the Nature and Scope of the Firm: An Adjustment Cost Theory', *Journal of Business*, 70(4) October: 489–514.

Wernerfelt, Birger (2015). 'The Comparative Advantages of Firms, Markets and Contracts: a Unified Theory', *Economica*, 82(326) April: 350–67.

Whinston, Michael D. (2003). 'On the Transaction Cost Determinants of Vertical Integration', *Journal of Law, Economics, & Organization*, 19(1) April: 1–23.

White, Lawrence H. (2012). *The Clash of Economic Ideas: The Great Policy Debates and Experiments of the Last Hundred Years*, Cambridge: Cambridge University Press.

Whittaker, Edmund (1940). *A History of Economic Ideas*, New York: Longmans, Green and Co.

Wicksteed, Philip H. (1894). *An Essay on the Co-ordination of the Laws of Distribution*, 1932 edition, Reprint No. 12, London: London School of Economics.

Wiggins, Steven N. (1991). 'The Economics of the Firm and Contracts: A Selective Survey', *Journal of Institutional and Theoretical Economics*, 147(4) December: 603–61.

Williams, Philip L. (1978). *The Emergence of the Theory of the Firm: From Adam Smith to Alfred Marshall*, London: The Macmillan Press.

Williamson, Oliver E. (1964). *The Economics of Discretionary Behavior: Managerial Objectives in a Theory of the Firm*, Englewoods Cliffs, N.J.: Prentice-Hall.

Williamson, Oliver E. (1970). *Corporate Control and Business Behavior*, Englewoods Cliffs, N.J.: Prentice-Hall.

Williamson, Oliver E. (1971). 'The Vertical Integration of Production: Market Failure Considerations', *American Economic Review*, 61(2) May: 112–23.

Williamson, Oliver E. (1973). 'Markets and Hierarchies: Some Elementary Considerations', *American Economic Review*, 63(2) May: 316–25.

Williamson, Oliver E. (1975). *Markets and Hierarchies: Analysis and Antitrust Implications*, New York: The Free Press.

Williamson, Oliver E. (1977). 'Firms and Markets'. In Sidney Weintraub (ed.), *Modern Economic Thought* (185–202), Philadelphia: University of Pennsylvania Press.

Williamson, Oliver E. (1979). 'Transaction-Cost Economics: The Governance of Contractual Relations', *Journal of Law and Economics*, 22(2) October: 233–61.

Williamson, Oliver E. (1985). *The Economic Institutions of Capitalism*, New York: The Free Press.

Williamson, Oliver E. (1993). 'Introduction'. In Oliver E. Williamson and Sidney G. Winter (eds.), *The Nature of the Firm: Origins, Evolution, and Development* (3–17), New York, Oxford: Oxford University Press.

Williamson, Oliver E. (1996a). *The Mechanisms of Governance*, Oxford: Oxford University Press.

Williamson, Oliver E. (1996b). 'Transaction Cost Economics and the Carnegie Connection', *Journal of Economic Behavior & Organization*, 31(2) November: 149–55.

Williamson, Oliver E. (2000). 'The New Institutional Economics: Taking Stock, Looking Ahead', *Journal of Economic Literature*, 38(3) September: 595–613.

Williamson, Oliver E. (2007). 'Transaction Cost Economics: An Introduction. Economics', Discussion Papers, No. 2007–3, Kiel Institute for the World Economy. Available from: www.economics-ejournal.org/economics/discussionpapers/2007-3 [accessed 27 April 2016].

Witt, Ulrich (1999). 'Do Entrepreneurs Need Firms? A Contribution to a Missing Chapter in Austrian Economics', *Review of Austrian Economics*, 11(1–2): 99–109.

Wolfe, J. N. (1954). 'The Representative Firm', *Economic Journal*, 64(254) June: 337–49.

Wolman, Leo (1921). 'The Theory of Production', *American Economic Review*, 11(1) March: 37–56.

Woodland, Alan (2011). 'General Equilibrium Trade Theory'. In Daniel Bernhofen, Rod Falvey, David Greenaway and Udo Kreickemeier (eds.), *Palgrave Handbook of International Trade* (39–87), Houndmills, Basingstoke, Hampshire, U.K.: Palgrave Macmillan.

World Bank (1995). *Bureaucrats in Business: The Economics and Politics of Government Ownership*, New York: Oxford University Press.

Yarrow, George (1986). 'Privatization in Theory and Practice', *Economic Policy*, 2 April: 324–77.

Yarrow, George (1989). 'Does Ownership Matter?'. In Cento Veljanovski (ed.), *Privatisation and Competition: A Market Prospectus* (52–69), London: Institute of Economic Affairs.

Yarrow, George (1993). 'Privatization in the UK'. In V. V. Ramanadham (ed.), *Constraints and Impacts of Privatisation* (64–80), London: Routledge.

Yeaple, Stephen and Warren Moskowitz (1995). 'The Literature on Privatization', Research Paper No. 9514, Federal Reserve Bank of New York, New York, June.

Yergin, Daniel and Joseph Stanislaw (1998). *The Commanding Heights: The Battle Between Government and the Market Place That Is Remaking the Modern World*, New York: Simon and Schuster.

Yu, Tony Fu-Lai (1999). 'Toward a Praxeological Theory of the Firm', *Review of Austrian Economics*, 12(1): 25–41.

Zame, William R. (2007). 'Incentives, Contracts, and Markets: A General Equilibrium Theory of Firms', *Econometrica*, 75(5) September: 1453–500.

Zenger, Todd R., Teppo Felin and Lyda Bigelow (2011). 'Theories of the Firm—Market Boundary', *Academy of Management Annals*, 5(1) June: 89–133.

Zingales, Luigi (2000). 'In Search of New Foundations', *Journal of Finance*, 55(4) August: 1623–53.

Zotoff, A. W. (1923). 'Notes on the Mathematical Theory of Production', *Economic Journal*, 33(129) March: 115–21.

Zouboulakis, Michel S. (2015). 'Elements of a Theory of the Firm in Adam Smith and John Stuart Mill'. In George C. Bitros and Nicholas C. Kyriazis (eds.), *Essays in Contemporary Economics: A Festschrift in Memory of A. D. Karayiannis* (45–52), Heidelberg: Springer Cham.

Index

Printed in the United States
by Baker & Taylor Publisher Services